Fifty Years in the
Sociological Enterprise

Let us celebrate the stray as the ambassador plenipotentiary of chance. And chance is the better gardener.
Charles Fenyvesi

Memoirs are almost always gilded documents, at least as fascinating for what they obscure as for what they illuminate.
Donal Hanahan

Why not call it 'How to Make It Without Doing Any of the Right Things?' Lewis M. Killian

Fifty Years in the Sociological Enterprise

A Lucky Journey

Charles H. Page

The University of Massachusetts Press   Amherst, 1982

Copyright © 1982 by The University of Massachusetts Press

All rights reserved   Printed in the United States of America

LC 82–7046   ISBN 0–87023–373–4

Library of Congress Cataloging in Publication Data

appear on the last printed page of this book.

Acknowledgment is made to the following publishers for permission

to reprint selections from copyrighted material:

Irving Kristol, "Memoirs of a Trotskyist," *New York Times,* January 23,

1977. Copyright © 1977 by The New York Times Company.

Charles H. Page, "Sociology as a Teaching Enterprise" in *Sociology*

Today, ed. Robert K. Merton, Leonard Broom, and Leonard S. Cot-

trell, Jr. (New York: Basic Books, 1959). Copyright © 1959 by

Basic Books, Inc.

Acknowledgments

SEVERAL SCHOLARS HAVE contributed substantially to the book with critical comment and with encouragement to a snail-paced author. Robert Bierstedt, Mirra Komarovsky, and Richard Martin read all the manuscript; John P. Hewitt, Paul Hollander, Alan M. Sica, and Randall G. Stokes read most of it. My indebtedness to them is much greater than a conventional acknowledgment suggests.

Lesser burdens have been carried by other readers, but they too have given important aid to both a book-in-process and authorial morale. Chapters 1, 2, and 3 were read by Lewis M. Killian, Michael Lewis, and Norbert Wiley, chapters 1, 2, and 7, by John W. Loy, and chapters 2, 3, and 7, by Thomas O. Wilkinson; chapters 1 and 2, by Norman K. Denzin and Hans Speier, chapters 1 and 4, by Helen Chinoy, William H. Van Voris, and Jacqueline Van Voris, chapters 3 and 5, by the late Morroe Berger, and chapters 3 and 6, by Joseph M. Goldsen and Richard Gruneau; chapter 4, by Daniel Aaron to whom I owe special thanks for editorial guidance, and by Adelaide Cromwell Hill, Renee Fox, and Elsa Siipola, chapter 5 by Allen H. Kassof and Wilbert E. Moore, chapter 6 by James L. McCartney and Peter I. Rose, and chapter 7 by William Julius Wilson.

The book has also benefited from frequently lengthy face-to-face sessions with men and women encountered in the journey. These include Mirra Komarovsky (on chapter 2, especially); Bob Bierstedt and Sidney Kaplan (on chapter 3); Helen Chinoy, Renee Fox, and Elsa Siipola (on chapter 4); Morroe Berger, Marvin Bressler, Suzanne Keller, Marion J. Levy, Mike Lewis, Robert A. Scott, and Melvin M. Tumin (on chapter 5), and Nicholas Jay

Demerath, Lewis Killian, Mike Lewis, Randy Stokes, T. O. Wilkinson, and David Yaukey (on chapter 7).

Full responsibility for what appears in the following pages, of course, is mine alone.

I am grateful to Sally Donahue for her expert typing of the final version of the manuscript; to my friend and neighbor Emma Kaplan, nonpareil in her profession, for tracking down sundry references; and to Mary P. Trott for generous help in the Smith College Archives.

The complicated process of turning the manuscript into a book was managed with great skill, and with toleration of an author's foibles, by luminaries of the University of Massachusetts Press: Pam Campbell, Ralph Kaplan, Mary Mendell, and Leone Stein; Richard Martin's contributions far exceeded his editorial responsibilities.

Finally, I owe an enormous and unpayable debt to my life's companion to whom this book is dedicated. Leonora has typed hundreds of pages masterfully, has listened with loving sympathy to the wails of a frequently bogged-down author, and has put up with his reading aloud of almost every paragraph without complaint.

Charles H. Page
February, 1982

Contents

Contents

1

An Introductory Rationale:

Claims and Disclaimers

WRITING THIS ACCOUNT of a long journey in the sociological enterprise has been an indulgence for more than
three years. A rationale is needed for such a bold undertaking. Thus in these introductory pages I will try to establish a
measure of solid ground for the publication of these personalized
and informal essays.

Let me begin, as authors of trivial articles in the sociological journals too often do, by citing scholars of prestige. Only a
few American sociologists have given us personal accounts of
their professional experiences. We have, for example, from the
first of the Fathers, *Young Ward's Diary* (edited by Bernhard J.
Stern), written in French, laden with mundane detail, and end-
ing in 1870—long before Lester F. Ward's sociological eminence
(the diary of his later years was destroyed, alas, by his second
wife). Charles Horton Cooley left us the modest, though often
sprightly, and revelatory *Life and the Student*. Pitirim Sorokin's
three autobiographical accounts tell us a good deal about both the
author's sturdy ego and his sociological convictions. My own mentor's autobiography, *As a Tale That Is Told*, includes Robert
MacIver's candid and at times highly critical appraisal of sociology itself. And on a smaller scale and from a later generation,
more sharply focused recollections have been provided by Paul
Lazarsfeld, George Homans, Talcott Parsons, Robert Bierstedt,
Joseph Fichter, and others. These scholarly confessionals, I believe, should enrich a social psychological history of American
sociology.

The present undertaking is not such a history; indeed it is

conceived as a "history" only in the most permissive use of the term. Nor does it have more than the slightest affinity with the autobiographical contributions cited above: those are the reflections of scholarly luminaries. The present writer, during a half century in the guild, has added relatively little to the literature and, as an occasional essayist, has generally avoided the hard labor of rigorous research. In this important respect, then, I have no insider's credentials for the task ahead; and on this count, as well as others, I write as a marginal.

Marginality is an important theme in the following pages— "Informal Essays by an ex-Marginal" was in fact the book's original subtitle. I do not use this term as a poor cloak for hubris, but in its double meaning: as on the outer edge of this or that and, more frequently, as a borderline or interstitial position. As a departmental chairman, as an editor, and as a sociologist who regards his field as both a scientific and humanistic discipline, I have been a marginal man.

Sociology's Coming of Age

But this two-sided status is only one of what are here claimed to be assets for the present venture in memorabilia. The most important of these by far is the fortuitous correspondence in time between the remarkable growth of sociology, in the academy and elsewhere, and the span of my activities as a card-carrier. In the 1930s, when for eight years I combined full-time teaching at the College of the City of New York with part-time graduate study at Columbia, sociology was in its childhood as a scholarly and teaching field; by 1960 it had reached the size, organizational complexity, reputability, and influence to justify perhaps its designation as a "major social and cultural institution."*

This transition, requiring only a few decades, was manifested in many ways: by the acceptance of sociology, at the undergraduate level, as a legitimate field of study in all but a handful of colleges and universities; by the breakdown of the hegemony of the "big two," Chicago and Columbia (to be joined by Harvard in the late 1930s), as major centers of graduate training and the seemingly never-ending proliferation of strong graduate departments; by the march of a growing number of sociologists into

* Justification for this bold phrasing is attempted in my essay, "Sociology as an Educational Enterprise," in *Sociology and Contemporary Education,* ed. Charles H. Page (New York: Random House, 1964), pp. 4–9.

government and business and even onto the airways; by awards to sociologists (almost unheard of in the earlier era) of such honorifics as Guggenheim Fellowships, distinguished professorships, and college presidencies, and, for some eminent scholars, membership in the American Philosophical Society and the American Academy of Arts and Sciences. More generally (and sociologically more impressively), there occurred the widespread diffusion in the educated public of sociological rhetoric and at least an elementary sociological perspective. In 1959, Talcott Parsons proclaimed (in extraordinary agreement with C. Wright Mills) that "a 'sociological era' has begun to emerge."*

Consider a minor but nevertheless indicative symptom of this great transition: the annual sociological jamboree. Sociologists of my generation, attending the massive end-of-August meetings of the American Sociological Association—with their elaborate programs, hectic hiring halls, multiple caucuses of dissidents, handouts at crowded publishers' parties, and all the rest—have nostalgic memories of the American Sociological Society's modest, midwinter assemblies of intimates in pre–World War II years. To have witnessed the changes from the ASS's *gemeinschaftliche* gatherings to the ASA's *gesellschaftliche* superconventions and to have participated in the events marking this development provide in themselves at least a modicum of rationale for the present indulgence.

This primary consideration, the happenstance of being born in 1909, is supplemented by several secondary circumstances, which are also largely the product of the play of luck—as should become clear in later parts of this book. (The role of the lucky break in what are generally viewed as successful careers has been underplayed in many biographical and autobiographical accounts. This neglect has been encouraged, as often noted, by preoccupation with the impact of cultural and structural forces upon individual lives.) Each of these circumstances warrants brief comment.

Teaching Sociology

As a teacher of sociology, my principal professional role over the decades, I have had the good fortune to be with students, undergraduate and graduate, in quite diverse but generally excellent schools. (A former colleague Marvin Bressler once observed

* "Some Problems Confronting Sociology as a Profession," *American Sociological Review* 24, no. 4 (August 1959).

that overexposure to first-rate students skewed my pedagogical perspective: as Bressler put it, I was "spoiled.") My early teaching years were spent in the CCNY of the 1930s, at that time an extraordinary hotbed of ideological, political, and intellectual activity, which presented both a severe challenge and enormous stimulation to a young instructor. Following this extensive and intensive apprenticeship (and prior to almost four years in military uniform), there was a stint in 1941–42 as the junior member of Columbia's graduate department of sociology which, although brief, was influential in several respects: it introduced me to the excitement and perils of graduate teaching, coping in seminars with such fine minds as those of David Aberle, Milton Gordon, Philip Selznick, and Benjamin Yinger. It gave me temporary colleagueship with Columbia's sociological powers-to-be, Robert Merton and Paul Lazarsfeld, both of whom joined the department that year. It lowered my self-esteem as a ping-pong player, for Lazarsfeld (my office mate) consistently trounced me. And, as a short-time but more or less full-fledged member of an elitist faculty, this stint induced what was to become a lasting and lamentable taste for hobnobbing with my superiors.

In 1946, like many ex-servicemen eager to try greener pastures, I deserted the subway circuit for New England and Smith College. Rather to my surprise, and in contrast with my biased views, here was no finishing school for daughters of the well heeled, but, with respect to both students and faculty, a splendid college, where (altogether contrary to my expectations) I was to teach for thirteen years. The joys and tribulations of these years, and problems confronted midst the female ivy, thus were a long-time concern. That such problems were not peculiar to the Seven Sisters, but pervaded both kinds of sexually segregated schools of the ivy tradition, I was to learn during five years at Princeton, where I joined the faculty in 1960 as the first chairman of an independent department of sociology. The rewards and frustrations of working with a group of distinguished colleagues, of facing Princeton's putatively blasé undergraduates in the classroom, and of teaching and learning from highly able (but conspicuously non-ivy) graduate students dominated those five years in Old Nassau.

The move to Princeton, I had assumed, would end my travels in the academy: a summit of sorts had been reached. But in 1965, deserting my proper station in the classroom, I succumbed to the powerful temptations presented by the new and exciting Santa Cruz campus of the University of California by becoming the first provost of Adlai E. Stevenson College. Less than three years later, however, I rejoined the teaching ranks at the then-mushrooming University of Massachusetts, where my terminal tenure of professing was blessed by close contact, in seminar room and elsewhere, with a large number of candidates for the Ph.D. As a member of the Department of Sociology at Massachusetts, I met, but did not conclude, my final class on May 14, 1975.

This account of academic positions depicts a seemingly conventional job record of a college teacher. As suggested earlier, however, not only were first-rate students, a school teacher's boon, in good supply in each of these colleges and universities, but these posts involved a relatively rare and rich diversity of both type of school and pedigree of student: graduate and undergraduate, male and female, ivy and non-ivy. This variety of teaching experience is reflected in several themes underscored in later chapters.

That teaching was my foremost occupational activity for many years (1931–1975), again, was no deviation for a sociologist. Most sociologists most of the time earn their keep, or claim to do so, in preparation for and performance in the classroom: they are instructors of sociological lore. There is full justification for this preoccupation, I have contended over the years, as long as sociology remains both a humanistic and scientific discipline, as long as it functions as a liberating and intellectually challenging subject of study, as long as it is taught by educated men and women, and as long as sociology is not overwhelmed by the utilitarian allurements of technological expertise.* This aside is an ancient's admonition, of course, and only one of many, readers are warned, that will intrude upon the pages of these recollections.

In the Chair

During my earlier years at City College, and in keeping with the convictions of perhaps most young teachers (then and now), I viewed the departmental chair in jaundiced terms: as the seat of ruthless manipulation of course assignments and of other tyrannies, as an agency of heartless administration, as a retreat for academic incompetents, and certainly not as an office I would ever occupy or to which I would ever aspire. But in 1951 at Smith College I became chairman of Sociology and Anthropology, brought

---

* Robert Bierstedt, in an eloquent essay, has written in partial agreement at least with this position; see "Sociology and General Education" in Page, *Sociology and Contemporary Education,* chap. 2.

about by the illness of Gladys Bryson, who had long headed the department expertly and humanely. In the course of the subsequent fourteen years in this position at Smith and elsewhere, my earlier conception of the chairman's role underwent considerable change. Moreover, my views concerning both sociology as an educational enterprise and the academy as a unique combination of bureaucracy and collegiality were no doubt strongly influenced by this prolonged tour in the chair.*

Eight of these fourteen years were spent at Smith in a small department (five or six sociologists and a lonely anthropologist), and here the tasks of the chair were both eased and complicated by the intimacy of departmental—and, at Smith, extradepartmental—life. In 1952–53, I faced a far different and more complex situation during a single year as chairman at New York's City College, where substantial changes had taken place since the 1930s. Following this short-lived, demanding, and frequently frustrating assignment, and after seven final years at Smith, I moved to Princeton. The stay at Princeton (1960–1965) brought rich rewards and unforeseen problems, as well as opportunities and challenges largely lacking in either a woman's liberal arts college of the ivy tradition or a (now) co-educational public school of the subway circuit.

Chairing these three departments, then, involved a diversity of academic and administrative experience (which was to pay dividends during the later provostship at Santa Cruz). But however great the differences between Smith and City College and Princeton, the three posts had in common an important attribute. They induced a perspective on various academic matters—educational administration, appointment and promotion, teaching and research, curricular development, interdepartmental projects and rivalries, and so on—that in some ways differed from the characteristic perspectives of academics who had no experience in the chair.

One attribute of this position, a structural feature, is a special kind of marginality, irrespective of type of school. For the occupant, whatever his personal allegiance, must function as both departmental colleague and representative of or at least messenger

---

* Some of these views are presented in the essays "Bureaucracy and Higher Education," *Journal of General Education* 5, no. 2 (January 1951); "Sociology as a Teaching Enterprise," in *Sociology Today,* ed. Robert K. Merton et al. (New York: Basic Books, 1959), chap. 25; and "Sociology as an Educational Enterprise."

for the administration: he or she must be something of a go-between. In this interstitial role, one is apt to be torn between loyalties—to one's colleagues "below" and the administrative powers "above." If one's ambitions are directed toward the latter, one may downgrade or neglect the interests and anxieties of the former. But this structurally encouraged possibility is by no means an inevitability: many chairmen and chairwomen give their first allegiance to the academic rank-and-file. And this preference, I have long believed, should be given top priority by all who hold this office.

Excursus in the Establishment

I would suppose that few academic men and women would take strong issue with these views on the departmental chairmanship. But many sociologists strongly disagree about the profession's "establishment": the elected officers and major committee members of the American Sociological Association, its handful of salaried officials, and the Old Boys (and Girls) whose long-time service carries some degree of prestige.

In 1957 I was elected to the Council of the ASA, and over the next decade my status as an establishmentarian was more or less confirmed by a number of important assignments. These included six years on the Council, during three of which the editorship of the *American Sociological Review* gave ex-officio membership on the Council's executive committee, and terms on such gate-keeping committees as those dealing with publications, awards, and nominations. (Although elected to most of these committees, my vote-getting deficiencies were indicated by two defeats for vice president of the ASA.) This experience may warrant extensive anecdotal report, but this brief excursus will be restricted to four nonmomentous episodes in the modern history of the establishment and some brief comment on its longer-range characteristics.

The first of these, an unanticipated action of the Council in 1959, was initiated by President Kingsley Davis's announcement of his frequent embarrassment concerning the initials of the American Sociological Society. This complaint, I first assumed, was the invocation of an ancient joke (no doubt needed toward the end of a long day's session) or, conceivably, the expression of a curious delicacy given the Society's unconcern since 1905 with its title's acronym. But my faulty perception was soon established by a serious discussion of the matter by distinguished members of the group, which included sober reference to the technical meanings of "society" and "association." A large majority of the Council voted for the replacement of ASS by ASA. Since 1960, then, the Association's membership has been unfettered with either burden: that of encouraging the jocular propensities of outsiders or insiders, or that of belonging to an organization with a title offensive to the niceties of the sociological lexicon.

A second episode, giving a different color to the Council's deliberations, occurred in 1961 under the chairmanship of President Paul Lazarsfeld. The Committee on Committees had presented a list of nominees for various offices to be elected by the Council; one of these was the ASA representative to the American Council of Learned Societies, the prestigious multidisciplinary organization which largely represents the humanities. No doubt the latter fact had affected the committee's nomination of a sociologist widely known for his breadth of learning, graceful writing, and his conception of sociology as a humane discipline. As the balloting was in process, however, the chairman of the meeting spoke strongly in opposition to this presumably highly qualified scholar and in favor of a "real scientist," as the chair put it, a sociologist with expertise in empirical and quantitative research. This surprising and what some of us viewed as ill-timed campaigning provoked sharp protest and had little effect on the Council's choice: the "nonscientist" was elected by a large majority.* This minor and soon-forgotten event in the establishment's proceedings failed to shake the profession's foundations, to be sure, but it provided one of many manifestations of the century-old tension between the scientific and humanistic aspirations of sociology.

Episodes of this kind may be little more than tidbits for those preoccupied with officialdom's closed-room affairs.† That both "establishments" and periodic efforts to reform or overthrow them, however, are permanent features of the sociological enterprise (as of many others) is suggested by past episodes of larger dimensions. Two of these, each marked by conflict between a supposedly entrenched elite and opposing Young Turks, stand out in my recollections.

---

* Robert Bierstedt's valuable contributions to the ACLS continued for many years.
† Although recent changes of policy have opened the Council's deliberations to observers, private meetings of establishmentarians, as with all such groups, are of course inevitable.

One memory goes back to the early 1930s when I first began to attend annual meetings of the national and Eastern sociological societies. In the relatively intimate gatherings of those years, a good deal of the gossip and at least some of the more formal shop talk centered on the alleged domination of sociology by the University of Chicago's renowned department: the creation of Albion Small, W. I. Thomas, Robert Park, and their successors. This charge was voiced loudly by dissidents in eastern schools, who focused their attack on Chicago's control of the *American Journal of Sociology,* then the official journal of the Society, and on the informal but powerful control of jobs by Chicago's sociologists. Here was a vulnerable target for the militant Young Turks of the time, who scored a major victory when, in 1936, the *American Sociological Review* was established as the profession's official journal under the editorship of Frank Hankins of Smith College. The fact that a few years later Hankins himself became president of the ASS, as did other easterners, illustrates a long-standing trend of shifting regional influence in American sociology. Successions of this kind also lend plausibility to a "natural life history" theory of establishments.*

Interpretation of a final and more recent historical case in terms of such a theory is tempting. Beginning about 1950, criticism of the ASS was mounting among both younger and older members of the organization who, in this case, had no regional identification. Their complaints, supported by what many of us believed to be considerable evidence, included the organization's minimal concern with serious social problems, its false neutrality in the name of scientific objectivity, overly rigid gate-keeping, and the publication of a dreary *American Sociological Review.* Interest in the study and amelioration of social problems, especially, led to a meeting of a small group of organizers in 1951 and within less than two years, under the leadership of otherwise such unlikely allies as Ernest W. Burgess and Alfred McClung Lee,† the

---

* Patricia Madoo Lengermann, in "The Founding of the *American Sociological Review:* The Anatomy of a Rebellion," *American Sociological Review* 44, no. 2 (April 1979): 185–98, gives a detailed account of this revolt in which she points up the impact of the Depression on the episode (a minor factor, in my view) and relates it to the contemporary extrinsic-intrinsic debate concerning the nature of scientific change.

† More than twenty years later Lee was to be elected president of the ASA as a candidate-by-petition, supported by many members of a new cohort of dissidents, as well as by veterans of the SSSP and others, in another revolt against the establishment.

Society for the Study of Social Problems and its journal *Social Problems* were launched. Antiestablishment sociologists—staunch supporters of democratic methods, open organization, and wide participation—saw in the SSSP a splendid opportunity to institute these progressive procedures, as inspection of the new society's governing code suggests. After only a few years, however, some sociologists were decrying what they viewed as replication of the targets of their earlier complaints: organizational and ideological conservatism, creeping bureaucracy, a conventionally edited journal. This uneasiness was not decreased by the conspicuous success of the SSSP and *Social Problems* and by a large movement into the former's ranks of luminaries of American sociology. Within a decade of its birth in 1952, the SSSP had become a major professional and scholarly association with the characteristic attributes of such a group, including of course an "establishment."*

The ASA has no doubt benefited substantially from being shaken by uprisings of antiestablishmentarians, a therapy beginning at least as early as the 1930s. But sometimes the charges of dissidents have reached extremes belied by the historical record, and sometimes distortions of the profession's officialdom have been as great as they became in accusations by the radical caucuses of the late 1960s. Not for forty years, for example, have sociologists from a single region or a single university monopolized the high offices and major committees of the ASA† (although the South has had few such posts). Of greater significance is the fact that the presidents, editors, Council members, and other officers of the Association have represented a wide diversity of theoretical orientation, specialization of field, intellectual style, political stance, and university affiliation—reflecting the multisided nature of sociology itself.‡

---

* For brief periods in the late 1950s and early 1960s, I participated in this group as a member of the SSSP's executive committee and the Committee on Publications.

† It might be argued that in recent decades three universities have had more than their share of presidencies: Columbia (Peter Blau, William Goode, Mirra Komarovsky, Paul Lazarsfeld, Robert Merton); Harvard (George Homans, Talcott Parsons, Pitirim Sorokin, Samuel Stouffer); Berkeley (Herbert Blumer, Reinhard Bendix, Kingsley Davis). These sociologists, however, were elected primarily on the basis of their scholarly contributions, not their school affiliations.

‡ As a member of the Council, I served under the following presidents: Robin Williams, Kingsley Davis, Howard B. Becker, Paul Lazarsfeld, Everett Hughes, and George Homans—a distinguished but motley sextet.

This diversity impressed me during the several years of my participation in the upper echelons of the ASA; it continues to do so. I was also impressed by the devotion to the profession and the sheer hard work displayed by most of my colleagues in their various official roles—a dedication rarely acknowledged by anti-establishmentarians, or recognized by the latter as an important reason for some cases of long-time tenure in office. This comment, let it be stressed, should be taken as in no way a qualification of my full enjoyment, in those years, of the side benefits of holding office: the freeloading, the after-hour companionship, the give-and-take with famed men and, to be sure, women of my vocation.

Editing Sociology

If the primary professional role of most sociologists is teaching, research and publication are essentials for those who make their mark beyond the classroom. Altogether unessential for such a career is the job of editing, which is often demanding and time consuming but carries only secondary status in the world of scholarship. For almost thirty years I no doubt spent far too many of my hours at the desk with editorial pencil in hand, giving evidence of yet another kind of marginality.

From 1952 until 1980 I was what commercial publishers call an "advisory" or "consulting" editor, misleading terms for the task of working with manuscripts and bringing misery to authors. Without previous experience, I began in this position at the gigantic firm of Doubleday, with fortune in my favor on two counts: the early 1950s were the start of a boom period in both sociology and the publication of its products; and I had the good luck to introduce the first paperback series in my field, "Short Studies in Sociology." After two years with Doubleday, in 1954, both the Studies and clothbound books were sold to Random House and, as a potentially valuable property in the view of officials at the latter firm, I became part of the package. But at the time no one guessed that I would be with Random House until 1980.

The move into editing books (and nonbooks) for a commercial publisher in 1952 was sudden and unanticipated. I was equally surprised five years later when an invitation to become editor of the *American Sociological Review* was conveyed by Donald Young, then secretary of the ASS. In accepting this important and challenging position, I sentenced myself to a three-year load (1958–1960) of multiple jobs: teaching, chairing, book editing, and a far different kind of editing of a scholarly journal.

But coping with the flood of manuscripts that came to the *ASR* and striving to broaden the journal's contents paid valuable educational dividends: eye-opening lessons in sociological research and writing, and indeed, in the psychology of sociologists.

My activities and views as a sociologist—as teacher, editor, and occasional author—have been influenced of course, perhaps profoundly, by experiences beyond the walls of the academy and beyond the boundaries of my vocation. Some of these will be referred to in the accounts that follow, but there will be no effort to pursue such outside affairs or to assess their impact on my professional life. If, as indicated at the outset, these recollections are only the crudest kind of "history," they are in no conventional sense "autobiography."

Such diverse activities as logging in Oregon and membership in what remained of the IWW (1926–1927), life guarding for six summers on the public beaches of Chicago (1926–1931), working for the National Refugee Service as field secretary (1940–1941), and four years of duty in this country and the far Pacific in the air branch of the navy (1942–1946) no doubt affected my academic pursuits and perhaps my sociological views. But to what extent and in what ways they did so is problematic—and of no concern in this book.

The chapters that follow are a memoir of a long-time worker in the vineyards of sociology. They deal with the sociological enterprise, especially in academia, and with a good many of its enterprisers. They are a personalized account, to be sure, but little more.

2

Columbia University, 1931–1942:

Robert MacIver and Company

DURING MY JUNIOR year at the University of Illinois, I began to flirt with the notion of teaching as a possible occupation. The idea struck my friends, including my profoundly sensible best girl, as rather silly. It was viewed by my bohemian and intellectual mother as absurd for she considered her son as eminently ineligible for a life with books and ideas: she thought that he might get by as a skilled worker or sporting goods salesman. But these skeptics had not been exposed to the powerful influence of that nonpareil teacher of undergraduates, William C. Casey.

An Important Preliminary: Bill Casey
and the Move to New York

Bill Casey, then in the Department of Political Science, offered mind-boggling courses which somehow brought together such unlikely companions as Graham Wallas's *The Great Society,* the medieval English manor, Walter Lippmann's *Public Opinion,* speeches of Woodrow Wilson, the Sacco-Vanzetti case, Pavlov's conditioned response, *Plunkitt of Tamany Hall,* and the success story of a mysterious "White Truck salesman"—all ingredients in a brilliant Caseological analysis. Casey's synthesis of devastating debunking, Veblenian irony, and rare erudition yielded an educational experience that stood far apart from the conventional curriculum. And his spectacular lectures gave vivid evidence that teaching need not be a dullish routine, but a creative and adventurous undertaking.

Bill Casey was a remarkable and paradoxical personality: severely critical of human follies, but warmly supportive of the jazz-age collegians whom he taught; a shameless Anglophile who purchased his distinguished clothing in London, but retained an indelible down-state stamp of his native Illinois; a frequent deviant from conventions of the professoriate, but a lover of ceremony and an impeccable gentleman who raised his hat to both men and women; a traditionalist in personal taste and manner, but a bold avant-gardist in his intellectual attainments. Such a man could hardly be a "model" in a youngster's aspirations, but Bill Casey uprooted for once and all my stereotypical and spurious ideas about the putative conventionality of academic life.

As a college senior, my misgivings about teaching had lessened, so much so that I pursued possible openings in the public schools of Illinois. But Casey, who had moved to the University of Chicago in 1930, proposed a more ambitious goal: graduate study in New York, where Casey himself had accepted an invitation to join Columbia's department of sociology. For a Chicagoan who had only recently given thought to a career in teaching, the prospect of tackling a renowned but unknown Columbia while trying to make a living in remote New York was both scary and exciting. My trepidations lessened, however, when Bill Casey endorsed the venture by recommending me for a job in a Manhattan private school and by assuring me of continuing psychological and, if necessary, material support. Thus, in the fall of 1931, two former Illini descended upon Gotham: one a sophisticated, wise, and already accepted member of the academy, the other a semi-educated and wide-eyed youngster.

My first day in New York is one of many illustrations in these pages of how sheer good luck at times far outweighs ability or diligence. Arriving in the early morning by bus with an overload of baggage but less than thirty dollars as a stake, I telephoned my single New York contact, a former Casey student. Samaritan Glenn McClelland* rescued me from the mounting crowd of Times Square, drove me to a friend's apartment in Greenwich Village for quick repairs, briefed me on the possible job at Birch Wathen School where McClelland taught and on Columbia where

* McClelland, my first friend in New York, fellow teacher at Birch Wathen School for two years, and codirector with me of an experimental summer camp on Monhegan Island in 1932, later became a successful careerist in the United States Department of State.

he was a graduate student, raised my spirits with his friendly encouragement, and sent me on my way. By midafternoon, the job was mine, Columbia had accepted me, I was installed in the fine Village apartment as a coresident, and, a bit later, I was enjoying a drink in a local speakeasy, standing side by side with the heroic figure of Heywood Broun, famed author of powerful pieces on the Sacco-Vanzetti case encountered two years before in Bill Casey's class. Fabulous New York, I concluded after the first few hours in the city, was my home forever.

My frequent but questionable claim to being a New Yorker is supported by full-time residence of little more than a dozen years: from my arrival until 1942, followed by a four-year absence while in uniform, plus several months in 1946 and the academic year 1952–53. But that first decade was jam-packed—occupationally, academically, culturally, and otherwise. Heavy teaching duties and prolonged pursuit of a Ph.D. could not prevent exploration of and indulgence in at least some of New York's exciting offerings: life in a fading Village bohemia, Harlem's great jazz sessions (my love of jazz had been Chicago-bred in the 1920s), the ground-breaking productions of the Group, Federal, and Mercury theaters (I had been an enthusiastic but wretched amateur actor in Illinois), the multiradicalisms of Union Square and elsewhere. Although these extracurricular activities were undertaken with no such end in view, they were no doubt educational for a student and teacher of sociology.

The two years at Birch Wathen, also instructive sociologically, were a breadwinning exercise, yielding the handsome salary of $900 the first year and $300 more the second. This income was supplemented a bit by such moonlighting jobs as coaching, tending bar, and tutoring. But there was little extra time, for my Birch Wathen assignments included the roles of classroom teacher in the elementary school (fifth grade the first year, seventh the second), teacher of ancient and European history in the high school, coach of three sports, and assistant in dramatics—a tidy program for an ill-prepared B.A. Yet this load did not strike me as excessive: to have a job of any kind in the early thirties was good fortune. And to share the classroom with Birch Wathen's talented youngsters was a splendid introduction to the joys of teaching.

Thus after a few months in New York my earlier skepticism of teaching as a career had vanished: the classroom had seduced me. I was far less sure about graduate study, however, and by no means confident of my ability to attain a Ph.D. The one or two courses at Columbia managed each term were parts of a program I then thought of as a long-odds gamble. But in the summer of 1933 a more or less successful passage through a tough, three-course schedule* was encouraging; and by 1939 the requirements for the doctorate were completed. Much of what went on during that decade of part-time participation in the activities of Columbia's Fayerweather Hall, sociology's headquarters then and now, has faded of course. But not all.

Graduate Study at Columbia

In the 1930s graduate study for the large majority of students had to be a part-time pursuit. The sociology department, as I recall, controlled one rotating fellowship every three or four years; this and a tiny number of residential scholarships almost exhausted its resources for student aid. There were no inside or outside research funds (no NSF or NIMH), no Bureau of Applied Social Research (BASR became a center of student employment only after World War II), and a single teaching assistant position (in Bill Casey's popular courses in the College). All but a handful of graduate students spent most of their time working or seeking work in the Depression decade, and therefore many courses were scheduled in late afternoon or evening. Small wonder then that withdrawals outnumbered completions of the Ph.D. and that ten years or more were often needed to complete the degree.

The formal requirements for the doctorate were quite conventional: twenty courses, two foreign languages, two or three days of written "preliminaries," an oral examination in both sociology (including statistics) and a minor from a related discipline, defense of the dissertation, and its publication. But there were soft spots in the program: the grade of "H" for auditing, or claiming to have done so, was acceptable in about a third of the courses; and quite a few of us who had convinced the faculty that we owned a degree of ability were excused from the rigorous preliminaries. More important, the program was loosely organized and highly permissive. The sociology of the 1930s had no established fields—we were expected to cover the sociological waterfront, to qualify as the kind of generalists so anathema to later generations of specialists. With one exception, there were no courses desig-

---

* These courses, taught by George Lundberg, Talcott Parsons, and Florian Znaneicki, receive special comment below.

nated as essential,* and sociological provincialism was lessened not only by the formal requirement of a substantial minor but by wide-spread elections from the other social sciences, psychology, philosophy, and history. In the absence of large research grants, no M.A. theses or Ph.D. dissertations served merely to give underpinning to the scholarly preoccupations of faculty; student research was individual enterprise. And no faculty members, in my memory, welcomed work by students that simply reflected or expanded upon their own research. This state of affairs—unbureaucratized, unfunded, sociologically unfocused—meant that students were largely on their own, unsupported by the organized and underwritten departments that flourished in a later era.

Yet, other kinds of support paid large dividends for both the morale and the scholarly efforts of graduate students in the thirties. Limited in number and only weakly constrained by formal regulations, we pursued our individual interests in the informal, warm, and intellectually nurturing social circle of the sociology department. All members of the faculty were available without prearranged appointment, and some of them—Bill Casey, Ted Abel, and the indefatigable Bob Lynd, for example—must have curtailed their own research and writing by giving seemingly limitless time and collegial companionship to students. These meetings were by no means confined to the offices of Fayerweather Hall: student-faculty sessions were commonplace in the cafeterias and saloons (beginning in 1933) of upper Broadway, in the inexpensive restaurants of southern Harlem, and in both faculty and student homes. And as a leavener of this extended shoptalk, there were numerous parties, planned and impromptu, at which whatever faculty-student barriers there may have been seemed to crumble altogether. Along with this pervasive informality, friendly intimacy, and periodic high jinks, and in keeping with the group's semifamilial norms, there were of course personal animosities, strong rivalries, severe anxieties, and shattering heartaches— among both students and faculty. But these were far outweighed, I believe, by the rich benefits of Columbia's community of sociologists and sociologists-to-be.

---

* The one required course, taught by Alva A. Tenney, which I illegally avoided, was reputed to have the sole and clearly utopian aim of keeping alive the dated view's of Tenney's teacher and long-time Columbia pundit, the pioneer sociologist Franklin H. Giddings. My circumvention of this course probably was a mistake: later, for my dissertation, I faced the dreary exercise of reading all of Giddings's prolific works.

Columbia's graduate students of the 1930s were a mixed group in terms of formal schooling, aspiration, direction of sociological interest, ideology and politics, and, of course, ability. Our ranks included some who were to become distinguished scholars and leaders of their profession; a few whose outstanding accomplishments at Columbia suggested future, but never realized, eminence; at least three whose well-established careers were ended early by death; and others who after receiving the doctorate left the field to gain prominence in government, journalism, the media, social work, or elsewhere. Our diversified national, regional, and educational backgrounds gave the group a rewarding degree of cultural pluralism, brought out in such memorable instances as the following:

—From England, with Oxford degree in hand, came Elizabeth Nottingham, whose historical and comparative studies of religion were to decorate sociological scholarship. At Columbia, we envied Betty's breadth of learning, gentle sophistication, and command of the mother tongue. But we held her in great affection, as we do today.

—Originally from Russia, came two young women whose beauty and brilliance were a frightening combination, at least for some of us. (Years passed before I dared to seek a date with either Mirra Komarovsky or Milla Alihan.) Unlike in temperament and sociological bent, these intriguingly accented cosmopolites presented us with both intellectual and personal challenge. Their contrasting talents were later to be realized in splendid careers: Mirra as an oft-celebrated scholar, teacher, and star of her profession;* Milla beginning as a hard-hitting critic of social ecology, but shifting her interests to become a successful analyst of problems faced by business and industry.†

—From India came Krishnalal Shridharani, a former youthful ally of Mahatma Gandhi. His volumes on nonviolence, India, and America were to bring him international fame.‡ Perceptive observer of all around him, good companion, and worldly-wise, Kris not only introduced us to fine Indian food, but demonstrated by deed that sociologists, if they will, can write graceful English.

* There is more about Mirra Komarovsky in my "Introducing the New President-Elect: Mirra Komarovsky," *American Sociologist,* June 1971.
† For many years, Milla Alihan has been president of Milla Alihan Associates.
‡ Krishnalal Shridharani returned to India after World War II to become one of his country's leading journalists and distinguished sociologists. Early death ended his brilliant career in midstream.

—The American hinterland sent several of us to Columbia, including Lee Deets of South Dakota and Robert Bierstedt of Iowa. Older than most of his fellow students, Lee had begun his studies in the final years of the Giddings regime, had returned to his native state to teach and do field research for a prolonged interval, and, as his dissertation, published the first important sociological work on the Hutterites. The much younger Bob Bierstedt, already equipped with a master's degree in philosophy from Columbia and primed in sociology by a year's study at Harvard, provoked our admiration and sometimes sour grapes with his intellectual precociousness, erudition, and critical prowess. While still a student Bob outstripped us all by writing bold critiques of books by the mighty Sorokin and the young but ascending Talcott Parsons, both published in the *American Sociological Review.**

—An unknown number of Columbia graduate students were native New Yorkers, perhaps the foremost among them Adolph Tomars, Harry Alpert, and George Simpson. Adolph, a polished graduate of Columbia College and learned in the fine arts as well as the social sciences, was a scintillating member of the group whose future scholarly accomplishments seemed to be assured, but whose great potential was never fully realized. From New York's City College (which soon was to send to Columbia a large supply of superior talent)† came a youngster who was a bit less promising than Tomars in the astigmatic view of some of us; but Harry Alpert's later feats as splendid scholar-teacher and as distinguished administrator in the National Science Foundation, UNESCO, and in the academy comprised a record rivaled by the careers of very few of his contemporaries. Many of us stood in awe of the brilliant, bombastic, and exceedingly articulate George Simpson, who as an undergraduate at Cornell had already begun the translations for which he was to become known as the "Durkheim Simpson."‡ At Columbia in the early thirties George played

* These papers, "The Logico-Meaningful Method of P. A. Sorokin" (1937) and "The Means-End Scheme in Sociological Theory" (1938) are reprinted in Bierstedt's *Power and Progress: Essays in Sociological Theory* (New York: McGraw-Hill, 1974); see pp. 1–7 for Bierstedt's delightfully candid account of the generation of these early essays.

† For example, Daniel Bell, Morroe Berger, Nathan Glazer, Alvin Gouldner, Seymour Martin Lipset, Peter Rossi, and Philip Selznick. Tomars, Alpert, and I taught at City College and thus functioned, in some measure, as talent feeders for Columbia.

‡ So as not to be confused with the "Simpson and Yinger" George *E.* Simpson.

the important role of a sociological enfant terrible in graduate student life.

Dissertations and Books

With the possible exceptions of the precocious George Simpson and Bob Bierstedt, the student luminaries, like the rest of us who sought the Ph.D., suffered the usual agonies provoked by the unknown terrors of the doctor's oral—exacerbated by a high failure rate on the first try. With the successful conquest of the examination, however, these anxieties were replaced by the several and oftentimes graver problems of managing a dissertation. The student was on his own, for the individualistic ethos discouraged or prevented theses in pursuit of faculty interests; there were no peel-offs from large-scale research projects, as in later years; there were almost no support funds; for many of us, there was the severe problem of finding time while working on demanding jobs; there was the Columbia requirement of publication. But all of this was viewed as normal in the thirties (we had no future reference points for invidious comparison), and dissertations, although sometimes prolonged for many years, were written and hard-earned degrees were awarded.

The publication requirement (to be dropped later at Columbia in keeping with practice elsewhere) posed a formidable financial problem for hard-pressed graduate students. The cost of printing alone and of supplying the university with almost 100 copies of a full-fledged book ranged between one and two thousand dollars. Some doctors-soon-to-be escaped this burden: a handful of superior dissertations in the social sciences—such as the volumes by Alihan, Alpert, and Wood, referred to below—were brought out in the Columbia University series, Studies in History, Economics, and Public Law; a few others—for example, books by Jones and Shridharani, also cited below—were published by commercial firms; and at least one ingenious author, Adolph Tomars, reduced printing costs by a half or more by publishing his study in Mexico. For the rest of us, however, moving the dissertation from typescript to printed page was an expensive business, unexperienced by later generations of graduate students.

But this requirement, while often imposing heavy indebtedness or exploitation of a working spouse, also had advantages for our generation, on two important counts. The fact that obtaining the degree guaranteed public exposure in the form of a "real book" strongly encouraged high self-standards of scholarly writing in our dissertational endeavors: to turn out a book became an exercise, in some measure, in intellectual craftmanship. Of course this kind of effort continued in many cases long after the demise of the publication requirement, as it does today, but close familiarity over the decades with graceless or even shoddy dissertations has convinced me of the educational value of what was in the thirties an unwelcome Columbia requirement. A second value of publication was more utilitarian, bearing directly upon employment in the academic marketplace. For a Columbia Ph.D. meant the inclusion of at least one full volume in a job-seeker's vita—oftentimes the sole such entry throughout the lifetime of academic men and women of whatever field.

Among the Columbia dissertations written in the 1930s were several impressive studies at least a few of which were destined to have long-lasting importance in sociology. Reflecting the multiperspectives and the permissiveness of the Columbia graduate program, these studies differ greatly in orientation, substantive concern, and methodology, representing a sociological potpourri. The following half-dozen volumes, each marked by the author's command of the scholarly craft, are illustrative. In alphabetical order:

—Milla Alihan's *Social Ecology* (1938), informed by the author's on-the-spot explorations at the University of Chicago, is a critical analysis of a major sociological perspective, in the 1930s headquartered at sociology's foremost academic and research center. Alihan's cogent and ungentle critique not only provoked powerful reactions among ecology's leading exponents, but remained for many years an important reference for all students of the urban community.

—Harry Alpert's *Emile Durkheim and His Sociology* (1939), the research for which was appropriately done in France, is a study in biography and the history of sociological theory which for decades, I believe, was the outstanding work on the great French scholar.* On the large shelf of excellent and fulsome books on Durkheim that have appeared in recent years, Alpert's dissertation retains an important place.

—Alfred Winslow Jones's *Life, Liberty, and Property* (1941) made extensive use of innovative techniques of field investigation in a provocative analysis of ideology and attitudes among managers and workers in the rubber industry. This vol-

* This appraisal holds notwithstanding Talcott Parson's detailed treatment of Durkheim in *The Structure of Social Action* (New York: McGraw-Hill, 1937), chaps. 8–11.

ume stands as a scholarly event in at least three areas of sociological concern: research methods, industrial organization and conflict, and social stratification.

　—Mirra Komarovsky's *The Unemployed Man and His
Family* (1940), like Jones's book, was a multisided addition to the
sociological literature. Hailed as "the greatest step forward in the
personal document method since *The Polish Peasant*,"* Komarovsky's volume on the husband's role, status, and authority among
families of the Depression not only gave ample evidence of her
prowess as an interviewer and analyst, but was a harbinger of the
widely acclaimed studies of both sexes she was to make during the
subsequent decades.†

　—Krishnalal Shridharani's *War without Violence* (1939)
was the first important sociological study of Gandhi's method of
Satyagraha and its accomplishments, enriched by the author's direct participation and graced by his reportorial artistry. Shridharani's analysis of nonviolence as a social strategy used far beyond
India's political struggles adds to the lasting sociological importance of this unusual doctoral dissertation.

　—*The Stranger* (1934) by Margaret Wood, already an established biologist and thus senior to most of us, was the forerunner
of her later *Paths of Loneliness* (1953). Making excellent use of
historical, anthropological, sociological, and fictional sources (as
she also did in her later work), in *The Stranger* Wood introduced
a Simmel-like treatment of the interconnections between an increasingly prevalent social type and the modernization of community life—long before alienation and anomie became staples
of social analysis in this country.

　These six volumes of course do not exhaust the meritorious
doctoral theses completed at Columbia in the 1930s.‡ But the

---

* Robert Angell in Louis Gottschalk, Clyde Kluckhohn, and Robert Angell,
The Use of Personal Documents in History, Anthropology, and Sociology
(New York: Social Science Research Council, 1945), p. 220.

† In addition to several fine articles in scholarly journals, these include the
volumes *Women in the Modern World* (Boston: Little, Brown, 1953), *Blue-
Collar Marriage* (New York: Random House, 1967), and *Dilemmas of Mascu-
linity* (New York: Norton, 1976).

‡ To cite only works of Columbians named above and below, there were,
for example, Lee Deets's *The Hutterites* (1939), John Innes's *Class Fertility
in England and Wales 1876–1934* (1938), Elizabeth Nottingham's *Methodism
and the Frontier* (1941), and George Simpson's *Conflict and Community*
(1937). These titles again illustrate the diversity of interests in Columbia's
department of sociology.

total number of dissertations was small—dropouts in the Depression decade were numerous, publication was often costly, and sociology itself was then an underdeveloped academic enterprise. Yet, each year we celebrated the arrival of two or three new volumes to be added to a growing list.

My own experience with the dissertation is another illustration of the role of luck in one's career, in this case on three counts: the topic, an unforeseen reduction of task, and publication. The choice of "social class" as a subject of inquiry was influenced no doubt by my political and ideological convictions (my mother was an active leftist and I had cast my first presidential vote for Norman Thomas in 1932) and by exposure to the Marxian canon (my small but growing library included, for example, all of Lenin). But I had also selected an area of study that had been almost ignored by American sociologists since the pre–World War I years—that is, since the extensive discussions of class and class conflict in the works of the American pioneers. Thus, in the writings of Ward, Sumner, Small, Giddings, Cooley, and Ross I hit upon a subject consistent with my own interests. It was also one that within a few years was to become a major preoccupation in American sociology, giving to *Class and American Sociology: From Ward to Ross* something of a "groundbreaking" reputation.* Moreover, only one or two of the Columbia sociologists attended to the outmoded works of the American Fathers; few were prepared to shoot down my dissertational effort. On April Fool's Day of 1939, however, at its defense in Fayerweather Hall's "delivery room," I faced an examining committee that included, among others, the eminent intellectual historian Merle Curti, the brilliant student of economic thought Joseph Dorfman, and a master of sociological Americana Willard Waller. But my good luck held.

Luck with the dissertation had been with me earlier. In 1935 or 1936 I had submitted a prospectus of what I then saw as a three-part study: the first on the pioneers was to be followed by an analysis of recent research and writing on class structure and change and, finally, a presentation of my own "developed" views on the concept of class and its theoretical utilities. With

* Written in 1939, what was perhaps an inkling of this possibility is noted in the introduction to the original edition of *Class and American Sociology* (New York: Dial, 1940), pp. ix–x; my retrospective comments are in "An Introduction Thirty Years Later" in the most recent edition (New York: Schocken, 1969).

what must have been maximum toleration of the author of such a ridiculously ambitious and pretentious plan, Professor MacIver approved it—without comment. About three years later, when with some self-satisfaction I said to MacIver "only one more chapter to go to finish part one," his astonishing response rocketed my spirits: another chapter, he opined, should complete the dissertation—and he added, with a twinkle, the observation that the projected parts two and three should give me something to do during the first decade or so of my postdoctoral years.*

Completing the dissertation was one thing, getting it published another. But again a teacher's kindly guidance converged with luck to my advantage. For Willard ("Pete") Waller, who had recently become consulting editor for the Cordon Company, recommended acceptance of the study; the ensuing contract assured its publication—or so I assumed. But in the summer of 1939 as I was preparing the manuscript for Cordon, an alarmed Pete Waller warned me of the firm's probable dissolution and urged me to seek termination of the contract, which I managed during a one-day emergency trip to New York from my summer hideout on Cape Cod. Within an hour or so after leaving the Cordon office, however, my depression vanished when, as a result of continuing to follow Waller's excellent counsel, *Class and American Sociology* was contracted by Dial Press. The book was published in 1940. Thus after nine years of part-time student status at Columbia, seven of these entailing full-time teaching at City College, my legitimacy as a sociologist was established.†

Faculty and Courses

During the 1930s Columbia's faculty in sociology was almost as mixed a group as the students—in background, sociologi-

---

* The second part of the project was begun in 1940, put aside during my four years in uniform, and thereafter faded away. But Milton M. Gordon, who in 1941 studied with me briefly at Columbia and many years later was my good friend and esteemed colleague at Massachusetts, ably carried out a similar project in *Social Class in American Sociology* (Durham, N.C.: Duke University Press, 1958).

† This foreshortened account of finding a publisher omits my obligation to Stanley Burnshaw, then head of Dryden Press, who, during that busy day in New York, gave a total stranger excellent advice about preparing manuscripts for publication and recommended *Class and American Sociology* to Dial Press. Pete Waller had urged that I discuss my publishing problem with Burnshaw—another example of Pete's wise counsel.

cal perspective, and scholarly interest. This heterodoxy, however, had only recently emerged, beginning in the late twenties. From 1894, when Franklin H. Giddings was appointed to the first chair in sociology, until his retirement in 1928, the department had been something of a one-man show, its diversification retarded by the domination of this Father of American sociology.* But in 1929, following a dozen years at the University of Toronto and two at Barnard College, Robert Morrison MacIver became departmental executive officer. And in 1931, after four years as secretary of the Social Science Research Council, Robert S. Lynd joined the department as full professor. Sociology at Columbia was powerfully influenced by these two strikingly dissimilar scholar-teachers. But there was no MacIver-Lynd duopoly.

Four members of the faculty were carry-overs from the Giddings regime: Samuel McCune Lindsay, Robert E. Chaddock, Alva A. Tenney, and Frank A. Ross. Professor of social legislation for more than three decades (until 1939), prominent in public affairs in this country and abroad, and president for twenty years (1910–1930) of Columbia's policy-oriented Academy of Political Science, Lindsay had limited interest in theoretical sociology, but this distinguished activist was held in respect and affection by colleagues and students alike. Chaddock, a leading statistician and demographer and a kindly man who somehow put up with our mathematical ignorance, was a mainstay of the department until his suicide in 1940. Joining the department in the same year as Chaddock (1911) and retiring in 1936, Tenney was the sole survivor from earlier years who remained a staunch follower of his mentor Giddings (rather to the distress of his modish students), but Tenney also introduced the study of communications which was later to become under Paul Lazarsfeld a major research field at the university. Editor of the *Journal of the American Statistical Association* (as the successor to William F. Ogburn who had been a member of the Columbia faculty in the 1920s) until his move to Syracuse University in 1937, Ross was a splendid teacher and a gentle guide through what for many of us—even at that kindergarten stage of quantitative analysis—were the perils of statistics.

* During Giddings's final years, Samuel McCune Lindsay, referred to below, was executive officer of the Department of Sociology. A brief history of the department, from the beginning until the early 1950s, is provided by Seymour Martin Lipset in R. Gordon Hoxie et al., *A History of the Faculty of Political Science, Columbia University* (New York: Columbia University Press, 1955), chap. 13.

These four were part of what for those years was a large group of Columbia sociologists—regular members of the department, assorted auxiliaries, and visiting scholars. The regulars included, in addition to MacIver and Lynd, Theodore Abel, Bill Casey, John Innes, William Robinson, Alexander von Schelting, and Willard Waller. Affiliated with other divisions of the university, but playing major roles in the graduate program, were Edmund deS. Brunner of Teachers College, George A. Lundberg, research associate, and Bernhard J. Stern of University Extension (later the School of General Studies). My principal teachers, in the classroom and elsewhere, were MacIver, Lynd, Abel, and Waller; but the education of a beginner was also enriched by study with all but one of the following sociologists:

—Bill Casey, whose guidance and support had brought me to Columbia at the time of his own appointment in 1931, as noted earlier, continued his extraordinary teaching in the College; his courses were a spectacular feature of the undergraduate program. Casey's office, with its huge library and warmed by Bill's hospitality, was located in Fayerweather where he also offered graduate courses in his own brand of "critical theory." Many, perhaps most, graduate students, however, viewed the latter as a wide deviation from even a many-sided sociology—and as no firm basis for, say, dissertational research. In the graduate faculty, Casey was additionally handicapped by what seemed to be a stubborn refusal to publish any of his extensive writing. This no doubt accounted for postponement of his promotion to senior rank until two years before his retirement in 1959.* At the age of eighty-seven, Bill died in 1978.

—John Innes, assistant to MacIver and junior member of the faculty, taught tough courses, one of which, in research methods, I was to inherit in 1941. But John's major contributions to the graduate program lay elsewhere: he was the chief initiator of newcomers into the life-ways of the group; an informal but splendid tutor of sociological neophytes; an effective liaison between faculty and students; for both, an unrelenting critic of shoddy scholarly workmanship. And, for some of us lucky ones, a warm friend.†

* This characteristic failure to promote a nonpublishing *scholar* (the correct term in this case) has not lessened Bill Casey's legendary status as a great teacher of lasting influence among hundreds of his former students.

† John Innes left Columbia in 1941, taught briefly at Ohio State University, and died after several years of government service in Washington, D.C.

—Bill Robinson, who gained junior faculty status when Frank Ross left Columbia in 1937, was a young sociologist of outstanding promise whose statistical expertise was extensively exploited by the graduate students. For Bill's face-to-face tutelage, given with great generosity and with friendly tolerance of our deficiencies, lessened widespread anxieties about an oft-dreaded requirement and enabled a good many of us to face the doctoral examinations with at least a modicum of confidence.

—Alexander von Schelting, called "Von" by his colleagues and a few brash students, came to Columbia as a visiting lecturer in the mid-thirties, remained for several years, and returned to Europe at the start of World War II. A shy bachelor and a strikingly handsome blonde with the non-American manners of the German academy, von Schelting had already published an important work on Max Weber.* My most vivid memories of Von are three: a small seminar in which we spent an entire term translating the first few pages of *Wirtschaft und Gesellschaft,* with debates about the meaning of each sentence or phrase; a friendly but prolonged confrontation during my oral examination about Marx's concept of "ideology," with Frank Ross in the adjacent chair whispering "shut up—he's killing time"; an all-night ramble in Harlem initiating Von into the wonders of jazz, reefers, and interracial frolicking. Von Schelting, clearly, was a full-fledged member of the group.

—Edmund deS. Brunner, although a professor at Teachers College (later he became a regular member of the Department of Sociology), was a major figure in Columbia's sociological establishment—but, to my loss, a scholar with whom I did not study. In the 1930s, Brunner had already won international prestige through his extensive research in America and Asia, several volumes and numerous papers on rural social life, and service with various federal and state governments. Throughout the decade and many years thereafter, this eminent rural sociologist was among Columbia's foremost scholar-activists.

—George Lundberg, whose *Social Research* (1929) had given a foretaste of his later powerful advocacy of a positivistic sociology, was a short-term but dynamic and influential Columbia sociologist while director of the ground-breaking study of leisure in Westchester County.† George's graduate course in methodology,

* *Max Webers Wissenschaftslehre* (Tubingen: J.C.B. Mohr, 1934).
† George A. Lundberg, Mirra Komarovsky, and Mary Alice McIrney, *Leisure: A Suburban Study* (New York: Columbia University Press, 1934).

his controversial role in the monthly "MacIver Seminar" (described below), and the many after-hour sessions with students and others were instructive and exciting events in the early 1930s. In later years, none of us who then had been Columbians was surprised that George Lundberg had become the field's most able and eloquent spokesman for a "natural science" of sociology.

—Bernhard Stern, who had been appointed initially in 1927, was a full-time lecturer throughout the thirties and in later years, giving courses on the family, medical organization, and social stratification, fields in which he published widely. As the only Marxist scholar among Columbia's sociologists, Stern performed a highly useful function in the graduate program (his course on "class" was the sole formal offering even remotely related to my dissertation subject), but he never became a member of the Department of Sociology. While Stern's Marxism and his open support of the political left may have brought about this exclusion, as some of us assumed in the reddish thirties, we had no firm ground for this antiestablishmentarian speculation. We did have good educational reason, however, to welcome an informed Marxist sociologist as a teaching member of the faculty.

Our teaching faculty included a large assortment of scholars from other fields—in keeping with the axiom that "a good sociologist must be more than a sociologist," and institutionally supported by the requirement of a minor in a related discipline. Thus a graduate program in sociology might have involved study with anthropologists, economists, historians, philosophers, political scientists, psychologists, or, in some rare cases, mathematicians. My own minor subject was political theory, represented at Columbia in those years almost solely by Robert MacIver. But, in addition, I attended an unprincipled miscellany of lectures and seminars: anthropological theory with Franz Boas, patterns of culture with Ruth Benedict, migration with Carter Goodrich, intellectual history with Merle Curti, social psychology with Gardner Murphy, revolutions with Vladimir Simkhovitch, and, as a postdoctoral eye opener in 1939, the first run-through with Ralph Linton and Abram Kardiner in their famous joint seminar on the psychoanalysis of primitive cultures. This pursuit of scattered academic riches was also a kind of preparation for the oral examination. On the examining committees were representatives of all departments in the Faculty of Political Science: Anthropology, Economics, History, Mathematical Statistics, Public Law and Government, and Sociology. Safeguards against parochialism were plentiful.

A precaution of another sort was the requirement in

statistics. Assurance that all Ph.D.'s in sociology possessed some degree of competence in quantitative analysis was largely the responsibility of three members of the department, Robert Chaddock, Frank Ross, and, later, Bill Robinson. But more often than not a watchdog role was played by the formidable mathematical statistician Harold Hotelling of Economics whose likely presence at the orals aroused in many of us a trepidation approaching terror. Like other unwise and overly fearful graduate students, I had postponed study of statistics until my final courses, and approached the orals practicing such magic as I knew to prevent Hotelling from attending the exercise; were he to examine me, failure was assured. My efforts had been to no avail, I assumed, when (after gentle questioning by Chaddock and Ross) Hotelling arrived about fifteen minutes before the conclusion of the scheduled three hours. But at that crucial point the chairman, Professor MacIver, probably with a mentor's compassion, declared the examination's termination. The resulting "Pass" was another confirmation of my lucky star.

Confrontation with the examiners, sans Hotelling, took place four years after my decision to continue part-time study for the Ph.D. This came about through a three-course program in the summer of 1933 taught by George Lundberg, Talcott Parsons, and Florian Znaniecki. If these courses could be survived, which I viewed as problematic, perhaps the goal of the doctorate was non-utopian. No doubt the permissiveness of the relaxed summer session was helpful on this score, but there were other favoring circumstances. Undergraduate study in psychology and philosophy had given me some background for Lundberg's behaviorism and logical positivism, and George's informal sessions in a West Side bar were doubly instructive. I had very little background for Parsons's course in theory—his lectures were largely from an early draft of *The Structure of Social Action*—but Talcott's generous "tutorials" during evening gatherings at the Innes's apartment were highly useful. Although Znaniecki's philosophical sociology was beyond me at times, his analysis of social action and the "humanistic coefficient" was consistent with my growing conviction—strengthened by my study with MacIver—that fundamental differences distinguish the natural and the social sciences. Whatever else I may have learned from these three remarkable scholar-teachers, their contrasting conceptions of the field were a lasting lesson in the theoretical and methodological diversity of sociology.

Beyond Fayerweather: Education from Abroad

In the 1930s, Columbia's department of less than ten members was the largest concentration of sociologists in New York. There were of course smaller contingents in other schools, but at the beginning of the decade the total number of the city's certified sociologists probably was less than that of the faculty of any one of several departments in American universities today. Following the rise of Nazism in Germany, however, New York's intellectual wealth in the social sciences (and in other fields) was significantly increased by the emigré scholars who arrived from Europe, some as members of the Frankfurt Institute of Social Research and others who joined the new "University in Exile" of the New School for Social Research. The fructifying influence of these newcomers upon both the theoretical and empirical work of American social scientists is an important part of this country's intellectual history.* And their impact upon at least some Columbians was substantial.

Exchange between Columbia sociologists and the Frankfurt group was assured by the Institute's new location on West 117th Street, a few doors from Fayerweather Hall. In 1934 these headquarters in a Columbia-owned building were made available by the university's conservative President Nicholas Murray Butler, with the backing of a number of Columbia's nonconservative faculty including Robert MacIver and Robert Lynd. (Following his account of the negotiations between President Butler and Max Horkheimer, Martin Jay concludes: "And so the International Institute for Social Research, as revolutionary and Marxist as it had appeared in Frankfurt in the twenties, came to settle in the center of the capitalist world, New York City.")† During its first year at Columbia, where the Institute was to reside for a decade, all but two of its most active members—Theodore Adorno who remained in Europe for several years and Erich Fromm who had come to the United States in 1932—joined the young and vigorous director Max Horkheimer in residence on Morningside Heights. Thus by 1935, among our nearby neighbors was a cadré of powerful scholars and social critics: Horkheimer, Leo Lowenthal, Her-

---

* As recorded, for example, in Donald Fleming and Bernard Bailyn, eds., *The Intellectual Migration: Europe and America, 1930–60* (Cambridge: Harvard University Press, 1969); see especially the essays by Paul F. Lazarsfeld, T. W. Adorno, and H. Stuart Hughes.

† *The Dialectical Imagination: A History of the Frankfurt School and the Institute of Social Research, 1923–1950* (Boston: Little, Brown, 1973), p. 39.

bert Marcuse, Franz Neumann, Friedrich Pollack, and Karl Witt-fogel.

Of the Columbia sociologists, MacIver and Abel, prompted no doubt by their concern with theoretical issues, and Lynd and Innes, in keeping with their radical sympathies, were especially interested in the work of these scholar-critics; Lynd would have welcomed their formal affiliation with the department. But Hork-heimer and his colleagues were eager to maintain the Institute's long-standing (since 1923) independence as a center of what came to be known as "critical theory" and related research. Moreover, they had no wish to become involved in the growing departmental division between MacIver and Lynd, both of whom were friends in the Columbia court. Beginning in 1936, however, lectures and seminars by Horkheimer, Lowenthal, and others were offered in the Extension Division of the university and on a less formal basis lively intellectual exchange developed between Columbians and members of the Frankfurt group.*

My all-too-limited exploitation of these educational op-portunities was restricted by a heavy teaching schedule and con-strained by minimal familiarity with the earlier work of the Insti-tute, which was limited to bits of information and rumor about how the Frankfurt theorists were bringing together my generation's foremost heroes, Marx and Freud. I did attend a few Columbia lectures and informal sessions at 117th Street, but with no appre-ciation of the Hegelianisms and other dialectical intricacies of Horkheimer and Company. In my youthful undertakings, how-ever, I incurred professional and educational indebtedness to scholars at the Institute of two quite different kinds.

The first of these, of no historical but only personal sig-nificance, was an invitation, in 1936, from Herbert Marcuse, an editor of the Institute's journal, the *Zeitschrift für Sozialfor-schung*. Even then Marcuse was an imposing figure—intellectu-ally, physically, and as a consumer of cigars—and his suggestion that I review a recently published volume on sociological theory

---

* This skimpy account refers to the years 1934–1940. Following his appoint-ment to the faculty in the latter year and the establishment of the Bureau of Applied Social Research, Paul Lazarsfeld, generally a strong supporter of the Institute, recommended affiliation of its "empirical wing" with the Bureau, a recommendation approved by the Department of Sociology. After pro-longed negotiation the invitation was declined in 1946, presumably because of Horkheimer's poor health. Details of this episode are presented by Jay, *Dialectical Imagination,* pp. 219–20.

was altogether unexpected. The possibility that my own words would appear in the heady *Zeitschrift* was also a rather fearsome prospect for, although I was already a college teacher of three years' standing, the review would be my first appearance on the printed page—and now a rereading of my comments on the work by Harold A. Phelps clearly reveals the limitations of a raw beginner.* This first effort at reviewing, however, was a foretaste of my large involvement with this marginal scholarly activity in later years, which was to bring me a measure of professional visibility.

My much greater indebtedness to the Frankfurt scholars, shared with many others, was also an introduction of sorts, but in this case to a body of theory and research of historical and sociological significance. Until two or three years after its re-establishment at Columbia in 1934, I had been only vaguely aware of long-standing efforts at the Institute to bring into a neo-Marxist interpretation of contemporary society a psychoanalytical interpretation of contemporary man—efforts, as I was to learn, revealed in works by Adorno, Fromm, Horkheimer, Lowenthal, and Marcuse. To try to encompass within a single theoretical scheme what were then usually viewed as irreconcilable conceptions of the human condition was a foolish and futile exercise according to the orthodox, whether disciples of Marx or Freud.

But in the mid-thirties two developments took place that aroused the interest of young Columbians (and others, of course) in the Institute's studies. On the one hand, at least a few American intellectuals of the left, including some academicians, were becoming increasingly critical of a Marxism that yielded no adequate explanation of what seemed to be the massive psychological appeal of the new "totalitarianisms" and thus were attracted by the synthetic neo-Marxism of the Frankfurt group, European leftists who had been close observers of the rise of Nazism. Of a quite different and less momentous nature, on the other hand, American social scientists—for example, Ruth Benedict and Robert Lynd at Columbia, John Dollard and others at Yale's Institute of Human Relations, and James S. Plant in *Personality and the Culture Pattern* (1937)—were giving renewed emphasis

---

* The review of Phelp's *Principles and Laws of Sociology* (1936) concludes with the ill-conceived statement: "He claims the major task of sociology to be 'the reorganization of its conceptual framework' but has produced rather an eclectic confusion of synthesis and anthology" (*Zeitschrift fur Sozialforschung* 6, no. 1 [1937]).

to an ancient truism by probing the interrelations of "culture and personality," "social structure and character structure," and similar versions of the interdependence of society and individual. For some of us, these separate developments, rooted in the strikingly dissimilar circumstances of European neo-Marxism and American academic innovation, were related reasons to explore both the earlier and ongoing work of the Institute for Social Research.*

These recollections, as I have suggested, are based on feeble contacts with only a few of the Institute's members in the 1930s. For younger sociologists in the 1980s they may seem to refer to a hoary and minor episode in the history of the Frankfurt School. For during recent decades—at least since 1953, the date of the publication of the seminal work *Character and Social Structure* in which Hans Gerth and C. Wright Mills sought to link theoretical perspectives of Marx and Freud (and of Weber and Mead)—critical theory here and abroad has become a conspicuous feature of the sociological enterprise. The present era is one in which the return of Horkheimer, Adorno, and the Institute to Frankfurt in 1950, with great fanfare, is itself sometimes seen as an ancient event;† in which Mills's *The Sociological Imagination* (1959) is often viewed as an early landmark in critical theory; in which Herbert Marcuse, for many years an ex-member of the Institute and as a teacher in American universities, functioned as a guru of the New Left; in which serious students of critical theory must

---

* During the late 1930s the Institute supported research related to its long-standing interests, for example, Komarovsky's *The Unemployed Man and His Family,* referred to above, which pursued a theme of the Institute's collective work, *Studien uber Autoritat und Familie* (Paris, 1936). Studies by associates of the Institute and published in this country in later years include, among others, the following volumes: Nathan W. Ackerman and Marie Jahoda, *Anti-Semitism and Emotional Disorder: A Psychoanalytical Interpretation* (New York: Harper, 1950); Theodor W. Adorno et al., *The Authoritarian Personality* (New York: Harper, 1950); Bruno Bettelheim and Morris Janowitz, *Dynamics of Prejudice: A Psychological and Sociological Study of Veterans* (New York: Harper, 1950); Erich Fromm, *Escape from Freedom* (New York: Farrar and Rinehart, 1941); Leo Lowenthal and Norbert Guterman, *Prophets of Deceit: A Study of the Techniques of the American Agitator* (New York: Harper, 1949); Franz Neumann, *Behemoth: The Structure and Practice of National Socialism, 1933–1944.* This exhibit suggests the magnitude and range of the Institute's contributions to the social sciences in the United States.
† A brief account of the post–World War II history of the Institute for Social Research is to be found in Jay, *Dialectical Imagination,* Epilogue.

cope with the dialectics and linguistics of the Institute's Jurgen Habermas; and in which, as a sure sign of legitimacy, graduate and even undergraduate courses in critical theory are offered in a good many American schools. None of this, surely, was foreseen at Columbia in the thirties.

Throughout most of the decade Columbians, including graduate students in sociology, had access to a second group of emigré scholars, the "University in Exile" of the New School for Social Research. In keeping with its establishment in 1919 as a haven for such native "refugee" academics as Charles A. Beard, James Harvey Robinson, and Thorstein Veblen, the New School's remarkable President Alvin Johnson had brought together a band of social scientists, most of them from Germany, who in 1933 began their tenure as a distinguished graduate faculty.* Thus, in addition to our immediate neighbors on 117th Street, in Greenwich Village on 12th Street a more distant but equally instructive array of lectures and seminars in the social sciences was available. The graduate faculty featured, among others, its first dean and eminent sociological economist Emil Lederer, a prominent socialist, whose *State of the Masses* (1940) nevertheless was a powerful challenge to the main-line Marxist interpretation of the rise and appeal of fascism; Max Wertheimer, leading Gestalt psychologist and anti-Freudian, who brought to the faculty his research collaborator, the world-famous musicologist Erich von Hornbostel; Freida Wunderlich, renowned authority on labor; and the sociologists Carl Mayer, Albert Salomon, and Hans Speier.

This assembly of notables at the New School was not an "old competitor" of the Frankfurt Institute at Columbia, as recorded in Martin Jay's volume. This suggests that the latter's neo-Marxism and Freudian coloration were anathema to the faculty of the University in Exile.† The two groups, to be sure, stood in sharp contrast: the Institute's members united by long-standing institutional ties and similar ideological convictions, the scholars at the New School representing a large diversity of background, theoretical orientation, and political viewpoint. But the depiction of this graduate faculty as joined in an anti-Marxist and anti-Freudian confrontation with the Frankfurt group is inconsistent

* The name "University in Exile," chosen by Johnson, was later changed to "The Graduate Faculty of Political and Social Science." The faculty's recruitment, financing, and so on are described in Johnson's autobiography, *Pioneer's Progress* (New York: Viking, 1952), chap. 31.
† Jay, *Dialectical Imagination.*

with my recollections—and has been strongly challenged by a major participant in the alleged rivalry, Hans Speier.*

As in the case of my limited study with the Frankfurt scholars, I took only small advantage of the educational opportunities presented by the University in Exile, but even so, again with long-range gains. Thus in lectures by Albert Salomon (and a year or two before the intensive course with Alexander von Schelting, referred to above) I struggled with Salomon's difficult but keen analysis of the theoretical methodology of Max Weber. From Max Wertheimer, in informal sessions, I learned a bit about Gestalt psychology, years before I encountered Kurt Koffka's powerful legacy at Smith College. Two or three lectures by Frieda Wunderlich taught me something about similarities and differences between the working classes of Europe and America. And in the late 1930s, an exciting seminar given jointly by Karen Horney and Erich Fromm (not as a Graduate Faculty course) stimulated what developed into a lasting interest in the sociological contributions and limitations of psychoanalysis. These were important lessons for a student of sociology.

But the finest long-range benefit derived from the University in Exile, altogether unforeseen in the 1930s, was my meeting with Hans Speier. Speier, as a fellow student of another promising youngster, Talcott Parsons, had received the doctorate from Heidelberg in 1928. His early studies in Germany of salaried workers and in social theory had already established his scholarly bona fides when he joined the New School Faculty in 1933. I first met Hans Speier a year later in the "MacIver Seminar" at Columbia where he gave an excellent paper on Karl Mannheim. The paper, as I learned decades later, was Speier's first piece in English, an experience he recently described as laden with anxiety; but at the time he impressed all of us with his erudition, analytical prowess, modest confidence, impeccable manners, and indeed what seemed to be his full command of our native language. These virtues were to decorate Speier's career: as a teacher at the New School until 1942 (and in 1947–48), as a communications and intelligence expert with the Office of War Information and the Department of State during World War II, as the head of the Social Science Division and later chairman of the Research Council of the Rand Corporation from 1948 until 1969, as a periodic

---

* Speier's criticisms of Jay's several instances of this depiction appear in his review of The Dialectical Imagination in the American Political Science Review 70, no. 4 (December 1976).

visitor to West Germany and author of such significant studies as *German Rearmament and Atomic War* (1957) and *Divided Berlin* (1961), as the Robert Morrison MacIver Professor of Sociology and Political Science at the University of Massachusetts from 1969 to 1973, and, all along, as the author of distinguished works in social theory, the sociology of knowledge, social stratification, political and military sociology, and the sociology of literature.* In 1948, thanks to Speier's colleague at Rand, Joseph Goldsen, my acquaintance with this rarely rivaled contributor to both scholarship and policy making was renewed. In the following years, including the period of our colleagueship at Massachusetts, I have had the good fortune to claim Hans Speier as my friend.

In the 1930s my contacts with members of the New School's graduate faculty, as I have suggested, were all too haphazard. But they did include casual meetings with three or four scholars who were brought to the faculty not long after its establishment in 1933. I recall brief encounters with the political philosophers Max Ascoli and Leo Strauss, so different in background and perspective but both men of great learning, and with the sociologist Carl Mayer whose more gentle disposition tended to obscure his intellectual strength. Many years later my acquaintance with a New School scholar was to be renewed and strengthened, for in 1964 at the Max Weber Centennial Congress in Heidelberg and during five additional weeks of travel in West Germany, Carl Mayer and I were companions as fellow guests of the Bonn government. A final instance of my later-day relations with the New School, recorded with no decent modesty, was a day-long session in the early 1960s with the School's graduate faculty followed by an invitation from President Henry David to become its dean. Had I accepted the post, the new dean would have been a far cry

---

* A large part of Speier's earlier work, originally published in Germany and the United States before 1952, appears in *Social Order and the Risks of War* (New York: George W. Stewart, 1952), and several of his subsequent studies are included in *Force and Folly: Essays on Foreign Affairs and the History of Ideas* (Cambridge: The M.I.T. Press, 1969). Speier's *Die Angestetlen von dem Nationalsozialismus* (Gottingen: Vendenhoeck and Ruprecht, 1977) is an enlarged revision of his early work on salaried workers; part of the original study was translated into English as a Works Progress Administration project at Columbia under the title, *The Salaried Employee in German Society* (1939). His most recent volume is a fascinating, autobiographical account of his experiences in Germany following World War II, *From the Ashes of Disgrace: A Journal from Germany, 1945–1955* (Amherst: University of Massachusetts Press, 1981).

from the brilliant Emil Lederer who graced that office in the 1930s.

During the 1930s and continuing into the 1960s, interrelations between the New School for Social Research and Columbia University were highlighted by Robert MacIver's important roles at the School. For several decades MacIver was President Alvin Johnson's frequent counselor and "long-cherished friend";* he was a member of the board of trustees for a great many years; he received an honorary degree (one of eight such awards) from the New School in 1950; and in his early eighties, in 1963–64, he was the School's president and subsequently its chancellor. But as a younger man, Robert MacIver was first and foremost a scholar-teacher at Columbia.

Robert Morrison MacIver

During my first year at Columbia (1931–32) I was enrolled in the Department of Public Law and Government, with no intention of seeking a degree in sociology, an unknown but suspect subject. But one of my courses, an exciting tour through political thought from Machiavelli to Laski and Lippmann, was taught by Robert MacIver, Lieber Professor of Political Philosophy and Sociology. MacIver's occasional references to sociology and to such sociologists as Max Weber and Vilfredo Pareto implied some scholarly reputability of the subject. This apparent endorsement by Columbia's ranking political theorist, together with the location of my undergraduate mentor Bill Casey in the department MacIver headed, encouraged me to change my major field. Thus, beginning in 1932 and continuing throughout my active teaching years and up to the present, I have been a student of Robert Mac-Iver's scholarly work and, in aspiration, a follower of his sociological wisdom.

---

* The phrase is from MacIver's autobiography, *As a Tale That Is Told* (Chicago and London: University of Chicago Press, 1968), p. 166; this volume includes several references to Alvin Johnson, among them passages from Johnson's personal letters which document their long and close relationship. Curiously, in Johnson's own autobiography, *Pioneer's Progress*, which is laden with accounts of his relations with contemporaries in the academy and elsewhere, there is not a single reference to MacIver—a reminder to this writer, and to the readers of the present recollections, that memory may be dangerously selective.

In the 1930s, for many of us at Columbia, Robert MacIver was a splendid teacher, as various testimonials have stressed.* Although not a spectacular lecturer nor a didactical virtuoso, MacIver brought to the classroom (and elsewhere) superior and wide-ranging scholarship, a masterful ability to expose the epistemological roots of theoretical issues, critical prowess and impatience with shoddy intellectual goods, a nonpolemical approach to views with which he disagreed, a kindly wit that tempered the inevitable ironies of all good social analysis, and, to our great benefit, the rare capacity to push students to maximize whatever talents they possessed. "The difference between good teaching and poor teaching," MacIver tells us in his autobiography, "is like that between a clear-shining lamp and a smoky, flickering flame. . . . teaching is a high art, the most essential, the most significant of all the arts, and the prime utility of civilization."† In many ways, MacIver was an exemplar of this lofty—but surely inflated— evaluation of the teacher's social role.

MacIver's finest and most lasting contribution as a teacher had little to do with the inculcation of his system of social and political thought, which could be readily gleaned by study of such seminal and beautifully formulated works as *Community* (1917), *Elements of Social Science* (1921), *The Modern State* (1926), and *Society: Its Structure and Changes* (1931). Rather, in keeping with the worthiest aim of teaching, MacIver spurred his students to exploit their own capabilities and concerns, to bring their best to whatever scholarly undertakings aroused their interests, to become their own sociologists or political scientists. The point is well stated by one of his outstanding students: "There is no 'MacIver school' in sociology. The reason is obvious: MacIver trained minds not disciples. He demanded no personal loyalty to him or to his system of sociology and expected none. In fact, he

---

* Published statements testifying to MacIver's impact as a teacher include the many acknowledgments in books written by his former students, and more fully, the assessments by Harry Alpert, Daniel Bell, Robert Bierstedt, Michael E. Choukas, Elizabeth K. Nottingham, Charles H. Page, Vahan D. Sewny, Sophia M. Robinson, and Adolph S. Tomars in Alpert, ed., *Robert M. MacIver: Teacher and Sociologist* (Northampton, Mass.: Metcalf Printing and Publishing Co., 1953). Several similar testimonials were presented at the formal celebrations of MacIver's seventieth and seventy-fifth birthdays in 1952 and 1957.
† *As a Tale That Is Told,* p. 20.

encouraged, delighted in, and drew deep satisfaction from the growing intellectual independence of his students."*

The intellectual maturation of some of the advanced and more fortunate students was fostered by their participation in a monthly symposium, the famous "MacIver Seminar." Faculty of the sociology department were regulars, supplemented by visiting professors such as the philosophical sociologist Florian Znaniecki and the philosopher Mortimer Adler, sometimes by nearby scholars (I recall, for example, Hans Speier of the New School and John Dollard of Yale), for a time by the brilliant and then bombastic exchange student Edward Shils from Chicago, and by a handful of Columbia's graduate students. During the first, course-credited year in the seminar (once admitted, most of us were permitted to remain), student members tested their mettle by presenting papers in this assembly, an awesome but instructive exercise. The far more important and exciting educational experience, however, was provided by the hard-hitting exchanges between senior scholars: among others, the outspoken critic of all "armchair theory" Bob Lynd, the doughty defender of the scientific faith George Lundberg (whose sometimes prone position on the floor signaled his dismissal of the ongoing discussion), and MacIver himself whose soft-spoken observations failed to mask their intellectual power.† A vivid and, in my memory, faithful depiction of the MacIver seminar has been written by a fellow participant, Harry Alpert:

> For many of us at Columbia the highlight of our studies was the Seminar which for many years met Sunday evenings in the delightful, informal atmosphere of the MacIver apartments on Riverside Drive and Claremont Avenue. Here we participated in a truly intellectual rough-and-tumble, with no holds barred. We rarely came away with a sense of finality; nothing ever seemed to be resolved ultimately. But our complacencies were severely shaken and our implicit assumptions and presuppositions were thoroughly exposed. Frequently our fuzziness and ignorance and our failure to consider possible alternatives were made painfully apparent. We learned and were grateful for this exposure to genuinely free aca-

---

* Alpert, *Robert M. MacIver: Teacher and Sociologist*, p. 1.
† MacIver's recollections of his own enjoyment of the "fast and furious, and at times rather heated" controversies are recorded in *As a Tale That Is Told*, p. 136.

demic discussion. No dogmas were foisted upon us, no single system propounded. Conflicting viewpoints were thoroughly and respectfully considered. Though seldom in full agreement intellectually, we soon developed a common, unanimously shared respect for MacIver's intellectual acumen and his tolerant, but discriminating regard for those with whom he disagreed. Above all, we felt that he warmly respected us and we were encouraged. The leadership he gave us, the sterling example he set for us, and the respect he showed us all contributed to our feeling that here, indeed, was a great teacher.*

And here too, as MacIver's students learned, was no academic recluse, no "ivory tower theorist" as his colleague Lynd sometimes charged, but a renaissance man of many interests and many talents. Superb social theorist, MacIver was also a powerful libertarian, an outspoken social critic, and a frequent participant in public affairs. Faithful to his boyhood indoctrination in the outdoor joys of the Outer Hebrides and to his Scottish background, he was an ardent lover of nature (and became an acclaimed expert on mushrooms), a fine fisherman, and an aficionado of the spirits of his native land. Of deceptively slight appearance, he was a vigorous and tough-muscled activist who relished the challenges of golf and the greater demands of figure skating. Trained in the classics and literature, he had once aspired to be a novelist, had tried his hand as dramatist, and remained an enthusiast of fiction and the theater. A strictly disciplined worker, most of whose mornings were spent in his well-protected study, MacIver, like other creative writers, mixed hard industry with generous play—bridge, poker, and games of almost any kind including a complicated Canfield of his own invention.† MacIver retained these twin capacities into his final years: "I like to play almost as much as I like to work, and I enjoy working after playing just as I enjoy playing after working."‡

In his many activities, formal and informal, MacIver won both the admiration and affection of students and colleagues, partners and opponents on the links or at the gaming table, men and women. For all of us who knew him, Robert MacIver's engaging personality enhanced his role as scholar-teacher.

---

* Alpert, *Robert M. MacIver: Teacher and Sociologist,* p. 1.
† "My Private Game of Patience" is described in Appendix 2 of MacIver's autobiography, *As a Tale That Is Told,* pp. 252ff.
‡ Ibid., pp. 25–26.

MacIver's scholarly writings have provoked a large literature of exegesis and critical assessment; they need little comment
in these recollections.* But two of his important contributions, as
both author and teacher, have been generally neglected; each
manifests MacIver's "linking" role in the history of social thought.
First, although his own social theory draws heavily on the works
of Tonnies, Max and Alfred Weber, Simmel, Durkheim, and
other predecessors, MacIver's analytical system and conceptual re-
finements represent a unique and provocative synthesis: his linkage of the "classical" sociological tradition and modern-day sociological concerns surpasses, I believe, the efforts of any of his
American contemporaries. Second, and here he has few if any
rivals, MacIver's sociology effectively bridges the "two cultures"
of science and the humanities by making ample use of both the
classics in which he was trained and modern literature to which
he was devoted: "I have always regarded our great novelists and
dramatists," he affirmed in later years, "as better social scientists
than many professional contributors to the field."†

The "great novelists and dramatists," as well as the ancient
classics, no doubt provided MacIver inspiration for his own literary artistry, but their strong appeal for him, it seems, was also
substantive. For such works point up major themes addressed by
MacIver's social theory: social codes and social order, power and
authority, inequality and social hierarchy, social and cultural

* My own efforts to summarize MacIver's principal contributions include the
brief statement in Alpert, *Robert M. MacIver,* pp. 6–8, and the more detailed
treatment in N. S. Timasheff and G. A. Theodorson, *Sociological Theory: Its
Nature and Growth,* 4th ed. (New York: Random House, 1976), pp. 319–24.
MacIver's sociological work is ably assessed by Harry Alpert in Morroe Berger,
Theodore Abel, and C. H. Page, eds., *Freedom and Control in Modern So-
ciety* (New York: D. Van Nostrand, 1954), chap. 13; more recently by Alpert
in David L. Sills, ed., *International Encyclopedia of the Social Sciences* (New
York: Macmillan and The Free Press, 1968), vol. 9; by Leon Bramson in
Bramson, ed., *Robert MacIver on Community, Society, and Power* (Chicago:
University of Chicago Press, 1970), introduction; and by Robert Bierstedt in
American Sociological Theory (New York: Academic Press, 1981), chap. 6.
His political theory is reviewed by David Spitz in Berger, Abel, and Page,
chap. 14, and in *MacIver's Politics and Society,* ed. David Spitz (New York:
Atherton, 1969), introduction. Summaries and evaluations of MacIver's work
are included, of course, in numerous textbooks.
† *As a Tale That Is Told,* pp. 214–15. MacIver's "linking" role in both re-
spects referred to above is noted in Robert A. Nisbet's *The Social Bond* (New
York: Knopf, 1970), p. 41.

change, and, and, as an ever-present focus, the interpenetration of the individual life and changing society. This is to say that MacIver's concerns, unlike those of so many contemporary sociologists, were "the great sociological issues of a rapidly changing world," as he once put it.* As a sociologist, he had little interest in either the tactics of social life or what he viewed as the obsession with methodology. On this score, MacIver's convictions were close to those of Robert Lynd.

Robert Staughton Lynd

Soon after he joined the Columbia faculty in 1931 Robert Lynd became a power in the sociology department, second only to MacIver. Although both men were deeply concerned with major social and political issues and with the relevance of social science for social practice, they differed sharply in background and schooling, intellectual orientation, sociological perspective, and in their views about the goals of graduate training. These differences, however, were well known to MacIver when he supported Lynd's appointment and were perceived as advantageous, not detrimental, for the development of a strong and diversified graduate faculty, one that would include both an eminent social theorist and a prominent exponent of field research. Yet, almost from the beginning of their colleagueship, a mounting antagonism between MacIver and Lynd emerged that sometimes disrupted departmental affairs and ultimately led to a permanent break between these two superior scholars.† (At the dinner celebrating MacIver's seventieth birthday in 1952, where Lynd and I were seated side by side during A. A. Berle's eloquent eulogy, he remorsefully told me that, rather than judging the celebrant to be a wrongheaded professional opponent over the many years, he should have realized that MacIver's humanitarianism and liberal creed were firm ground for a strong collegial alliance.) Lynd's Columbia appointment, it was rumored at the time, was prompted by what certain university authorities viewed as

* From an unreferenced passage, quoted in Howard W. Odum, *American Sociology: The Story of Sociology in the United States through 1950* (New York: Longmans' Green, 1951), p. 194.

† MacIver's own account of this affair is presented in *As a Tale That Is Told*, pp. 137–38. Below I question MacIver's depiction of Lynd as a "primarily utilitarian" educator who advocated "professional service" as the overriding goal of graduate training.

a sociology department overweighted on the side of abstract theory: the new position would bring "balance" to the program. Lynd, although not yet forty and inexperienced in graduate teaching, had strong credentials as a research-oriented and "down-to-earth" sociologist. He had recently completed four years as executive officer of the Social Science Research Council, he had written a fact-laden critical report on "The People as Consumers" for President Hoover's Commission on Recent Social Trends, he served on the Consumers' Advisory Board of the National Recovery Administration, and, most important, he was the co-author (with Helen Merrell Lynd) of *Middletown* (1929), the acclaimed and widely influential study of the "culture" of an American community. These accomplishments gave firm support to Robert Lynd's first (and only) academic appointment: a full professorship in Columbia's graduate faculty.

The several contributions of this newcomer to Columbia's social science program in the 1930s (and later) were impressive— as a proponent and exemplar of field research, as a promoter of graduate training in empirical methods, as an advocate of cross-disciplinary study and scholarship, as an affable and seemingly indefatigable counselor of graduate students. And during these years, Lynd's sociological perspective, shaped in part by the momentous events of the decade, took on a much sharper focus than the inclusive approach of his earlier *Middletown,* a kind of "social anthropology of contemporary life."* *Middletown in Transition* (1937), at least an equally influential work, gave special attention to the community's business-dominated power hierarchy and its structure of social classes, features of Middletown reported but not emphasized in the original study. Economic and political control, class and class conflict, and, especially, the phenomenon of power became Lynd's principal sociological concerns in the thirties and remained so thereafter.†

As sociologist and academic man, Lynd was seen by many of his colleagues and students as something of a deviant, and on

---

* The phrase is from Clark Wissler's foreword to *Middletown: A Study in American Culture* (New York: Harcourt, Brace, 1929), p. vi. The Lynds' "six main-trunk activities," presumably subsuming "all the things that people do" in Middletown (p. 4.), represented a modification of Wissler's nine-category "universal culture pattern."

† In the late 1930s, Lynd introduced a graduate course on power and in subsequent years planned to publish a book on the subject; the volume, to which many of us looked forward eagerly, unfortunately had not been completed at the time of Lynd's death in 1971.

several counts. He expressed little interest in, and appeared to have little knowledge of, the sociological classics; he once startled some of us by asking whether or not he "should read that fellow Weber." Of the earlier American social scientists of giant stature, he gave first rank to the unorthodox Thorstein Veblen. Among his favorite contemporaries were such pioneers in the study of culture and personality as Edward Sapir and Margaret Mead, the experimental social psychologist Gardner Murphy, and the exponents of sociological psychiatry, Lawrence K. Frank, Karen Horney, and James S. Plant. To be sure, there was no "main line" in the sociology of the thirties (or, contrary to a commonly held view, in the sociology of any period), but Bob Lynd's students were exposed to what were then unconventional and innovative ideas about behavior and society that were rarely met in the classrooms of the times.

During his initial years at Columbia, in his formal courses, Lynd, for at least some of us, was both an effective and a frustrating teacher. On the one hand, his lectures and class discussion were enlivened by a rare, nonacademic, earthy style, by colorful and instructive illustrations drawn from his research and professional background, and by powerfully stated personal conviction. On the other hand, probably in part as reflection of his lack of classroom experience, Lynd's lecture notes consisted of huge stacks of five-by-eight cards filled with quotations from scholarly works which he would read relentlessly until interrupted by brash student plotters—we had learned early on that to get Lynd away from his cards was to replace dreary recital with stimulating and rewarding give-and-take between professor and pupil. Quite apart from this challenging game, which involved only a few of us, most students in his popular courses found Lynd's major achievements as a classroom teacher in these early years to be revelation and inspiration: his informative and forceful lessons aroused their interest in the pressing problems of a troubled society.

Bob Lynd's greatest strengths as an instructor, however, were not on display in the classroom, but in informal sessions during open-ended office hours and as a commentator on and keen critic of student work. His close reading of a course paper, a master's essay, or a doctoral thesis would often provoke a document of Lynd's observations almost as lengthy as the one submitted—sometimes to the distress of its author. But our training as sociologists and our self-assurance as professional beginners were enhanced by the meticulous attention Lynd gave to our writing efforts and by the many hours of informal discussion in his office where we were treated in collegial, not master-pupil, terms. Lynd's great generosity, his disdain of "professorialisms," his eagerness to learn from his students were important but too often unrealized desiderata of effective graduate teaching—as I was to appreciate more fully in later years.

In the thirties, Bob Lynd was an unusually conscientious teacher-scholar of seemingly inexhaustible energy and a bear for work. He was also a stickler for very high standards, not only with respect to his own and others' academic output, but also with regard to personal deportment. On this score the more fun-loving among us were sometimes unwitting victims of what appeared to be a curious ambiguity in Lynd's relations with students. The friendly, "man-to-man," and free-wheeling sessions, which we greatly prized, were at times offset by Lynd's private but strong disapproval of what he judged to be intolerable disregard of conventional norms of conduct (some of us, alas, did not conceal our enjoyment of youthful follies). In a recent memoir on a later period, Lynd is depicted aptly as "the saint, the moralist, who set the goals" of Columbia's sociology department.* His moralism, in my perspectival view, handicapped Lynd's otherwise splendid guidance of budding sociologists.

Lynd's moralism, it may be surmised, was the psychological basis of his powerful reformistic bent and his deep concern with the inequalities and injustices of social life. For a brief period in the thirties, Lynd was strongly attracted by the political left, and this ideological flirtation, I suspect, was also anchored in his moral convictions. But in later years, Lynd, always the moralist, not only condemned scholarly work that appeared to be influenced by the changing Communist party line, but expressed his repugnance of such violations of academic canons in student recommendations and departmental personnel actions.† In the mid-thirties, however, when so many academics were tempted by the nonrevolutionary, collaborationist program of the American CP, Lynd's short-lived dalliance with the left was consistent with his moral concerns.

Lynd's status as a leading social scientist and social critic

* Seymour Martin Lipset, "Some Personal Notes for a History of the Department of Sociology at Columbia," mimeographed (Stanford: Stanford University, 1977).
† Lipset supplies information on this score in the paper cited above, and contrasts Lynd's strong antileftism with the presumably less concerned position of his colleagues Robert Merton and Paul Lazarsfeld.

was assured by the publication of *Middletown in Transition* in 1937. In the following year he delivered the prestigious Stafford Little Lectures at Princeton University, the first sociologist to be invited to do so. The lectures, revised in the light of extensive discussion in which I had the good fortune to participate with such senior seminarians as Marie Jahoda and Paul Lazarsfeld, were published in 1939 as *Knowledge for What? The Place of Social Science in American Culture.* This hard-hitting volume decried the cultural conformism of social scientists, challenged them to break loose from both traditional, abstract theory-building and the more recent preoccupation with frequently pointless data-gathering, took strong issue with the positivist conception of value-free social science, and called for the replacement of the latter's established disciplinary divisions by policy-relevant study of the pressing "problem areas" of social life.

Knowledge for What? was widely hailed, especially by graduate students and younger teachers, and widely criticized, not only by defenders of current orthodoxies, but by scholars who shared many of Lynd's values, including his colleague MacIver. In what he much later called "a rather injudicious action,"* MacIver published a long review of the book praising Lynd for his "vigorous, challenging style," a "lively vision of the American scene," a "vivid sense of the tangle and frustration of human affairs," and an awareness of the "dangers of narrow specialization." But in most of the essay MacIver charged his fellow Columbian with grievous scholarly delinquencies: the view that cultural anthropology should be the guideline for all social science; the identification of institutions and "culture" with the behavior of individuals, disregarding the reality of social relations and social systems; almost total neglect of classical works in the social sciences, the "enduring systems of thought"; a utilitarianism blind to the search for knowledge for its own sake. Lynd, in the same issue of the journal publishing the review, answered these accusations under the caption "Intelligence Must Fight," elaborating the principal arguments of *Knowledge for What?*, emphasizing the "leap-frog" relationship between theory and practice in all science, and concluding that social scientists must "find in the struggles of men to live more abundantly the values that motivate their work."† This public debate between Columbia's foremost

* *As a Tale That Is Told,* p. 137. Here MacIver identified his review of *Knowledge for What?* as the "breaking point" in the prolonged difficulties between him and Lynd.

† *Survey Graphic* 28, no. 8 (August 1939): 496–99.

sociologists stands, I believe, as an exciting intellectual event in the history of American social science—a debate concerning issues that persist today.*

Soon after the 1930s, the later history of Columbia's sociology department was significantly affected by the opposing orientations of Robert MacIver and Bob Lynd. In 1941, both Robert K. Merton and Paul F. Lazarsfeld (who had been a part-time departmental lecturer for two years) became members of the faculty, and the appointment of each of these sociological giants-to-be had the backing of a contending senior professor. MacIver, eminent theorist and long-time advocate of study of the urban community, strongly supported Merton who had already displayed great promise in both of these areas. Lynd, as an exponent of empirical research and technical professional training, pushed the candidacy of Lazarsfeld whose work in methodology and communications research had gained considerable attention. Within a very few years after both of these young scholars became assistant professors, the MacIver-Lynd controversies were replaced by Columbia's collaborative sociological regime of Bob Merton and Paul Lazarsfeld.

Theodore Abel

During the years of rivalry between MacIver and Lynd, Columbia's sociologists became increasingly divided between support of one or the other, and in 1939 matters came to a head with the issuance of lengthy statements by each of the protagonists on the desirable future of the department. Lynd and younger advocates of empirical and quantitative research openly challenged the man who had been chairman for more than a decade. MacIver's allies included the more theoretically oriented sociologists: Bill Casey, the relative newcomer Willard Waller, and MacIver's earliest Columbia colleague, Theodore Abel.† Abel, who a few

* Historically, *Knowledge for What?* was the first major work in what became a series of important radical critiques of orthodox or "main-line" sociology, extending over several decades. Lynd's book, published in 1939, was followed twenty years later by C. Wright Mills's *The Sociological Imagination* and, after another decade, by Alvin Gouldner's *The Coming Crisis of Western Sociology* (1970). This periodic display of powerful criticism was also highlighted by the apposite and provocative work of a nonradical: P. A. Sorokin's *Fads and Foibles in Modern Sociology and Related Sciences* (1956). These four volumes constitute an appropriate reading list for those interested in an American version of "critical theory," circa 1940–1970.

† MacIver's account of this "active revolt," as he called it, is presented in *As a Tale That Is Told*, pp. 137–38.

years later was to serve as its executive officer, had joined the department as a lecturer in 1929 and, until his move to Hunter College in 1952, his contributions to both our sociological education and our adult maturation were an important part of Columbia's graduate student life.

I first glimpsed Ted Abel surrounded by starry-eyed co-eds in the "Theta" sorority house during my junior undergraduate year at Illinois where he was a visitor, although we did not meet at the time. But I was impressed by and decidedly envious of this stranger's military bearing, his handsome Slavic features, his slightly accented but impeccable English, and most of all by his ease and urbanity, gifts that few midwestern youngsters possessed. I was unaware of what I would have then viewed as Abel's lowly academic pedigree, and I would have scoffed at the notion that this sophisticated Polish-American would soon become my esteemed teacher and thereafter a lifelong friend.

At Columbia, shortly after my unforeseen switch of major fields from political science to sociology, I followed Bill Casey's advice by electing a course of Ted Abel's, without the usual briefing by fellow students. I soon learned, however, that study with this newly appointed (in 1933) member of the graduate faculty was a rewarding educational exercise for those who invested time and thought in his courses. More permissive than most teachers, Abel conducted his classes as if he took for granted both our interest in the subject and our intellectual maturity: he treated us as sociological colleagues, providing in this respect what I have believed for many years to be an excellent model for graduate instruction. His permissiveness, however, in some ways extended to himself; as a teacher, for example, he prepared few formal lectures or any discernible "lesson plans" in favor of extensive background reading that added to his readiness for discussion wherever it might lead. But Abel also had the keen intelligence, idle curiosity, and nonconformist temperament to make the classroom an intellectual adventure.

Abel's courses were eye openers, especially for a newcomer to sociology. They dealt with subjects that at the time were rarely pursued in graduate programs: theoretical perspectives of the German "systematic" sociologists; social change and social movements, long before these topics became standard academic fare; society and personality, a course in which we faced the unusual and challenging task of trying to write autobiographies of sociological relevance. When only a bit of Simmel's work was available in English, Abel introduced us to the "formalism" and essayistic brilliance of this unconventional scholar. He exposed us to German phenomenology, years before the influence of Edmund Husserl and Alfred Schutz was to spread among American sociologists. In the wake of his friend and fellow Pole Florian Znaniecki, he demonstrated in the classroom and in his research how the study of individual life histories can be major contributions to sociological scholarship.*

Ted Abel's own earlier experiences were unlike those of the other Columbia sociologists—or those of American academics generally. Of what was rumored to be (he was silent on the matter) upper-class or aristocratic family background, he had been an active member of the wartime Polish cavalry and had had superior training in philosophy and science before migrating to the United States. As an educated mid-European he had command of several languages and he impressed all of us, of both sexes, as an elegant "man of the world." These attributes, together with his generously displayed personal warmth and his contagious joie de vivre, gave Ted a unique place in the sociology department: he was a worldly and wise counselor, a delightful companion, a firm friend.

Willard Walter Waller

From the beginning of my part-time and prolonged graduate study, Robert MacIver, Bob Lynd, and Ted Abel were the principal teachers of record without whose guidance through the sociological labyrinth I would have floundered. But the completion of this account of the most influential of my mentors must include some comment about that extraordinary man and scholar Willard "Pete" Waller.

With the strong support of Abel and MacIver, Waller came to Columbia in 1937 as an associate professor at Barnard Col-

---

* Abel's principal books include his Columbia doctoral thesis, *Systematic Sociology in Germany* (New York: Columbia University Press, 1929), a critical analysis of the theoretical formulations of Georg Simmel, Alfred Vierkandt, Leopold von Wiese, and Max Weber, and the first study of its kind published in the United States; *Why Hitler Came Into Power* (New York: Prentice-Hall, 1938), based in large part upon analysis of "original life histories" of 600 of Hitler's followers, an important but rather neglected example of "human-documents" research; and *The Foundations of Sociological Theory* (New York: Random House, 1970), a major part of which is an assessment of the contributions of Durkheim, Weber, and Simmel to contemporary sociological theory.

lege—a move, as he put it, to the "sociological major leagues."* By that date I had completed the course work for the doctorate and had survived the orals, but during my remaining years at Columbia (1937–1942) Pete Waller played a major role in both my sociological and my general education. I audited Waller's graduate courses in American sociological theory and the family; his erudition and critical acumen were brought to a meticulous reading of my dissertation; most instructive were the many informal sessions, in our homes and elsewhere, highlighted by Pete's intellectual brilliance and sociological imagination.

These qualities were appreciated by most of the Columbia sociologists who reportedly would have invited Waller formally to join the graduate department had not Lynd strongly opposed the appointment in favor of a "quantitative" scholar.† But Waller, while not officially of mandarin faculty status, soon became a compelling figure in the university. Graduate students, as well as Barnard undergraduates, were impressed by his wide learning, penetrating perceptions, originality, and sharp wit. A persistent iconoclasm, a cynical stance, and at times a candor approaching recklessness failed to conceal Waller's social idealism, human compassion, and personal warmth. His manifest interest in students and their work and his hearty camaraderie were an important source of Waller's appeal, but so was the inventive nature of his thought, nourished by his close study and effective use of the writings of Charles Horton Cooley, George Herbert Mead, John Dewey, and Sigmund Freud.

Waller was an innovator, with respect to both his substantive interests and his style of work. In the 1920s he had been a graduate student at what was then this country's only sociological center of distinction, the University of Chicago, and in 1926 he went to the University of Pennsylvania where, although welcomed

* Waller's appointment involved a loss of academic rank: he had been a full professor at Penn State, as well as chairman. That such a loss when moving to Columbia in the 1930s and later was not necessarily viewed as "downward skidding" is illustrated by both Waller's case and that of Robert Merton who as a full professor at Tulane accepted an assistant professorship at Columbia in 1941.

† Lynd's opposition to Waller is recorded by William J. Goode et al., in "Willard W. Waller: A Portrait," the introduction to Goode, Frank Furstenburg, Jr., and Larry R. Mitchell, eds., *Willard W. Waller on the Family, Education, and War* (Chicago: University of Chicago Press, 1970), p. 82. Waller offered graduate courses, as noted above, and was elected to the Faculty of Political Science in 1940.

as a representative of the "Chicago school," Waller ignored that perspective when writing a psychoanalytically colored, controversial doctoral thesis, *The Old Love and the New* (1930). This off-beat study made considerable use of his personal observations and his own experience with divorce and remarriage, and on this count exemplifies the kind of "data source" that he exploited with great skill in most of his later sociological work. Thus in *The Sociology of Teaching* (1932), destined to become a classic, Waller's earlier experiences as a high-school teacher were drawn upon heavily; and in the ground-breaking volume, *The Family* (1938), the "dynamic interpretation" of familial relationships, processes, and problems is vividly and amply illustrated with perceptive observations from what Waller took to be the "field." Like David Riesman and Erving Goffman more recently, Waller saw the social world around him as an ever-present opportunity for sociological (and, in his case, psychological) interpretation.

In the late 1930s (and even today) Waller's national reputation as an unconventional and creative sociologist was largely based upon his unprecedented volumes on teaching and the family, his numerous book reviews, and a handful of articles.* During those years at Columbia, however, in both the classroom and informal sessions with graduate students, Waller's favorite subjects were two varieties of organizational analysis. Waller referred to one of these—an impressive anticipation rather than an adumbration of Erving Goffman's work on "total institutions"—as the study of "institutions of segregated care," including both voluntary and compulsory organizations (public and private schools, general and mental hospitals, reformatories and prisons, convents and monasteries). Waller's analysis of their inevitably contrasting and conflictive inmate and supervisory "cultures," of the dynamic relations between the two, and of the interconnections of both with the outside world was masterful. In 1941 plans were underway, under Waller's direction, to use his conceptual scheme in a volume of comparative studies to which he and several "Wallerites" were to contribute; World War II dispersed us and, alas, this important sociological innovation never reached the printed page.

* Notably, "Insight and Scientific Method," *American Journal of Sociology* 40, no. 3 (November 1934); "Social Problems and the Mores," *American Sociological Review* 1, no. 6 (December 1936); "The Rating and Dating Complex," *American Sociological Review* 2, no. 3 (October 1937). Waller's bibliography is included in Goode, Furstenburg, and Mitchell, *Willard W. Waller,* pp. 355ff.

Waller's other favorite theme during his early years at Columbia embraced the organization and dynamics of university and college education, with special emphasis on prevailing patterns in sociology. For some time he had been a participant in academia—at Chicago, Pennsylvania, the University of Nebraska (briefly), Penn State, Columbia—and had made detailed notes for a volume on the subject, only a fraction of which has survived.* But again, as in the case of his analysis of "institutions of segregated care," Waller's perspicacity as an observer, his Veblenesque bent to expose institutional realities, and his role as an innovator were put on display. This work, mostly unpublished, foreshadowed such revelatory books as Logan Wilson's *The Academic Man* (1942), in which Waller's "germinal ideas" are acknowledged, and Theodore Caplow and Reece McGee's *The Academic Marketplace* (1958). Moreover, Waller found his own guild to be a fascinating subject for study, particularly university centers of power and influence (he often expressed both admiration for and criticism of the University of Chicago's baseball-like "farm system" which in the 1920s and '30s spread over many schools in this country and Canada), as well as the relationship between different kinds of academic settings and the amount and nature of the sociological output. On the latter count, Waller was an early contributor to that branch of *Wissenssoziologie* that in later years mushroomed into the extensive navel-gazing known as the "sociology of sociology."†

The "discovery" of Willard Waller in the 1970s was not surprising in view of the affinity of much of his writing with recent trends in sociology. Inspired by the perspective's founders Cooley and Mead, Waller was a forerunner of what came to be known as symbolic interactionism: the development of self and personality, the psychodynamics of social relations, and the problematics and tensions of group life were among his central interests. And his analyses of social roles—teacher, husband and wife, divorcée, widow and widower—were conceptual, though not terminological, anticipations of later studies of "role making," "role

---

* These perceptive observations, "Notes on Higher Education," are included in Goode, Furstenburg, and Mitchell, *Willard W. Waller,* chap. 19.

† My own forays into this area, which insufficiently acknowledge my indebtedness to Waller, include "Bureaucracy and Higher Education," *Journal of General Education* 5, no. 2 (January 1951): 91–100; "Sociology as a Teaching Enterprise," chap. 25 in Robert K. Merton et al., eds., *Sociology Today* (New York: Basic Books, 1959); and "Sociology as an Educational Enterprise."

taking," "role set," and "role strain." Similarly, there is a pronounced phenomenological element in Waller's work: his persistent concern with the emergence of social order from ever-present change, disorder, and conflict is consistent with both Berger and Luckmann's "social construction of reality" and ethnomethodological principles. (Long before Erving Goffman and Harold Garfinkel, in their different ways, were to employ their "shock" techniques, Waller frequently posed outrageous or absurd situations, for his students and others, as a method of exploring basic realities of social interaction.) Finally, and in keeping with an ancient but continuing tradition, Waller was "a man bent on stripping the mask from others and exposing the false facade of social institutions"*—a self-styled social realist.

But Waller's "realism," as I have suggested, only faintly obscured his humanistic ideals, one of which, frequently declared, concerned the presumably achievable educational and social functions of sociology itself. Waller saw sociology not only as an aspiring science, but also as a humane and even artistic enterprise of great educational and thus social potential. He believed that sociology should become an important part of formal schooling and as such that it should contribute significantly to the training of socially useful and ethically constrained men and women. In this respect, Waller stood shoulder to shoulder with his senior colleague and fellow humanist Robert MacIver.†

These pages about Waller and his contributions as scholar and teacher have been strengthened by rereading the introduction to a collection of his writings by William J. Goode, Frank Furstenburg, Jr., and Larry R. Mitchell, cited above. On one count, however, my own recollections (and those of his Barnard colleague Mirra Komarovsky) are inconsistent with this generally excellent "portrait" by Goode and his co-authors. They depict Waller's final years at Columbia, 1940–1945, as a period of intellectual sterility

---

* The phrase is from Goode, Furstenburg, and Mitchell, *Willard W. Waller,* p. 25. This generally excellent (but see below) "portrait" refers to most of the similarities noted above between Waller's work and recent trends in sociology. See esp. pp. 41, 49, 76–77, and 109.

† Waller was a great admirer of MacIver (whom he saw as "one of the few really original minds of the day") and of his sociological system, but was quite critical of what he viewed as MacIver's disregard of the psychological components of social behavior. These points are amply documented in Waller's letter of January 9, 1937, to James Van Toor, then editor of Farrar and Rinehart, Inc., publisher of MacIver's *Society: Its Structure and Changes;* the original letter is in my personal files.

for Pete, with "disastrous," though perhaps temporary, "results for his academic work." During these years, to be sure, Waller was the editor of and contributor to a nondistinguished volume on war, author of a weak booklet on war and the family and of numerous journalistic publications on veterans; he became something of a celebrity on the lecture circuit and radio; he was rejected in an attempt to enter the military and gave some time to governmental service; and his minimal output of sociological scholarship at this time was further reduced by his newly assumed roles of commercial advisory editor and, briefly, of publisher.* But Waller was only one of many academic men and women who became heavily involved in the hectic activities of this prewar and wartime period, and there is no evidence, in my view, that his scholarly powers suffered a collapse. At least until the spring of 1942, when I left Columbia to join the navy, and notwithstanding his own involvements, Waller remained an intellectually exciting and splendid sociologist whose major creative work, as many of us were convinced, was yet to come. Pete Waller's sudden death in 1945, at the age of 46, was of course a tragic blow for his family and friends, and a great loss to the field to which he had already given sociological riches.

Afterword: A Brief Stint with the Elite

In 1940–41 a leave of absence from my teaching post at City College permitted me to become field secretary of the National Refugee Service, an exciting break from teaching. The leave was extended for a second year so that I could accept a lectureship in the graduate Department of Sociology at Columbia—an appointment far beyond my aspirations. Thus, in 1941–42 (until April when I began a long tour in military uniform), and as their less than confident junior colleague, I shared Fayerweather Hall with such scholars as the old hands Robert MacIver, Bob Lynd, Bill Casey, and Ted Abel, and the newcomers to Columbia Paul Lazarsfeld and Bob Merton (Pete Waller was headquartered at Barnard College). This short stint with a sociological elite was both demanding and instructive.

My regular teaching assignment consisted of a seminar on class structure and change, elected by only a handful of adven-

---

* Details concerning these activities, as well as the depiction of Waller's alleged "intellectual 'suicide,' " are presented in Goode, Furstenburg, and Mitchell, *Willard W. Waller*, pp. 72–76, 96–108.

turers, and a heavily populated course on methods of social research, for which my qualifications were few. And for a month or so I "substituted" for absentee Bob Merton, coopting as class lecturers Pete Waller, the anthropologist Ralph Linton, and the brilliant graduate student Philip Selznick. But as a long-time teacher of highly able and boldly challenging undergraduates at City College, my classroom anxieties were more or less under control—I survived. There were other duties, including the time-consuming but enlightening job of representing the department, as its exploitable junior member, on numerous and diverse examining committees: I read, and sometimes made bold to query the authors of, doctoral dissertations in history, economics, and political science, as well as sociology.

During most of the years of my long association with Columbia (1931–1942) I taught full time at City College. Some of the features of that remarkable institution of the 1930s, and some of my adventures within it, are the subject of the following chapter.

3

City College in the Thirties:

Seedbed of Modern American Sociology

I HAVE OFTEN referred to the City College of New York of the 1930s as my "first academic love." At none of the schools where I later taught—Columbia, Smith, Princeton, Santa Cruz, Massachusetts—could there have been the combination of circumstances that so powerfully stamped the eight years (1933–1941) at CCNY: the widespread miseries and utopian products of the Great Depression, the accomplishments and defeats of a political New Deal, the burgeoning of rightist and leftist social movements, the spectacular organization of militant labor, the ascendancy of "writers on the left," the rise of a socially conscious theater centered in New York, and so on.* In the midst of all this was a tuition-free college with a large number of ideologically and intellectually engaged students and faculty, divided by a running battle of "furious theologies," but united by a common foe, an ultraconservative prexy. And not least, there was the happy circumstance of my own youth. For these exciting years, it is all but impossible to separate sociology at City College, or the larger life of the college, from the social drama of New York and the momentous events of the greater society.

The Move to City College: Fortune Smiles Again

In 1933 my qualifications for a faculty post at CCNY, or any other college, were minimal at best. At the time of the ap-

_____

* Eric Hoffer, speaking at Adlai E. Stevenson College, University of California, Santa Cruz, in 1966, in response to a then-popular cliché of many youngsters, stated that he trusted no one who had not been an adult during the 1930s. Oftentimes I have been tempted to agree with Hoffer's sally.

pointment in the spring of that year I was a green teacher of elementary and high-school students in a private school, I had not
completed the courses for the Columbia M.A. (a degree never obtained—the diploma fee was twenty-five dollars), I had avoided
sociology as an undergraduate and had only the vaguest notion of
how to teach the subject, and I had barely reached the age of
twenty-four. Moreover, teaching jobs in all fields were few and
far between in those early Depression years, and sociology was
decades away from its great blossoming into a more or less reputable and popular academic offering. This combination of skimpi-
est of credentials, the dismal economic situation, and the shaky
status of my recently chosen vocation made the odds on getting a
teaching position at the college level about a thousand to one.
Once more, however, lady luck was in my corner.

Even in today's marketplace, with its institutional safeguards against ascriptive discrimination, old-boy influence, and
cronyism, these unfair practices in academic appointments persist—and so does mere happenstance, which played the major role
in my move to CCNY. On a spring day in 1933 I was visiting
Columbia's Fayerweather Hall when Robert MacIver received a
telephone call from Professor Samuel Joseph, senior sociologist at
City College; to fill a sudden vacancy in his department he was
seeking an "advanced" graduate student with training in political
science as well as sociology. Although I was little more than a
beginner with a flimsy record of only six or seven courses, it included some work in the two fields. I could claim to have won
my teaching spurs at Birch Wathen. And, of crucial importance,
I happened to be on the spot when Joseph reached MacIver. Thus
I became a candidate for what then struck me as the exalted position of tutor of government and sociology in New York's most
exciting school.

MacIver's recommendation was essential, to be sure, but it
by no means assured me of the job. There was first a lengthy inter-
rogation by Professor Joseph, assisted by a fellow student at
Columbia, Adolph Tomars, and conducted in the nonacademic
setting of John Wanamaker's restaurant;* I got by. The second
interview was far more awesome: in this case the interrogator and

---

* As I was to learn later, this restaurant was Joseph's ill-chosen headquarters
for fairly frequent off-the-record meetings concerning departmental policy
and personnel at City College. I was invited to none of these sessions which
were controlled by the "Joseph-Tomars axis," to use an invidious phrase of
those years.

final authority was Frederick B. Robinson, president of City College. Robinson was widely known as a syndicated columnist for the Hearst newspapers, a political conservative, and an energetic busybody in the life of CCNY—he made unannounced visits to classrooms, frequented the handball courts, and created passable oil paintings which decorated his office. My recollection of the dreaded session is hazy, yet I do remember that he asked me, if I could, to distinguish between "sociology" and "socialism" and, in keeping with a widespread view, Robinson expressed some skepticism about the intellectual merits of the former. This experience must have left a shaken and inarticulate youngster, but the president's tolerance exceeded my expectations: I got the job.

Initiation in a School of Business

The job, as I have noted, was "Tutor of Government and Sociology," a nonimposing title perhaps in need of explanation. In those years many members of the faculties of New York's public colleges (CCNY, Hunter, Brooklyn) held the rank of tutor, the equivalent of instructor in most schools, which was assigned to those of us who had not yet surmounted the general and oral examinations for the Ph.D. But tutors were full-time teachers and often, as in my case, carried large responsibilities. Sociology at City College was then a division of the Department of Government, accounting for the dual designation in the title and the fact that my duties included a heavy load of instruction in two academic disciplines. The job involved teaching the courses offered in sociology plus several sections of a required course in American government at CCNY's School of Business and Civic Administration located on Twenty-third Street at Lexington Avenue.* This lofty position paid the beginning annual salary of $1,200.†

---

* This was the location of the "Free Academy," chartered in 1847, which was named "CCNY" in 1866, "City College" in 1929, and "City College of the City University of New York" in 1961. Thus the School of Business and Civic Administration (since 1954, the Bernard M. Baruch College) occupied the original site of what in recent years has become the enormous, multicampus CUNY.

† The starting salary at City College matched that of my second year at Birch Wathen School and remained at the same figure during my first year and a half at CCNY—raises at City went into effect only midway in the second academic year following the initial appointment. Thus, from September 1932, until February 1935, my annual salary of $1,200 was supplemented by various moonlighting jobs, as noted earlier.

"Twenty-Third Street" differed strikingly from the main or "Uptown" branch of City College on several counts. Uptown was a college of liberal arts (plus engineering), Twenty-Third Street a business school, its name decorated with the largely euphemistic "Civic." Its students, drawn from all the boroughs of New York, faced a curriculum heavily loaded with such utilitarian courses as accountancy, business law, and various offerings in applied economics. Uptown's student body (and almost all the faculty) in those years was strictly male, whereas teaching and life in general at Twenty-Third Street were enhanced by a sizable minority of career-seeking women, not husband-seeking "co-eds." The very large majority of Uptown's male students were recent high-school graduates and this concentration of raw youth stood in contrast with the wide age range of Twenty-Third Street's men and women, a good many of whom were older, and no doubt wiser, than the school's sole teacher of sociology. (During my first year two students in the same course were father and son, a somewhat disconcerting situation for a twenty-four-year-old instructor.) And the status of sociology itself was far different at the two branches: an introductory course in sociology was a requirement Uptown for one of the liberal arts degree's* guaranteeing a large captive audience, and a major in the field was permissible and even popular; at Twenty-Third Street there were only two sociology courses, both electives, and there was no major in a subject defined as widely marginal for future members of the world of business.

The dean of this business school was Justin H. Moore, a friendly man of conservative bent who nevertheless had written a reputedly "sexy" novel and who, following the lead of President Robinson, made surprise visits to the classrooms of untested teachers. He once appeared in my American government course when, in feeble imitation of my mentor Bill Casey, I was struggling to show the relevance of Pavlov's salivating dogs for the study of public opinion; the dean must have had some second thoughts about his approval of my appointment.

Moore headed a faculty most of whose members taught "business" courses and whose names have long been forgotten, but there were others. For example, the historians could boast of the impressive teacher Henry David; for a brief period, the

* There were at least two such degrees: the B.A. and the Bachelor of Social Science (B.S.S.), and a required course for the latter was introductory sociology.

leftist Jack Foner who, with his brother Phil, subsequently lost his job because of alleged membership in the Communist party; and the conventional and dignified Raymond Lisle, then studying for a law degree, who was to become a distinguished member of the U.S. Foreign Service. There were a few psychologists, including the experimentalist Alexander Mintz, who in middle age married a young Twenty-Third Street student; and Eugene Horowitz (later Hartley), who a few years later wrote influential studies in social psychology. Among the many economists were Bernhard Ostrolenk, an agricultural specialist whose excellent courses in that subject were generally viewed as curious academic fare for city-bred City College students; Louis Mayers, a lovely man and true intellectual who taught the unpromising subject of business law; and "Steamboat Bill" Fulton, conductor of a hilarious curricular roadshow ("*air* is free, ain't it?"), who eventually retired from CCNY with the unusual rank of "Instructor Emeritus."

Two stalwart members of the faculty, the school's one political scientist John Larkin and the historian Henry David, were my closest colleagues and strongest supporters during those initiatory years in academic life. Larkin, an assistant professor who had recently completed the doctorate at Harvard, was the senior representative of the Department of Government and Sociology at Twenty-Third Street, my immediate superior, and companionable office mate (our tiny quarters were far more commodious, I was to learn, than the sardine facilities uptown). Larkin taught the upper-level electives in government, I managed the introductory and urban courses in sociology, and the several sections of the required course in American government were divided between us. The latter subject was altogether new to me, but with the help of Charles Beard's excellent text, a casebook on Supreme Court decisions, and especially John's kindly guidance I somehow managed. My survival at Twenty-Third Street was due in large part to John's sustaining friendship and his generous toleration of what were no doubt the many follies and clearly the too-frequent rashness of a turned-on raw beginner.*

My introduction to Henry David was brought about by students who took courses with both of us and who at times would interrupt my classroom efforts with the comment, "But Mr. David disagrees." This challenge was disconcerting for David was well

* Following his several years at City College, John D. Larkin's successful career as a political scientist and administrator was pursued at the Illinois Institute of Technology.

known as a brilliant young scholar, a tough but splendid teacher, and a severe critic; I found him an intimidating paragon. Soon after we met, however, Henry and I became the closest of colleagues, political and ideological allies (marching together on May 1), occasional basketball teammates (he barely put up with my abysmal play), and much more; our friendship was to be life-long. In those Depression years neither of us had great expectations, and in no way could we foresee what was to be Henry's extraordinary professional career.* But his wide-ranging and superior scholarship was already on display: as co-author with Harry Elmer Barnes of the two-volume work, *A History of Western Civilization* (1935) and as author of the definitive study, *The History of the Haymarket Affair* (1936), his Columbia dissertation.† As a fellow graduate student at Columbia and as a teacher at City College, Henry was about three years ahead of me, but at Twenty-Third Street we shared in equal measure both the hectic life of a business college on the subway circuit and, to our good fortune, a fair number of highly able and nonbusiness-oriented students.

A good many of these deviants from the Twenty-Third Street norms, in the hope of becoming social scientists, elected such courses in that area as the limited curriculum provided, including the scanty offerings in sociology. Therefore, as I was the school's only teacher of the subject, they were among my classroom captives. In several cases their aspirations were to be fulfilled: Louis Lister and Jack Loft, with Columbia doctorates, in economics; the late Bernard Peck, following three years as a combat pilot in World War II, in social psychology; Jack Alterman, trained in sociology and political science, in governmental ser-

---

* While still an undergraduate at City College, Henry David faced a difficult choice of possible careers: his artistry as a violinist competed strongly with his already evident scholarly bent. He has served on the faculties of CCNY, Queens College, Columbia University, the New School for Social Research, as Pitt Professor at Cambridge University (where his son Paul David, the economist, subsequently occupied the same chair), and, most recently, at the Lyndon B. Johnson School of Public Affairs. David's talents as administrator and research director have been brought to executive positions with the BBC (during World War II), the National Manpower Council, the National Academy of Sciences, and as dean of the graduate faculty and later president of the New School for Social Research.

† My own dissertation, *Class and American Sociology*, benefited from David's expertise in economic history and, more generally, from his persistent encouragement.

vice; Herbert Lahne, another Columbia Ph.D., in economic history. There were others, including an unusually bright youngster, Joseph Goldsen, who became, and remains, a cherished friend. Joe's varied and outstanding career as a social scientist, policy analyst, and administrator has been managed without the union card of a graduate degree.* These young, intellectual, and activist students, notwithstanding the educational constraints of a business college, were as able as the best of their contemporaries in liberal arts. And they prepared me for the rigors and rewards of CCNY's Uptown campus.

During those three years at the School of Business and Civic Administration I was unaware of a widely held and elitist belief among members of the Uptown liberal arts faculty: that being sent to Twenty-Third Street was banishment to the Siberia of City College, a punitive device employed by authoritarian chairmen. Thus, in the spring of 1936, upon receiving a "Main Campus" teaching schedule for the following fall, and in what my future Uptown colleagues must have viewed as a sign of utter innocence or worse, I entered a formal protest, misconstruing the reassignment as punishment for my delinquencies at the downtown center. The protest failed, and with great reluctance to leave my Twenty-Third Street companions, I faced the move uptown. Of course, I could not have known that soon I would be sharing classrooms with several of the foremost sociologists and other intellectual leaders of future years.

The Thirties: A "Golden Age" at CCNY

Recently a colleague remarked that "it must have been a great experience to have taught at CCNY in the 1930s," expressing a frequently voiced speculation, often tinged with envy. Over the years there has grown a multisided legend: that of a City College of that period with a student body of unsurpassed brilliance and passion for learning, disdainful of the "collegiate" preoccupations of other campuses, and activated by a widespread militant radicalism in short supply elsewhere. To be sure, this

---

* Since graduating from CCNY (B.B.A., 1937), positions held by Joseph Goldsen include research assistant for Norman Bel Geddes, vice president of Leo Nejelski and Company, communications analyst (with Harold D. Lasswell) for the Library of Congress during World War II, long-time member and for several years head of the social science division of RAND, and coordinator of area and international studies at Yale University.

portrayal is a distortion of the historical reality, but there is good reason for the rise of such a legend: City College in the thirties was in fact an exceptional school of outstanding accomplishment. To teach there at that time was indeed a "great experience."

In earlier years, especially before World War I, CCNY had been something less than a first-rate center of "higher learning," at least according to conventional academic standards. Chartered in 1847 as the Free Academy and the first tuition-free college in the United States, it served a small number of the sons of immigrants throughout the century and beyond, with a good many courses in the limited curriculum pitched at the high-school level, compulsory study in the English language (as an infamous cultural lag, a required course in public speaking persisted until after World War II!), a nonimpressive faculty, and, faced by the wretched conditions of working-class life, a large quota of student dropouts. In the twentieth century, however, beginning in 1903 with the presidency of John Finley, standards greatly improved and by the thirties CCNY surely was the outstanding public college in this country.* During my years there admission was generally restricted to the top 10 percent of high-school graduates (a far cry from the "open door" of later times), the curriculum was extensive and fairly demanding, and the faculty, as will be specified shortly, included more than a few scholar-teachers of superior ability. On these counts, City College had arrived in the educational major leagues.

In striking contrast, the physical plant of the college, on Convent Avenue two miles north of Columbia in a dreary section of Manhattan, and the facilities for students and faculty were in no sense "major league." The main building, an ornate Gothic in gray stone, housed the School of Liberal Arts: classrooms, offices, laboratories, a huge auditorium, administrative quarters, and so on. The men's lavatories provided conventional urinals but, to the distress of overly shy occupants, young and old, featured fully exposed toilets unprotected by partitions or doors. Office space was minimal: unlike the cubicle I had shared with

---

* The several accounts of the early years of City College include S. Willis Rudy, *The College of the City of New York: A History, 1847–1947* (New York: The City College Press, 1949) and Sherry Gorelick, *City College and the Jewish Poor: Education in New York, 1880–1924* (New Brunswick, N.J.: Rutgers University Press, 1981). Irving Howe presents a brief but excellent description in *World of Our Fathers* (New York: Harcourt Brace Jovanovich, 1976), pp. 280ff.

John Larkin at Twenty-Third Street, my "office" consisted of a pair of drawers in one of a half-dozen desks jammed into a small room occupied by the entire sociology faculty—including the chairman who enjoyed the luxury of a whole desk, a prerogative of his position. There was some equipment: an ancient hand-operated mimeograph machine, for which we cut our own stencils and which we tried our best to keep in repair, a rickety typewriter of about the same vintage, a single telephone strategically located on the chairman's desk. But these limitations and this lack of privacy, for most of us, were not seen as frustrating obstacles to our principal preoccupation: teaching the sons of New York's nonprivileged who sought a college education.

Moreover, there were adaptations to these rugged circumstances which in some small measure partook of Toynbee's "virtues of adversity." In the absence of office space, for example, conferences with students took place on benches in the spacious hallways of the college or in the less private and far noisier basement cafeteria or, weather permitting, on the concrete seats of nearby Lewisohn Stadium—wherever, face-to-face communication between student and teacher was managed. A rarer improvisation was induced by the inadequate collection and the crowded condition of the small college library which led some of us to open our homes and individual libraries, such as they were, to frustrated but eager young scholars.* These and other such adjustments in those years were generally viewed as part of the normal life at City College.

In spite of the adversities, one is tempted to look back upon the thirties at CCNY as indeed a Golden Age. Any such depiction is hyperbolic, to be sure, but there is little doubt that the City College of that period was an extraordinary center of learning for both students and faculty—largely the consequence, as indicated earlier, of the historical conjuncture of several circumstances. In addition to the pervasive Depression, large-scale social and political movements, and the other impinging events of the decade, there was the important fact of a predominantly Jewish student body, many of whom were second-generation Americans and sons of socialists and labor unionists. These young men differed greatly in academic attainment, intellectual prowess, temperament, and aspiration, but a large number shared an unusual combination of propensities: tough-mindedness, an idealism

---

* Among others who studied from time to time in the Page apartment were the future sociologists Morroe Berger and, later, David Matza.

thinly disguised by a proclivity for criticism, a high regard for scholarly and intellectual accomplishment rooted in religious and ethnic tradition, this or that variety of political radicalism, and, not least, a strong achievement drive. Students possessing this pattern of traits were a severe challenge for an immature instructor; while they pushed me to the wall at times, they were a joy to teach. It was also a joy to learn from them.*

Some or even most of these students, as Irving Kristol has suggested, may have seen the City College faculty as a collection of dull teachers playing no part in a real "intellectual community."† We were a mixed lot, certainly, and our ranks included mediocre scholars, dull teachers, academically disinterested tenure-seekers, and at least a few out-and-out incompetents—on this score, the faculty of CCNY was not unique. Moreover, the passage of state legislation in the mid-thirties, which granted tenure after three years of service and promotion to the instructorship, and was retroactive, guaranteed jobs for the inferior, as well as the first-rate. But my own recollections of that faculty differ in some important respects from Irving Kristol's.

There were both senior and junior scholar-teachers of recognized ability in various fields at City College. Philosophy, for example, could boast of the altogether contrasting Morris R. Cohen and the equally well-known Harry Overstreet, together with two younger and highly able colleagues of the political left: Abraham Edel (brother of Leon whose biographical studies were to win renown) and Lewis Feuer who in later years gained wide repute as controversial scholar and severe critic of radical student

* With shameless immodesty, I quote from Harry Alpert's "testimonial" letter of March 24, 1975: referring to the early 1930s, when Harry and I first joined the faculty at City College, he wrote, "Into this strange—and wonderful—academic setting . . . there came this goyische jock. . . . Any enumeration of Charles Page's achievements must include the fact that he was appreciated as a teacher and human being by what must have been the most severely critical student body in the world."

† Because of the poor facilities, the heavy teaching loads, and the abysmally low salaries of younger faculty, Kristol maintains that "the very best professors left, if they could," but notes that such moves were restricted by the Depression. "But the fact remains," he continues, "that for the bright, inquiring student, City College was a pretty dull educational place. The student who came seeking an intellectual community, in which the life of the mind was strenuously lived, had to create such a community and such a life for himself" ("Memoirs of a Trotskyist," *New York Times Magazine*, January 23, 1977, p. 56).

movements. In history, a diversified department, in addition to the distinguished author J. Salwyn ("Jack") Schapiro, whose friendship and wise counsel I prized, there were several notables-to-be: Moses ("Moe") Finkelstein, then a Stalinist, who became the eminent Cambridge classicist M. I. Finley; the prolific Europeanist Louis L. Snyder; Richard Morris, renowned for his learned and mile-a-minute observations at faculty gatherings, who later occupied a Columbia chair in American history; and Henry David. During my years there, psychology at City was strengthened by the surprising move of a seasoned Gardner Murphy from Columbia and by the appointment of a young Kenneth Clark whose subsequent fame reached far beyond his academic status. The large Department of English, as I recall, was oversupplied with routineers, but its ranks included some of the most able members of the faculty: Edgar Johnson, fine literary historian and foremost Dickensian; the irrepressible Theodore ("Teddy") Goodman, acclaimed as an unrivaled instructor of neophyte writers by former students who later made their mark; Edward ("Eddie") Mack, author of unsurpassed books on the English public schools; John C. ("Jack") Thirlwall, powerful teacher of both modern and Biblical literature.* And of course there were others, among them the remarkable John Hastings, cartographer. In Hastings's famous course (which I had the good fortune to audit) students were excited by a display of teaching prowess and erudition in geography, economics, anthropology, and sociology. Hastings, in my experience, was one of the very few academics who has ever managed successfully a one-man multidisciplinary course of true distinction.

Towering above all others—as teacher, man of learning, and, in Irving Howe's phrase, "culture hero"—was Morris Raphael Cohen, graduate of CCNY in 1900 and member of the Department of Philosophy from 1912 until 1946. Cohen's contributions to generations of City College students (Ernest Nagel and Sidney Hook, both class of 1923, among them), to his field, and indeed to America's higher culture have been reported at length and need little comment here.† This "stray dog" of a philosopher, as

---

* Jack Thirlwall, a fellow unionist and boon companion, remained my close friend throughout his lifetime.

† An excellent depiction of Cohen and his contributions is presented by Irving Howe in *World of Our Fathers*, pp. 283–86. Two books that tell us much about this remarkable man are *Portrait of a Philosopher: Morris R. Cohen in Life & Letters* (New York: Harcourt, Brace, and World, 1962) by his daughter Lenore Cohen Rosenfield and Cohen's autobiography, *A Dreamer's Journey* (Boston: Beacon, 1949).

Cohen himself once put it, had studied with Harvard's William James, Hugo Munsterberg, Ralph Barton Perry, and Josiah Royce, but he was no one's disciple and disdained all philosophical and ideological systems. Cohen was a superb logician, a skeptical critic, a questioner, a seeker of truth. He was also a master of Socratic method which he used without mercy: "It was a terrifying, even sadistic method of teaching, and only the kinds of students that came to Cohen could have withstood it. . . . Cohen's ferocity in the classroom was quite impersonal. 'For most of us,' recalled historian Richard Morris, 'to be corrected by Socrates seemed neither a surprise nor a disgrace.' "* These observations by Howe and Morris are consistent with my own mixed memories of Professor Cohen's chairmanship of the oral examining committee for honors candidates in the social sciences on which I served for a year or two and, more extensively, are supported by the testimony of numerous students who faced the perils of his regular courses. They also suggest the Janus-faced reaction to this extraordinary teacher: he was held in great esteem, of course, and in great affection, for his knowledge, wisdom, and logical prowess, and for his understanding of youthful defiance of authority (at seventeen Cohen had declared himself "not only a reformer but revolutionist");† but he was feared, and hated at times, for his ruthless critical exercise of the minds of the bright "boys" of CCNY.‡

The City College students of the 1930s "inherited" Morris R. Cohen from earlier decades. They took pride as well in City's other famous alumni—among them Felix Frankfurter, Lewis Mumford, Upton Sinclair, and New York's senator, Robert F. Wagner, plus such diverse talents as the financier Bernard Baruch, the lyricist Ira Gershwin, the learned sports writer John Kieran, the anthropologist Robert M. Lowie, the actor Edward G. Robinson. Such exemplars of outstanding accomplishment encouraged a good deal of "ancestor worship"§ in the college, but their greater

---

* Howe, *World of Our Fathers,* pp. 284–85.
† Ibid., p. 283.
‡ Many of the students, as recent and unusually young high-school graduates, were in fact boys; and for Morton Gottschall, the generally beloved dean of the college, all of them were "my boys." In the classroom, however, they were "young men" and so treated, although very few, if any, of the faculty could approach Morris R. Cohen's expertise in stimulating their intellectual maturation—on this score, he was a ruthless teacher at times, but unsurpassed.
§ This phrase is used by Meyer Liben in "CCNY—A Memoir," *Commentary,* September 1965, pp. 64–70; this article is an excellent portrayal of City College in the early 1930s.

contribution, I believe, was the reinforcement of an extant achievement drive, sometimes channeled into unconventional or revolutionary activities, which withstood the debilitating circumstances of the Depression years. In any event, the students at CCNY, no less than the sons of affluence in the ivy schools, were amply provided by their forerunners with a worthy—and challenging—legacy.

The graduates of City College of the thirties surely surpassed the record of accomplishment of their predecessors. Although severely handicapped by the economic conditions and limited opportunities of the period, and in a good many cases forced to postpone, prolong, or forego the advanced study to which they aspired, an impressive number (as indicated, for example, by the listings in *Who's Who* and similar publications) more than made their mark, and in a variety of fields. Several professions other than sociology were enriched by the achievements of men who were undergraduates at City between 1930 and 1940. There were the future Nobel Prize winners in medicine and economics, respectively, Arthur Kornberg and Kenneth Arrow; there were such renowned scientists-administrators of later years as the biochemist Philip Handler and the physicist-oceanographer William Nierenberg; there was Jonas Salk, class of 1934, who moved into international fame as the husband of my one-time intended, the remarkable Donna Lindsay; there were the future distinguished men of letters Irving Howe and Alfred Kazin; there were Irving Kristol and Melvin J. Lasky who were to become enormously successful editors of leading intellectual journals in England and the United States; there was at least one young actor, Lee J. Cobb, who was to grace both stage and film for many years. And of course there were others.

To depict a "Golden Age," however, is a shaky case of looking backward, supported by the later achievements of a small minority and inflated by disregard of certain realities of City College life in the 1930s. I suspect that relatively few alumni, thirty years or more after graduation, would share the conclusion of Meyer Liben's memoir: "The *main thing* about City College as I lived it is that it was a place where young people were learning, and where the process of learning had a certain excitement, and led to further learning, further growth."* As in most colleges, for the majority of students, surely, "learning" was only one activity among many, and not necessarily the "main thing." With-

* Ibid., p. 70, my emphasis.

out co-eds (girls were a rare sight Uptown), with almost no Greek letter nonsense, with a valiant but tiny and inexpert football squad, City nevertheless possessed a vigorous "collegiate" life actively pursued by the nonaffluent, sexually segregated, subway riding, city dwellers who attended that unique public school. These students were loyal and uninhibited supporters of the best basketball team in town, coached by the great Nat Holman, which with unrivaled and spectacular ball-handling—the "famed City razzle-dazzle"—electrified full houses at Madison Square Garden.* They took pride in a several-times national championship fencing team and in a worthy team of wrestlers coached by Alfred "Chic" Chaken, who was later killed in the Spanish Civil War. Almost all of them, it sometimes seemed, were first-rate at ping-pong; and many—in keeping with the college's brainy reputation—played the less agonistic game of chess with a skill few of their teachers could match. And of course there were other activities and interests, including the splendid concerts in Lewisohn Stadium highlighted, in the limited view of some of us, by the music of George Gershwin and its superb rendition by that champion of chutzpa, Oscar Levant. But surpassing all of this, as an intense preoccupation of City's most visible students, was political and ideological involvement.

The "Red Decade"

The political ferment at City College in the thirties has received lengthy and diverse commentary—in individual memoirs, in scholarly works, in investigatory documents, in later-day polemics, in fiction. The observations that follow make little use of these reports and assessments; they are largely the recollections from years long past of a one-time participant and, as such, necessarily are highly selective, skewed by personal experience and ideological bias, and inconsistent with accounts of others. But all of us who lived through and were in some measure politically active during the "red decade" at CCNY, as students or teachers, carry vivid, though no doubt faulty, memories of what was an exciting, and even at times a traumatic, adventure for our generation.

---

* Among the several members of varsity basketball teams who were in my classes, all able students as I recall, was the backcourt star "Red" Holzman who years later became the coach of the New York Knickerbockers' most famous teams.

Although most City College students (and most of their teachers) were not political leftists, nor indeed political activists of any kind, a large majority of the intellectually serious and academically successful, at least in my experience, were radicals of one sort or another. Meyer Liben, editor of the student newspaper *Campus* in the early 1930s, lists several of the political and ideological camps represented at City: "radicals ranged from right-wing Socialists . . . to splinters from the Trotskyist left-wing. In between was a bewildering variety—Austro-Marxists, orthodox Communists, Socialist centrists, and Socialist left-wingers, Kautskyites, followers of the Independent Labor Party in England, the Lovestonites, Brandlerites. . . ," and, in keeping with my own youthful disposition (though not my convictions) even a handful of Anarchists.* Prominent in this leftist array were three groups: the Socialists of the tradition of Eugene V. Debs and supporters of Norman Thomas and of political democracy (to whom I gave my political allegiance); the more militant, more tightly organized, and far more disciplined Communists and their Young Communist League (YCL), the revolutionary "steel instruments" of Lenin and Stalin; and the much smaller but clearly visible and highly articulate Trotskyists, certain of whom receive special mention below. There was also a contingent of "independents" and another of what might be called mobile Marxists, remembered by a fellow activist as "exasperating left-wing individualists who either could not bring themselves to join any group or else insisted on joining them all in succession."† Among the independents, as well as in each of the big three, were young men of superior talent who were to become distinguished alumni of their college and intellectual luminaries of their society.

One of these achievers, Irving Kristol—City College class of 1940 and my short-time student, later an editor, subsequently a member of the professoriate, and in recent years a foremost voice of the "neoconservatives"—in "Memoirs of a Trotskyist" has given us a nostalgic and informative report on his undergraduate years as an anti-Stalinist Marxist.‡ As Kristol points out, the

---

* Liben, "CCNY—A Memoir."
† Kristol, "Memoirs of a Trotskyist," p. 55.
‡ Ibid. Kristol's piece provides a good deal of the content of this and the following paragraphs, together with my own memories of frequent visits to the alcoves in the City College cafeteria. As a socialist of sorts, I was more or less accepted in Alcove No. 1, but viewed with grave suspicion by the Stalinists in Alcove No. 2.

"conglomeration" of socialists of various kinds, Trotskyists, and independent leftists, united by their common opposition to the Communists and (although this is not noted by Kristol) by a general ideological allegiance to a multisided Marxism, included several students who later became men of prominence. These doughty opponents of the much larger and line-following Communists, who occupied Alcove No. 2 in the college cafeteria, assembled in Alcove No. 1, their headquarters for political plotting and the planning of protests (for example, for Free Speech, against ROTC), for skimpy lunches and expert ping-pong, and especially for extended debate concerning the "correct" interpretation of the political, economic, and cultural scene in the light of the sacred Marxist texts and such heterodox journals as *Partisan Review*, V. F. Calverton's *Modern Monthly*, and the Trotskyist "theoretical organ," the *New International*. This seemingly never-ending debate, together with the preparation for it that, at least for a few students, oftentimes equaled or exceeded the work done for courses, was an important scholastic experience: a powerfully motivated exercise in documentary analysis and theoretical disputation. Thus Kristol recalls:

> Alcove No. 1 was the place you went to if you wanted to be radical *and* have a theory as to the proper kind of radical you should be. When I say "theory," I mean that in the largest sense. We in Alcove No. 1 were terribly concerned with being "right" in politics, economics, sociology, philosophy, history, anthropology, etc. It was essential to be "right" in all of these fields of knowledge, lest a bit of information from one should casually collide with a theoretical edifice and bring the whole structure tumbling down. So all the little grouplets that joined together to make Alcove No. 1 their home were always in keen competition to come up with startling bits of information—or, better yet, obscure and disorienting quotations from Marx or Engels or Lenin or Trotsky—that would create intellectual trouble for the rest of the company.*

Kristol's account may give the impression that the intense intellectualization of City's leftist students was a near-monopoly of the Trotskyists and their anti-Stalinist allies, and that their Communist enemies, a "dreary . . . bunch," were apt to be mindless followers of a tightly controlled and shifting party line. In

* Ibid., p. 54, Kristol's italics.

my own memory, this contrast is overdrawn—as Kristol himself notes, his Trotskyists were bounded by the parameters of a "Marxist scholasticism," and some of the others in Alcove No. 1 were mobile Marxists or even renegades from Alcove No. 2. It is more significant that in the 1930s the leftist movement generally— which embraced Socialists, independents, the various splinter groups, *and* Communists—was marked by an intellectualism that was almost entirely lacking decades later in the "New Left" of the 1960s. To be sure, the anti-Stalinists, in addition to studying the sacred Marxist classics, read in the *New International* such diverse and brilliant contributors as James Burnham, Dwight Macdonald, and Max Schachtman, and in *Partisan Review* such worthies as Paul Goodman, Sidney Hook, Philip Rahv, and Meyer Schapiro. But the Communists, notwithstanding the constraints of the line as set forth in the *Daily Worker* and the *New Masses,* not only studied the complex writings of Marx, Engels, and Lenin (sometimes in the classrooms of the Workers' School), but had their own high-powered intellectuals—Lewis Farina (Lewis Corey), R. Palm Dutt, John Strachey, and others. Moreover, many of us on the left, both students and teachers, encountered in such nonpartisan journals as the *New Republic* and the *Nation* authors as learned and stimulating as Kenneth Burke, Malcolm Cowley, and Edmund Wilson.

This display of name-dropping might suggest that all or most radicalized City College students in the thirties were omnivorous consumers of leftist and other critical literature, which of course was not the case. But many of them were very serious young intellectuals, and on this score they differed sharply from the sons and daughters of largely middle-class parents who about thirty years later rejected rational and scholarly critiques of capitalist society in favor of an expressive "counterculture" that emphasized a mixed bag of themes: paradoxically, communal sharing *and* an anarchistic individualism; a self-centered search for personal identity; technological primitivism in the midst of a highly rationalized economy; the alleged social evils of all bureaucracies; and their own "alienation" from all "bourgeois" institutions, including family, school, economy, and polity. This alienation (affirmed by such otherwise ill-grouped writers as Erich Fromm, Herbert Marcuse, Charles Reich, and Theodore Roszak), together with the anti-intellectualism of rebellious youth of the sixties, stands in sharp contrast with the radicalism of their predecessors at CCNY. Again, to quote Kristol:

At City College in the 30s we were familiar enough with the word ["alienated"] and the idea behind it. But for us it was a sociological category and referred to the condition of the working class. *We* were not alienated. By virtue of being radical intellectuals, we had "transcended" alienation (to use another Marxist term). We experienced our radicalism as a privilege of rank, not as a burden imposed by a malignant fate. It would never have occurred to us to denounce anyone or anything as "elitist." The elite was us—the "happy few" who had been chosen by History to guide our fellow creatures toward a secular redemption.*

The student radicals of the thirties included, not only Kristol's Trotskyists and other anti-Stalinists—his "happy few"— but nonalienated Marxists of all brands, by no means least the Communists and fellow travelers. As I have suggested, these competing groups were important educational agencies where, for a good many students, intensive social analysis and hot debate overshadowed their classroom exercises. The subjects confronted in the alcoves and elsewhere, moreover, transcended the conventional academic curriculum: the "dictatorship of the proletariat" in the Soviet Union, the fascist takeovers in Europe, the worldwide economic depression, Franklin Roosevelt and his New Deal, the powerful movements of Huey Long and Father Coughlin, the defeats and victories of organized labor, the growing menace of large-scale war. These were, or should have been, concerns of courses in history and the social sciences; they were profound concerns of Marxists and independent leftists of whatever variety. It is not surprising, then, that emerging from their ranks were several scholars and writers who, as graduates of radical circles of the thirties, continued over the years to be ardent students of the structure and dynamics of modern society.†

Perhaps the least radical and least doctrinaire of these young activists was Daniel Bell, whom I remember as a superior student and, while still an undergraduate, as a very busy working

* Ibid., p. 50, Kristol's italics.
† Kristol, referring to Alcove No. 1 of the Trotskyists et al. as an "authoritative educational milieu," in alleged contrast with Alcove No. 2 of the Stalinists, notes that this early training perhaps "is why so many went on to become professors—getting paid, as it were, for continuing to be interested in the things they had always been interested in" (Ibid., p. 55). Kristol's thumbnail sketches of several of his contemporaries who became well-known professors are drawn upon in the paragraphs below.

editor of the *New Leader*. Among his other accomplishments, Dan Bell appeared to have full command of Marxist literature and made devastating use of this knowledge in both the alcove debates and in the classroom. As a nonaffiliated independent, however, and even then a broad-gauged intellectual, he was critical of all rigid ideologies and skeptical of both academic and political orthodoxies. But his serious study of Marxist writings and his polemical exchanges with able Marxist fellow students must have been an important educational preparation for his impressive career: at the University of Chicago, as the first labor editor of *Fortune,* as a scholar and writer of great distinction at Columbia and Harvard.*

An equally prominent sociologist, Seymour Martin Lipset, son of a trade unionist and socialist father, may have been a mobile Marxist, but he was substantially more. His role in Alcove No. 1, as depicted by Irving Kristol, was that of an "intellectual bumblebee, whose function it was to spread the pollen of ideological doubt and political consternation over all [the alcove's] flowering ideologies." Marty Lipset was less of a "bumblebee" than Dan Bell in my classroom, which to be sure was a far less exciting place than the alcoves, but he was an excellent student and a promising social scientist. That his early engagement with Marxism, as was true in a number of other cases, was a rich educational asset is suggested by Lipset's splendid professional and scholarly record as a professor at Columbia, Berkeley, Harvard, and Stanford, and as a prodigious author of widely acclaimed works in political and historical sociology, social stratification, and social movements.

That sociology, more than other academic fields, has been enriched by the contributions of alumni of the left at City College in the 1930s is a claim to be examined shortly. But this radical background was an important part of the educational milieu of

* Three contrasting commentaries on Daniel Bell's voluminous writings are Ron Chernow, "The Cultural Contradictions of Daniel Bell," *Change,* March 1979, pp. 12–17; Peter Steinfels, *Neoconservatives: The Men Who Are Changing America's Politics* (New York: Simon and Schuster, 1979), chap. 7; and Bell's own comments in the preface of *The Winding Passage: Essays and Sociological Journeys 1960–1980* (Cambridge, Mass.: ABT Books, 1980). An exhaustive bibliography of Bell's publications has been compiled by Douglas G. Webb, author of a reported study, *From Socialism to Sociology: The Intellectual Careers of Philip Selznick, Seymour Martin Lipset, Nathan Glazer, and Daniel Bell, 1932–1960;* unfortunately, this work was unavailable when the present chapter was underway.

men of distinguished accomplishment in various areas of intellectual endeavor, predominantly in the social sciences but also in the humanities. To cite an outstanding case, Irving Howe,* a participant with Kristol, Bell, and Lipset in the ideological disputations of Alcove No. 1, was a Trotskyist leader as an undergraduate. As founder and editor of *Dissent,* however, for many years Howe has been a nonsectarian socialist and, as a splendid scholar and teacher, an eminent literary historian and critic whose *World of Our Fathers* (1976), in my view, surpasses all but a very few works in sociology itself as a comprehensive study of one of America's principal ethnic groups.† On this score, although no doubt he would disclaim the association, in addition to his achievements in literary scholarship, Irving Howe has bona fides as a sociologist.

Howe, the "theoretician" of the Trotskyists, Bell, precocious iconoclast, and Lipset, "intellectual bumblebee," were not the only anti-Stalinist student leftists of the thirties who were to become noted scholars in later years. Of those who passed through my own classes, for example, were Morroe Berger, Nathan Glazer, Peter Rossi, and Philip Selznick—all destined for highly successful careers as sociologists.

The left at City College, however, with its sharp divisions and internecine struggles, extended considerably beyond these undergraduate elitists and included, in addition to a substantial number of students of varying academic ability, a minority of faculty and even a handful of administrative and library personnel. Most of the faculty radicals, as in my own case, were young-

---

* Preceding Howe by several years was Alfred Kazin (CCNY, 1935) who became an equally famous man of letters. Like "everyone else [he] knew in New York [Kazin] was a Socialist," but he was primarily a self-styled "literary radical, indifferent to economics, suspicious of organization, planning, Marxist solemnity and intellectual system building." See Kazin's *Starting Out in the Thirties* (Boston: Little, Brown and Co., 1965), pp. 3–4. I first knew Alfred Kazin as a City College student; much later we were colleagues for a year at Smith College.

† The then-editor of the ASA publication *Contemporary Sociology*, Bennett Berger, agreed with my suggestion that *World of Our Fathers* should receive a long review, or a "Review Symposium," but to the date of this writing (March 1978) nothing had appeared in the leading review journal in the field. The fact that major contributions to our subject are made by "outsiders" rarely gets attention in sociology's major journals—a reflection perhaps of the provincialism associated with academic success, long marked, for example, in history and psychology.

sters with the rank of tutor, instructor, or in rare instances, assistant professor. And most of us, at least in my memory, were either unaffiliated "socialists" of ill-defined ideology or, especially from the mid-thirties until the Nazi-Soviet pact in 1939, more or less faithful travelers, but not members, of the Communist party.

The Communist party at City College (and, in New York, at Brooklyn College) during the 1930s has received extensive attention in reports of investigatory bodies, in memoirs and fiction, and in at least one large-scale scholarly study.* I have drawn upon this work in some small measure in an effort to link personal recollection of City's Communists and their activities, a subject still in dispute in the 1980s, with the documented historical record.

Within a year after my arrival at CCNY in 1933 a CP "fraction" was established at the college, led by Morris Schappes, a tutor in English who also wrote many of the unsigned pieces in the *Teacher-Worker,* a lively and sometimes amusing monthly issued by the local party unit. By 1938 (the year that Frederick B. Robinson, a powerful enemy of the left, was dismissed as president) the CP had achieved considerable influence in college affairs—with no more than fifty comrades on the faculty and staff, probably less than 3 percent of the students in the affiliated YCL, but with a much larger contingent of fellow travelers and periodic sympathizers. Some of this influence derived from a well-organized and ultimately successful campaign in support of Schappes himself, who after eight years on the faculty was threatened with dismissal in 1936; some from the skillful manipulations of party members in the Instructional Staff Association (ISA), a group of junior faculty with such nonrevolutionary objectives as salary increases and regulation of tenure, in which Communists dominated a misnamed "Caucus for Democratic Control"; and some from the party's yeoman work in "front" organizations, especially the League Against War and Fascism (we in the league were what the FBI later called "premature antifascists"), and, for a few years, in the Teachers Union. In these various spheres—in the ISA's push for academic tenure and the safeguarding of academic free-

---

* Robert W. Iversen, *The Communists and the Schools* (New York: Harcourt, Brace, 1959), in which the case of City College is discussed at length in chaps. 4–7 and 9. Some attention is given to the college in Nathan Glazer, *The Social Basis of American Communism* (New York: Harcourt, Brace, and World, 1961), chap. 4. Both studies are volumes in the series entitled "Communism in American Life," edited by Clinton Rossiter.

dom, in antiwar and antifascist programs, in the developing unionization of teachers—Communists and their fellow travelers were enormously industrious and generally effective functionaries, and were often seen as the most dedicated among us, dedicated to goals widely shared by both faculty and students.

The influence of individual Communists, then, had little or nothing to do with the Marxist-Leninist "theoretical" orientation of the party or indeed with any kind of socialist doctrine. In their teaching, moreover, Communists on the faculty were rarely found (though sometimes so accused) to be using the classroom for indoctrination or recruitment: their party politics was exercised elsewhere.* Several members of this group were able young scholars and excellent teachers—for example, Philip and Jack Foner in history; and among the larger number of fellow travelers and sympathizers were such academic stars as the philosophers Abraham Edel and Lewis Feuer. There were spokesmen for the party line, though only a tiny few as card-carriers, in most large departments, notably in History and English, but none in the then-small Department of Sociology.

My own relations with Communists at City College were fairly extensive, yet only once was I urged to attend their meetings with a view to party membership; the recruiter was Arnold Shukatoff, a tutor in English who had masterminded the defense of Morris Schappes. In connection with this drawn-out case, involving the interrelated presumption of job security based on long-time service and the protection of academic freedom, and in the ISA and especially the Teachers Union, my most active fellow participants included both identifiable CP members and a larger number of their staunch supporters. These faithful followers of the line no doubt privately condemned the undisciplined ideology, the liberalism, and the lack of "realism" displayed by a good many of us, but their criticisms were muffled during our work together in the union and elsewhere. It was our seemingly common endeavor in the American Federation of Teachers, particularly, that revealed fully the fundamental irreconcilability of doctrinaire communism and democratic principles.

The history of New York City's Local 5 of the AFT during

---

* As Iversen stresses (*The Communists and the Schools*, pp. 6off.), indoctrination in the classroom was inconsistent with Communist party policy as expressed by Earl Browder and other CP leaders. Iversen also notes (p. 142) that recruitment of teachers into the party was sometimes accomplished by their students—a *reversal* of "the common conception of campus indoctrination."

the "red decade," marked by the ascendance of the CP within the organization and its subsequent decline, has been amply recorded elsewhere.* The observations below are largely the recollections of a non-Communist union activist, but a reminder may be in order about the strength and composition of the AFT in the thirties. Of the 850,000 teachers in the United States at the beginning of the decade, some 5,000 were union members (there had been twice this number in 1920—before the "Red scare" years) and a fourth of these were New Yorkers with a large proportion of Jews who, in the face of long-standing discrimination, had been entering the teaching profession in large numbers. By 1935 more than 2,000 of the 30,000 teachers in New York were members of Local 5, and a year later another 1,000 had joined. Until about mid-decade three groups—the Socialists, Lovestonites, and Communists—vied for political leadership, although these Marxist rivals were generally cooperative in pursuit of the union's goals. But in 1936 the loyal fellow traveler (and sociologist of sorts) Jerome Davis was elected president of the AFT and by 1938, following a period of rapid party growth, the Communists had achieved substantial power in the national organization and were almost in full control in the New York local.† During the next two or three years, however, Communist power and influence were dealt heavy blows—by the Nazi-Soviet pact in 1939, by sudden shifts or reversals in the party line obviously reflecting Soviet direction, by the assassination of Trotsky in 1940, by a heavy-hitting "counteroffensive" of the Committee for Cultural Freedom (led by John Dewey and, among others, the one-time Communist sympathizer Sidney Hook), and, in 1940–41, by the investigations of the New York State legislature's Rapp-Coudert Committee resulting in the expulsion of several members of the party from the faculties and staffs of Brooklyn, Hunter, and City Colleges.

* Notably in ibid., chaps. 1–9, passim. Also revelatory are the (greatly contrasting) volumes by the anti-Communist Nathan Glazer, *The Social Basis of American Communism,* esp. chaps. 3–4, and the long-time and highly able "unofficial" Communist of Hunter College, Bella Dodd, *School of Darkness* (New York: Kennedy, 1954). Dodd became an "open" party member in 1944 and was on the National Central Committee of the CP. She was distressed by the expulsion of Earl Browder in 1945, and was herself expelled in 1949.
† The "almost," based upon personal participation, is a qualification of what I view as the overstatement of Nathan Glazer who, in a reference to the same period, notes that the "New York Branch, the Teachers Union, was *fully* dominated by the Communists" (*The Social Basis of American Communism,* p. 138, my italics).

Several years before these events, in the mid-thirties, I joined the Teachers Union, but initially did little more than pay my dues to Local 5. In 1938, however, with the establishment of Local 537 for college personnel, I became an activist: a recruiter of faculty colleagues, an eager participant in all too many union meetings, a partisan of both worthy and dubious causes—from the drive for tenure legislation for the city colleges to support of Jerome Davis in his dismissal from Yale's School of Divinity. For a year or so I was a member of the executive committee and secretary of the CCNY chapter of the union (the secretaryship was something of an anomaly in view of the Communist's generally successful effort to secure this strategic office in organizations in which they sought control). As a union busybody I worked closely with party members and fellow travelers and, for a time, without much difficulty: we seemed to be striving for common goals. But toward the end of 1938 and increasingly so in the following months it became apparent that Communists would use almost any means—stacking meetings, vilifying "enemy" colleagues, distorting reports, and so on—to gain domination and to impose the vagaries of the party line upon the union. Deploring these practices and faced with what often appeared to be a CP policy of "rule or ruin,"* a good many of us—mild liberals, unaffiliated socialists, anti-Stalinist radicals—resigned from the Teachers Union before the end of the "red decade."

To these recollections of competing Marxisms and their proponents' activities at City College in the thirties, two final observations: one of some contextual importance, the other a comment on the later-day views of ex-radicals. The first refers to the fact, recorded in a large literature, that many American intellectuals turned toward the left early in the decade, giving strength to campus radicalism among both students and teachers.† Thus by 1932 there were at least a dozen John Reed Clubs (the first club, in New York, had been launched by the *New Masses* in 1929) located in university centers where writers, a few professors,

---

* This policy also seemed to be manifest in the New York division of the American Labor Party, in which the Communists had achieved considerable power by 1938–39. My wife, Leonora, and I, as active members of the ALP at the time, were direct observers of the distressing practices referred to above.
† Daniel Aaron has given us a splendid account of intellectuals and the Communist party in *Writers on the Left* (New York: Harcourt, Brace, and World, 1961); for the 1930s, see esp. part two on "The Appeal of Communism."

and graduate students gave close attention to Marxist-Leninist lore. In the same year, among the fifty-two signers of the manifesto "Culture and Crisis," which endorsed the Communist ticket in the presidential election, were such prominent authors as Sherwood Anderson, Malcolm Cowley, John Dos Passos, Sidney Hook, Lincoln Steffens, and Edmund Wilson; and in 1934 appeared Hook's article on "Why I Am a Communist," in which this later-day target of a newer left, while condemning the atrocities of the Stalin regime and the dogmas of the CP, concluded that "only communism can save the world from its social evils. . . . *the time has now come to build a new communist party and a new communist international.*"* The intellectuals' denunciations of a seemingly bankrupt and clearly exploitative capitalism and the advocacy of communism by some of them, however, were less the result of rigorous analysis (or, as sometimes argued, of their being dupes) than the invocation of the social ideals of brotherhood, egalitarianism, and human justice—so important in the continuing, world-wide appeal of "Marxist" socialism itself.† In the thirties this appeal affected thousands of Americans—intellectuals and academics, to be sure, but also other idealistic men and women who were moved to support a program that appeared to promise a more humane society. (These included, in my own immediate circle, my mother, a Debsian Socialist of long standing, who, with no blessing from her son, was a member of the Communist party from about 1934 until several months before the Nazi-Soviet pact in 1939; and my wife's younger sister and two of her cousins, a daughter and sons of staunch Republicans, who became card holders soon after they had graduated, between 1933 and 1937, from schools of the ivy tradition and remained in the party for several years.)

The careers of certain former leftists provide the basis for an all-too-popular cliché: the alleged transition of most ex-radicals from left to right. That this is only one pattern of conversion from

---

* *Modern Monthly* 8, no. 3 (April 1934): 165, italics Hook's. This article, subtitled "Communism Without Dogma," was in reply to pieces on "Why I Am Not a Communist" by Bertrand Russell, John Dewey, and Morris R. Cohen.

† Here the words of a great scholar, written a half-century ago, are apposite: "When men paint up on the walls of their public halls or inscribe on the membership cards of their unions 'Labor is the sole source of wealth' they are not expressing a casual economic doctrine; they are making a fervid declaration of right" (A. D. Lindsay, *Karl Marx's Capital* [London: Oxford University Press, 1931], p. 116).

youthful to later-day ideologies is evidenced by the biographies of City College radicals of the thirties. The careers of four of the graduates of Alcove No. 1—Irving Kristol, Daniel Bell, S. M. Lipset, and Nathan Glazer—illustrate a rightward move over the years; today they are widely referred to as "neoconservatives." Yet, to lump together these four (along with Daniel Patrick Moynihan, Robert Nisbet, Samuel P. Huntington, James Q. Wilson, and others) is apt to be misleading.* The ex-Trotskyist Kristol, to be sure, is a self-styled Burkean conservative. Bell, always an independent thinker, as a mature scholar advocates a mixed economy, political democracy, and cultural conservatism. Lipset, the onetime "intellectual bumblebee" of Alcove No. 1, although affiliated with Stanford's conservative Hoover Institute, has espoused democratic socialism for many years. Glazer is a critic of what he views as discriminatory affirmative action and has decried some of the consequences of open enrollment at his alma mater, but his political stance is much closer to Bell's or Lipset's than to Kristol's. Notwithstanding these important differences, however, and as Peter Steinfels brings out in the volume cited above, these four City College graduates share a "neoconservative" style. They have also been depicted as united "Men of the Right" or as "bourgeois apologists" by present-day radicals. These stereotypes are as ungrounded as the presumed conservative destiny of most "Men of the Left."

The fallaciousness of this presumption is made abundantly clear by the careers of the other City College alumni. As undergraduates, two of the Trotskyist leaders were Irving Howe and Philip Selznick. Howe was a founder and for decades has been co-editor of the Socialist journal *Dissent,* and is a prominent member of the Democratic Socialist Organizing Committee (DSOC). Throughout his academic career in sociology and legal studies, Selznick's politics, like Howe's, have been a good way left-of-center, as they are today. A third ex-Trotskyist, the "main-line" sociologist Peter Rossi, also supports the DSOC. Another leading figure in Alcove No. 1, the always-independent Morroe Berger, remained a social democrat and an enemy of all political dogmas, left or right. The late Alvin Gouldner, a Stalinist at City College, was a hero of the New Left in the sixties, subsequently disavowed

---

* In *The Neoconservatives,* Peter Steinfels depicts similar beliefs and a common "style" among the subjects of his excellent study (in chaps. 3 and 4). But he also points up differences in their political and economic views, especially between those of Kristol, Moynihan, and Bell (in chaps. 5, 6, and 7).

the latter's anti-intellectualism, but remained until his death in 1980 a scholarly eminence in radical sociology.

Of these nine proponents of one or another kind of radicalism during the "red decade," all but two have been card-carrying and superior sociologists for many years. And the exceptional Irving Howe and Irving Kristol, with their conflicting ideologies, are more able sociologists than many members of the professional guild, in my unorthodox opinion. As undergraduates, however, they and other first-rate students encountered a less-than-distinguished program of formal instruction in the field.

City's Sociological Enterprise

At the School of Business and Civic Administration on Twenty-Third Street, my first three-year post at CCNY, I taught in both fields represented by the joint Department of Government and Sociology. But about the time of my move Uptown in 1936 a separate Department of Sociology and Anthropology was formally established, and that year I became a full-time teacher of a subject of questionable repute in the School of Liberal Arts. Sociology at City, as elsewhere in the thirties, was years away from its flowering in the academy, it ranked far below such traditional departments as history and philosophy, and its newly achieved status as a full-fledged department was viewed with some concern in faculty circles. In those years, moreover, the large majority of the sociology faculty itself consisted of a handful of youngsters, heavily involved in graduate study while teaching five-course programs, whose future scholarly and professional careers were problematic.

The one member of the department with established professional credentials was the chairman, Samuel Joseph, whose doctorate had been awarded by Columbia in 1914. Born in Russia himself and an escapee from religious persecution, Joseph's dissertation on Jewish immigration was something of a groundbreaking work; and decades later he published a study on the Americanization of Jewish immigrants.* Before joining the City

* The dissertation, *Jewish Immigration to the United States from 1881 to 1910*, Columbia University Studies in History, Economics, and Public Law, vol. 59, no. 4 (New York, 1914), although largely a study in demography, a province of sociology at Columbia, was directed by Franz Boas of anthropology—according to Joseph, because of Franklin H. Giddings's alleged anti-Semitism. The later work is the *History of the Baron de Hirsch Fund* (New York: The Jewish Publication Society, 1935).

College faculty in 1928, Joseph had taught the children of immigrants, first in the preparatory school that he founded and headed and later in public high schools. Teaching was a role he seemed to prefer to scholarly research or careful preparation for his classes at CCNY. At City, as an associate professor (his rank at retirement) and in the face of considerable opposition, he nevertheless succeeded in his ambition to create an independent department, which he chaired throughout my tenure. But Joseph was much less successful as a teacher of "what must have been the most severely critical student body in the world."* Whatever his classroom problems may have been, however, Professor Joseph's seniority and his genuine affection for young people, especially the sons of first-generation Americans, gave him a measure of protection against what was often unconcealed disparagement by City College students.

No such protection was enjoyed by four other members of our small department, all of whom were near beginners as teaching sociologists and all of whom combined demanding faculty duties with graduate study at Columbia. The senior among us was Adolph Tomars whose appointment at CCNY preceded my own in 1933 by a year or two. Tomars was an excellent student and young scholar of high promise. But his effectiveness as a teacher of bright City College students was greatly reduced by a susceptibility to an all-too-common pedagogical affliction: heavy reliance upon one-time carefully constructed lecture notes that scarcely changed from year to year—alert students, with malicious glee, could anticipate even his time-worn jokes. If, on this score, Tomars was a countermodel of his slightly younger colleagues, Harry Alpert, my exact contemporary at City, set an example of scholarly and teaching expertise that challenged the rest of us. A graduate of the college himself with an insider's empathy, Harry brought knowledge and wisdom, rigorous standards, sensitivity, and spontaneity to the classroom, as he did elsewhere in his later distinguished and well-known career. Little known beyond local circles, then or in subsequent years, was another City graduate, Arthur Ellis, an engaging and friendly man whose single claim to educational fame, at least as I remember, was his superior skill as a gadgeteer: Ellis created an answer sheet designed for a remarkable grading rack upon which thirty or more papers could be scored with minimal time and effort—of little use to those of us for whom "objective" examinations were anathema. For several

* Harry Alpert, letter of March 25, 1975.

years this mixed foursome of Tomars, Alpert, Ellis, and Page, together with Chairman Joseph, managed most of the instruction in sociology at City, supplemented by part-time specialists in criminology and social work, occasional visitors, and by two or three seldom seen auxiliary teachers in the evening division of the college.

The caliber of this instructional staff, with Harry Alpert as its only superior representative in the classroom, no doubt contributed substantially to my own proclaimed success as an undergraduate teacher*—the competition was generally weak. In this respect, the departmental milieu at City College provides another instance of a running theme in these recollections: the important role of sheer good luck in reputedly successful careers.

Although the sociology department was hardly an educational showpiece in a college sometimes referred to as the "proletarian Harvard," it was the center of some unusual achievements, one of which was the Social Research Laboratory, an innovation made by Samuel Joseph in 1929. The SRL, in unconventional linkage with regular departmental courses, pioneered in the promotion of supervised field investigation by undergraduate students who worked as part-time volunteers in a large variety of New York's welfare and research agencies and, in some measure, brought together abstract formulations of the classroom and concrete experience in the field. Joseph was the nominal director of the misnamed Laboratory, but the day-to-day supervision of the SRL, during most of the 1930s, was managed by a succession of junior faculty appointees (fellows and tutors). These included two young men who in later years were to be numbered among America's leading sociologists: Harry Alpert and Louis Schneider, each of whom in his initial professional post received the handsome annual salary of $1,000. But these future scholars of distinction, together with others who held this position,† added substantially to the educational wealth of the Department of Sociology.

---

* During the mid-thirties, one year the students named me the "best teacher" at City College—a wonderful kudos, of course, but one with no warrant in a school with a good many excellent teachers on its faculty, including the nonpareil Morris Raphael Cohen.

† Among them: Henrik Infeld, the author of important comparative studies of cooperatives in Israel and elsewhere; and William Henderson, a protégé of Willard Waller (see chap. 2) who, as an Air Combat Intelligence officer in the U.S. Army, was killed during the early months of America's participation in World War II.

In contrast with the curricular giantism of many departments a few decades later, at City College in the thirties there
were no more than a dozen offerings in the subject, including one
or two in anthropology. But "Sociology 5" was a guarantor of
heavy departmental enrollments, for this introductory course
was required for the most popular degree (the B.S.S.) in liberal
arts—in all likelihood a unique stipulation in American colleges
at the time. In addition to this assurance of a large captive audience, a limitation of class size of about thirty students (there were
no huge lecture courses at City) demanded numerous sections of
introductory sociology, which were distributed unevenly among
all full-time members of the department. One semester my own
fifteen hours of teaching consisted of five sections of Sociology 5,
imposing upon the students what must have been something less
than stimulating instruction. Usually, however, my program was
enhanced with a course in urban sociology and for a couple of
years I taught the two sections of "Methods in Social Research,"
with its supervised "laboratory" raising my assignment to seventeen hours—then considered to be only a bit beyond the normal
load. (For readers who might question an essayistic sociologist's
qualifications in research methods, I should add that in those years
it was generally assumed that *any* doctor of philosophy or near-
Ph.D. was equipped to teach *any* undergraduate course in sociology—an assumption long since undermined by specialization in
our multifarious field.) The course in methods proved to be a
double blessing: in directing student projects, it alerted me to the
complexities and hazards of serious field research; and it provided
a measure of preparation for my subsequent—and unanticipated—
teaching stint in Columbia's graduate department.*

It was introductory sociology, however, that offered the
severest challenge and contributed most to my education as a
classroom teacher. And the fact that during my tenure at CCNY
I taught forty or so classes of Sociology 5 provided a ground of
sorts for someone's sally in later years, that I was the "Mr. Chips
of American sociology"—a not unkindly canard. The challenge—
forcefully presented by the bright and often skeptical City College students—was to try to show how study of sociology can offer
fresh perspectives on the world around us and on the larger society—and indeed can bring some light to the existential task of
locating oneself in that changing world. In the pursuit of such

---

* As noted in chap. 2, one of the courses I taught at Columbia was "Problems
in Social Research."

lofty and, in the eyes of some of my colleagues, unrealistic goals, each instructor was given free reign as to textbook (if any), other readings, and course papers, constrained only by the college regulation of a scheduled final examination. In my own sections one year the semester's readings consisted of the following unharmonious quartet: Robert MacIver's *Society,* the Lynds' *Middletown in Transition,* Nikolai Bukharin's *Historical Materialism,** and John Steinbeck's *Grapes of Wrath*—a far larger and more demanding assignment than undergraduates of a later day, or their teachers, would tolerate. But City students in those years, while differing greatly in sociological interest, diligence, and academic performance, regarded 1,500 to 2,000 pages as no wide departure from the college norms. Under such circumstances, however great a challenge, teaching was enormously rewarding.

The main job of teaching five classes of sociology, while a greedy consumer of time and energy, was supplemented by other activities at City, including the unionization efforts referred to above. For the sociology faculty, ranking only behind instruction was the ever-present academic exercise of departmental politics— in our case a nonpacific process. The precise nature of the issues that divided us is long forgotten, but I have a clear memory of the combat alignment: Chairman Joseph and his faithful ally Adolph Tomars versus Harry Alpert and me. In preparation for the confrontations in department meetings, there were extensive strategic preliminaries on both sides involving clandestine sessions at Joseph's Wanamaker headquarters and, my wife reminds me, many evening hours of telephoned exchanges between Alpert and Page. Although our concerns had less to do with sociology and college education than with the alleged administrative machinations of the chairman, I had no doubt at the time, with respect to all matters, that academic virtue was arrayed against professional malfeasance. That this conviction was foolishness should have been made apparent by my own unseemly and noncollegial deportment in departmental gatherings; the chairman, oftentimes confronted with the inexcusable bumptiousness of a callow youth, probably had reason to rid himself of a troublesome (and, for several years, untenured) colleague. But an index of Samuel Joseph's tolerance was the mildness of his punitive measures—for example,

---

* This work by the Soviet Union's one-time leading intellectual, originally published with the subtitle "A System of Sociology," proved to be more enlightening for my students (and easier to read!) than Engel's orthodox and more "scientific" *Anti-Duehring.*

assigning me for a term a schedule of five sections of Sociology 5 unrelieved by an elective course or, to cite Joseph's harshest punishment, during my final semester at City, the imposition of a program split between the Uptown and Twenty-Third Street branches of the college. Compensating many times over for these burdens, however, were the rewards provided by my students.

Of the large number of future sociologists who began their study of the subject at CCNY, there were several students in the late 1930s and early '40s whose later careers give support to the hyperbole of City College as a "seedbed of modern American sociology."* Consider the following array of later-day notables: Daniel Bell (class of 1938), Morroe Berger (1940), Nathan Glazer (1944), Alvin Gouldner (1941), Seymour Martin Lipset (1943), Peter Rossi (1943), and Philip Selznick (1938); and to these may be added, from the same cohort, such able teachers, scholars, and administrators as Meyer Barash, Murray Hausknecht, Bernard Kutner, William Spinrad, Herman D. Stein, and Leonard Weller. At one time or another at City, I confronted each of these sociologists-to-be in the classroom. Since then their works have added greatly to my own education, the enhancement of my professional status has been a latent function of their achievements, and over the years continuing friendship with almost all of them has been a lasting reward of my first college teaching job. At this point in these recollections, the early exploits and later accomplishments of three of these one-time students warrant special comment.

Morroe Berger

In almost every one of my classes at City College one or two students stand out from the others as brilliant youngsters who offered more to their teacher than they received. Thus I had the opportunity to learn from Joseph Goldsen, Louis Lister, and Jack Loft during my apprenticeship at Twenty-Third Street, and in later years Uptown a dozen or more superior students were also my tutors without intention. Prominent among them was the extraordinary Morroe Berger, class of 1940.

But my earliest impression of "Mr." Berger (academic custom in those days precluded first names) held no such promise and indeed was disconcerting. During the first several meetings

---

* There are other, but fewer, distinguished sociologists who were undergraduates at City College in the subsequent decade, for example, Irving L. Horowitz, class of 1951, and David Matza, my student in 1952–53.

of the introductory course in which he was enrolled this distressingly silent student appeared to be enduring, quietly but painfully, my attempts to elucidate the virtues of a sociological approach and to stimulate discussion by the skeptics whom I faced. Following class one day, however, in our initial private talk Berger displayed a thorough grasp of MacIver's *Society* and the other readings assigned for the entire semester, considerable knowledge of the all-too-many authors whose names I had already dropped in the classroom, critical acumen far beyond his nineteen or twenty years, and, to my delight, a serious interest in sociology itself. From that unexpected and welcome occasion until his death in 1981, Morroe Berger was both friend and teacher.

Only by unwarranted post hoc reconstruction can it be claimed that Morroe's feats as an undergraduate (or those of other students) clearly presaged his later accomplishments as scholar, teacher, and administrator. But there was no question that here was a first-rate student whose rare combination of interests and talents gave promise of a successful and multifaceted career. He was a college junior when he and I first met, and Morroe was already deeply involved in four socially and culturally important fields: leftist politics as an anti-Stalinist independent and critical activist in Alcove No. 1; the study of literature, including the works of the unlikely bedfellows Henry Adams, John Dos Passos, Thomas Mann, and Ignazio Silone; jazz music, some of the best of which nearby Harlem provided in the thirties; history and the social sciences. Evidence of both Morroe's independent radicalism and his early scholarly bent is to be seen in one of his contributions to an unusual student journal, published in 1939.

> The books that have influenced me in the study of history fall into two broad categories. The first could be called: "and sudden insight." The second marked the consolidation of something of a comprehensive formal system of many loose ideas derived from countless sources.
>
> In the first class is Veblen's *Theory of the Leisure Class,* in which I found basic insights into the nature of ruling classes in history; Thomas Mann's *Magic Mountain,* which taught me among other things metaphysics, anthropology, some geology, and the meaning of a philosophy of history; Henry Adams' *Education,* which somehow made me feel the *humanity* of history and historical characters.
>
> In the second, belongs Marx's *Capital* (vol. 1, only parts 2 and 3) . . . need I say what it taught me? Complementing it

was Veblen's *Theory of Business Enterprise.* In a general way
I had known the importance of what they were saying before
I approached them directly. But the direct communication of
their ideas emphasized for me the necessity of precise qualification and the valuelessness of loose generalizations.*

In view of the fact that his principal academic interests lay
within the fields of history, literature, and economics (his undergraduate major) Morroe's decision to pursue graduate study in
sociology came as a surprise to his teacher of this less sturdy subject. The decision was consistent, however, with his admiration
of the work of Robert MacIver, who together with Morris R.
Cohen, John Dos Passos, and Ignazio Silone, was one of the "great
thinkers and writers" to whom he recently expressed a lifelong
indebtedness.† Accordingly, I assumed that Columbia, MacIver's
university, would be Morroe's unhesitant choice for a graduate
school, but it was only after prolonged discussion of almost all
possible alternatives that Morroe made what seemed to be the agon-
izing decision to elect Columbia.

Graduate study at Columbia for Morroe was interrupted
by more than four years in the army which involved language
training at Princeton and subsequent duty in the Middle East, a
preliminary preparation for his then-unforeseen role as sociology's
foremost authority on the Arab world. But the prolonged military
service failed to detract from his excellent record at Columbia,
culminating in a dissertation that established Morroe's bona fides
as a political sociologist. *Equality by Statute* (1952, revised 1967)
was the initial volume in what was to become an extensive bibliography marked by a versatility matched by very few American
social scientists.‡

* The *Chronicle* ("An Undergraduate Journal of History, Published by the
History Society, College of the City of New York"), 4 (Winter 1939): 7. The
quotation is from a symposium on "Books that Shaped Historical Thinking,"
the contributors to which included, among others, Abraham Edel, Philip
Foner, Sidney Hook, Max Lerner, J. Salwyn Schapiro, and a young instructor
named Page, as well as the two students Morroe Berger and Melvin J. Lasky,
both of whom, together with Irving Kristol, were editors of the *Chronicle.*
† In the preface to *Real and Imagined Worlds: The Novel and Social Science*
(Cambridge: Harvard University Press, 1977), p. vii.
‡ In addition to works on Arab societies and in political sociology, Berger's
publications include, for example, two volumes in the sociology of literature
and scholarly contributions to such diverse and atypical subjects as jazz music,
military rhetoric, and belly dancing. There is commentary about these accomplishments and others in chap. 5.

During the postwar years until 1952, when he joined the Princeton faculty, Morroe's multiple talents, which had been evidenced earlier at City College, were amply demonstrated: in free-lance journalism, involving frequent pieces in the *New Leader* and New York's *Herald Tribune* and *Times;* in part-time teaching of the famous contemporary civilization course at Columbia and of sociology at New York University; in social research for *both* the American Jewish Congress and the rival American Jewish Committee, providing a strange background for a scholar who a few years later would be persona grata in Arab political and academic circles; and, preceding all of this, in a display of matrimonial perspicacity when Morroe, while still in uniform, joined forces with a lovely lady, Paula, at a splendid celebration which my wife, Leonora, Robert MacIver, and I, also in uniform plus yarmulke, were privileged to attend in March 1943.

Since these wartime years, Morroe Berger's achievements, like those of other former students heralded in these pages, have been a source of unearned pride for me—and indeed, as I have noted earlier, the ground for a degree of conferred prestige. Standing high among the others is Philip Selznick.

Philip Selznick

My recollections of Phil Selznick as an undergraduate at City are less vivid than my memory of Morroe Berger. Nevertheless I remember him as among the half-dozen or so most able students of the thousands who have journeyed through my courses. Of the class of 1938, Phil met the introductory requirement a year or two before my first encounter with Morroe; he did so quietly and, considering his Trotskyist convictions at the time, probably with a skeptical or even jaundiced view of a MacIverian brand of sociology. But his powerful intellectual bent and scholarly potential were apparent—Selznick's later outstanding career in the academy came as no surprise.

At CCNY—and indeed in greater New York—Phil was an important figure in Trotskyist circles. As a teacher, however, I was only vaguely aware of his political convictions and activities, extracurricular preoccupations that probably served Phil educationally (as they did other sociologists-to-be) more richly than a course or two in sociology. His early absorption of Marxist literature and intense participation in Trotskyist party affairs, although he then viewed them in quite different terms, were an important preparatory exercise, surely, for his later seminal studies of organizational phenomena: *TVA and the Grass Roots* (1949), an analysis of the dilemmas of leadership in democratic planning which established "cooptation" as a highly useful conceptual tool in the social sciences; *The Organizational Weapon* (1952), a "study of Bolshevik strategy and tactics" which must have been informed by Phil's earlier adventures as a Trotskyist; and *Leadership in Administration* (1957), in which simplistic psychological interpretations are replaced by a sophisticated sociology of both bureaucratic decision-making and innovative leadership in formal organizations.

The TVA volume was Phil's doctoral dissertation, which joined the list of distinguished works written by Columbians.* One of the several rewards of my own brief association with Columbia's faculty in 1941–42 was the re-establishment of my acquaintance with Phil, but in this instance on a far different basis from that of being his undergraduate instructor. For Phil as a registered student and I as an auditor were fellow participants in a remarkable course on institutional analysis where for several weeks we were spellbound by the lectures of the man who, through his published essays as well as in the classroom, was to become sociology's foremost teacher. We were saddened, however, when illness prevented Bob Merton's completion of the course—a blow for all of us in the class, but a misfortune with the consequence that Phil and I became working colleagues. As a legitimized member of the faculty, I was asked by Chairman MacIver to "complete" the course, a terrifying assignment that I managed after a fashion with the help of a powerful threesome: Willard Waller, the anthropologist Ralph Linton, and Philip Selznick. It was clear that we could not follow closely in Merton's theoretical footsteps or begin to approach his brilliant analysis of the functionalist perspective. But each of us lectured on a topic more or less consistent with the substantive content of Merton's course: Waller on "institutions for the care of segregated persons," Linton on status and role, Page on unintended effects of the democratization of informal groups, and Selznick on organizational aspects of the Trotskyist party in New York. In this non-Mertonian medley, Phil Selznick was the star.

In the years since his student apprenticeship, Phil's pro-

* Several of these from the 1930s are depicted in chap. 2. The three-year delay of the publication of *TVA and the Grass Roots* (Berkeley and Los Angeles: University of California Press, 1949) was "a wholly incidental consequence of the war years" (p. v).

fessional achievements, like those of other City College graduates who subsequently pursued the doctorate at Columbia, are solid evidence of his membership in sociology's elite. Following successful teaching on the faculties of Minnesota and UCLA,* and only after extended negotiations between the University of California's reluctant Los Angeles and the developing Berkeley departments, Phil joined the latter's small band of sociologists, largely through the efforts of S. M. Lipset, Reinhard Bendix, and Robert Nisbet.† These young plotters sought to convert sociology at Berkeley from what had long been a tiny department of "social institutions" under the domination of the eminent Frederick J. Teggart into a modern-day and diversified center of research and teaching staffed by scholars of distinction. That their efforts were successful is known to all sociologists: for a quarter of a century Berkeley has been—and continues to be—a powerful sociological stronghold. Perhaps less well known is the part played in this institutional success story by City College's alumni: from the early beginnings, by Marty Lipset and Phil Selznick; for six or seven years until 1969, by Nat Glazer; and from a later City cohort (class of 1953), by David Matza—who today, unlike the emigrés to Harvard, Lipset and Glazer, but together with Selznick, continues his affiliation with Berkeley's department.

Over the decades Phil Selznick's own important role, both at Berkeley and in the larger world of sociology, has been many sided. In the formative years, he and his colleagues in their search for a senior scholar to head the department made the fortunate choice of Herbert Blumer, under whose wise and permissive

---

* While still at UCLA, Selznick's *The Organizational Weapon* was published, joining such volumes in the RAND series as *The Operational Code of the Politburo* by Nathan Leites, *Air War and Emotional Stress* by Irving L. Janis, and *Soviet Attitudes Toward Authority* by Margaret Mead. At RAND Selznick worked closely with Hans Speier (see chap. 2, above) and Paul Kecskemeti, and with a fellow alumnus of City College, Joseph Goldsen (see the first section of the present chapter). The Selznick-Goldsen association at RAND is only one illustration recorded in these recollections of talented "old boys"—from CCNY and later from Princeton—coming together professionally long after their student days. In the fall of 1980, Selznick, Goldsen, and I held a reunion in San Francisco.

† Nisbet and Lipset have long since left Berkeley; Bendix moved to the Department of Political Science in 1972. But in the summer of 1950, as a visiting teacher, I was privileged to attend several meetings with these conspirators in which planning for sociology's future at Berkeley was underway—and which included the "capture" of Selznick from UCLA.

leadership Berkeley's sociological enterprise achieved deserved fame.* During the time of troubles in the mid-sixties when the department, like the university itself, became polarized and suffered the anguish of the breakup of long-time friendships, Phil's collegial devotion and tireless efforts contributed to the group's survival as a distinguished academic entity. In the quite different realm of innovative scholarship, Phil established and directed the Center for the Study of Law and Society and published, among other works, the provocative volume *Law, Society, and Industrial Justice* (1969). In collaboration with Leonard Broom, his former colleague at UCLA, he assembled and partially wrote an introductory textbook that in its many editions probably has been read by more undergraduates than any other work in sociology. In any event, as he once remarked, this publishing bonanza has assured Phil Selznick a style of life undreamt of by the young Trotskyist revolutionary at City College in the 1930s.

Alvin W. Gouldner

In what turned out to be my final semester of teaching at City in the prewar years, Chairman Joseph, for reasons long forgotten, penalized me with the worst of all possible schedules, a program split between the Uptown campus and the School of Business and Civic Administration. The almost daily subway trips between the two centers, the stand-up, ten-minute "luncheons," and the return, if only part time, to a reputedly academic Siberia at Twenty-Third Street, I was convinced, were an overly severe punishment for a tenured doctor of philosophy, whatever his delinquencies. But I survived and at least on one count was the benefactor of Professor Joseph's imposition. For among my students at the School of Business was a lively young redhead named Alvin Gouldner.

I do not recall why Al Gouldner was taking a degree in business administration (B.B.A., class of 1941), but in firm memory he joins Morroe Berger and Philip Selznick as one of the very best of my City College students, uptown or downtown. Al, like

* Twenty sociologists who hold or have held senior rank in the Berkeley department include Robert Bellah, Reinhard Bendix, Judith Blake, Herbert Blumer, John Clauson, Kingsley Davis, Wolfram Eberhard, Nathan Glazer, Charles Glock, Erving Goffman, Gertrude Jaeger, William Kornhauser, S. M. Lipset, Leo Lowenthal, David Matza, William Petersen, Neil Smelser, Arthur Stinchcombe, Guy Swanson, and Harold Wilensky—an extraordinary parade of sociological talent.

Phil, was a Marxist, but he followed the line of the Trotskyists' left-wing enemies, the Communist party of Lenin, Stalin, and Earl Browder. This ideological and organizational commitment, however, did not prevent Al (as it did in at least a few other cases of potentially first-rate students) from amassing an excellent academic record—or from enlivening the classroom with spontaneity, wit, and intellectual versatility. There or in more private sessions Al's enthusiasm for learning as such and his propensity for the free play of ideas seemed to be a far cry from the demands of a revolutionary "steel instrument." His proclivities as an undergraduate, I believe, foreshadowed Gouldner's later achievements as an outstanding scholar, a foremost exponent of a radical sociology, and the author of a shelf of dazzling works.

Like other City College student radicals of scholarly bent, Al Gouldner's Ph.D. in sociology was obtained at Columbia where his teachers included MacIver and Lynd of the earlier regime and the younger stars Lazarsfeld and Al's principal mentor Merton. Politically, Al did not succumb to the cooling-out process so characteristic of graduate study (he remained a follower of the Communist line for several years after graduation from City), but his achievements at Columbia were those of a talented young scholar, not a doctrinaire. Especially in his work with Merton* Al became a student of the non-Marxist sociology of Max Weber, which he put to fruitful use in the two books derived from his dissertation, *Patterns of Industrial Bureaucracy* and *Wildcat Strike,* both published in 1954. The former, an excellent case study of a gypsum plant, joined Selznick's *TVA and the Grass Roots* and Peter Blau's *The Dynamics of Bureaucracy* (1955) as Mertonian dissertations that for many years functioned as influential models in the sociological analysis of organizational structure and change—one of the several fields in which Gouldner was to become a leading figure.

Beginning in 1947, his academic positions included posts at the University of Buffalo, Antioch, Illinois, and Washington University in St. Louis where he became the Max Weber Research Professor of Social Theory in 1967. During the preceding two

---

* Gouldner's close relationship with Merton (whatever their theoretical and political differences may have been) continued for almost forty years. Thus, for example, Merton became "Special Advisory Editor" of *Theory and Society,* the journal established by Gouldner in 1973; and Gouldner contributed to Merton's festschrift with the essay "Sociology and Everyday Life," in Lewis A. Coser, ed., *The Idea of Social Structure* (New York: Harcourt Brace Jovanovich, 1975), pp. 417–32.

years he had lectured extensively abroad (in West Berlin, Stockholm, Jerusalem, and Warsaw) and, on leave from Washington from 1972 to 1976, he was Professor of Sociology at the University of Amsterdam. Al's years in Europe corresponded with the upsurge of Marxist, structuralist, and critical theories that strongly influenced his own work.

Al's publications are vast, thematically diverse, and controversial. After his early books, *Patterns of Industrial Bureaucracy* and *Wildcat Strike,* there were an introductory text (with Helen Gouldner), expertly edited books on leadership and applied sociology, and a brave but successful venture into classical history, *Enter Plato* (1965). Already well known as a keen critic of mainline sociology,* the publication of *The Coming Crisis of Western Sociology* (1970) established Gouldner, following the late C. Wright Mills, as the foremost radical sociologist in the United States—and set off some hot debates. This volume was followed by a series of critical studies in the Marxist tradition: *The Dialectic of Ideology and Technology* (1976), *The Future of Intellectuals and the Rise of the New Class* (1979), *The Two Marxisms* (1980), and the posthumous *Marxism and the Sociology of Intellectuals* (1981). These recent publications, like *The Coming Crisis,* are marked by impressive displays of learning in both classical and contemporary social theory, relentless social criticism, preoccupation with the sociology of sociology, and polemical propensity.

Along with this monumental output, Al displayed unusual professional perspicacity by founding and editing two contrasting journals. In 1963 *Trans-Action* (later *Society,* edited by Gouldner's co-founder, Irving Horowitz) appeared, clearly demonstrating that socially and sociologically important work need not be written either pretentiously or only by insiders. And ten years later, from Amsterdam, came *Theory and Society* whose contributions to "renewal and critique in social theory" are exciting additions to international sociological scholarship.

This extraordinary record—as teacher, editor, and especially as author of publications matched in quality and quantity

---

* Gouldner's critical prowess is exhibited in both his books and papers. The latter include, for example, "Anti-Minotaur: The Myth of a Value-Free Sociology," *Social Problems* 9 (Winter 1962): 199–213; "Reciprocity and Autonomy in Functional Theory," in *Symposium in Sociological Theory,* ed. Llewellan Gross (New York: Harper and Row, 1959); and the distressingly personalistic piece, "The Sociologist as Partisan: Sociology and the Welfare State," *American Sociologist* 3 (May 1968): pp. 103–16. Several of Gouldner's most important papers are brought together in *For Sociology* (1970).

by very few of his contemporaries—fully warranted, in my view, Al Gouldner's election to the highest office that American sociologists can bestow (he was president of the Society for the Study of Social Problems in 1962). His radicalism and critical stance may have hindered Gouldner's nomination; if this be so, ASA committees have been at serious fault. Probably Al's greater handicap was his widespread reputation as an alienator of colleagues and a man of violent temper; and on this score too I would fault my fellow sociologists. For surely the governing consideration in awarding the presidency of the association should be the sociologist's scholarly work, irrespective of difficult personality or unconventional deportment.

Firebrand from his City College years, Al died in 1980 at the age of sixty without having received this honorific. Far more important than any such office, however, were the testimonials of his fellow sociologists who hailed Alvin Gouldner's contributions to scholarship and indeed to the intellectual life of his times.*

Educational Background, Generations, and
Sociological Work: A Historical Note

The cases reported in the preceding pages—of Daniel Bell, Morroe Berger, Nathan Glazer, Alvin Gouldner, Seymour Martin Lipset, Peter Rossi, and Philip Selznick—point up the role of City College in the education of important members of a generation of American sociologists. These cases also illustrate the function of City as a feeder for Columbia, where all of these future leading lights received the doctorate (and where Bell, Berger, and Lipset at different times held faculty positions). Thus a reliable history of American sociology during the second half of this century, if it is undertaken, surely will record the CCNY-Columbia avenue into the higher reaches of the field. And such a history might note that the scholarly work of these sociologists, in thematic focus and intellectual style, not only reflects the influence

---

* The testimonials include, for example, the obituary in *Footnotes* (March 1981) by Charles Lemert and Robert K. Merton, a fine appreciation of Gouldner's contributions and of Gouldner himself, "warts and all." On March 22, 1981, Merton, Erving Goffman, Norman Birnbaum, and Cornelis Disco spoke movingly at a special session in memory of Gouldner at the annual meeting of the Eastern Sociological Society; similar sessions were held at meetings of other regional societies. At the time, plans were underway for a session on Gouldner's scholarly work at the 1981 meeting of the American Sociological Association in Toronto.

of their Columbia mentors, but carries marks of their earlier schooling in the classrooms and especially the alcoves of City College. This kind of exploration of interconnections between educational background and "mental production" could be revealing, but only if pursued with caution.*

In the research and writing of the City College-Columbia sociologists, most notably in the studies of Bell, Gouldner, and Lipset, we encounter the themes of class structure and change, social and political movements, shifting ideological patterns, revolution and counterrevolution—and these weighty subjects were major concerns of many undergraduates at CCNY in the 1930s. Clearly, however, there are other prominent sociologists of the same generation with similar thematic interests from strikingly dissimilar and diverse backgrounds, social and educational.† Yet to a greater degree than in the sociological work of most of their contemporaries, the publications of the graduates of City and Columbia are colored by the academic and ideological events of their younger years—or so I would contend. There are great differences of course between the theoretical and political views of Bell, Gouldner, Lipset, and the others, but their like talent for *both* sustained scholarship and disputation retains the flavor of the intellectual controversies in which they were once engaged at City College.

This observation is far less firmly grounded than the more general predication that the sociological work of scholars who were students in the thirties and forties—whether at CCNY, Columbia, or elsewhere—was strongly influenced by the events and concerns of those momentous decades. As academic sociology burgeoned in the postwar years, around the work of sociologists of that generation—legatees of the great Depression, ideological confrontation, and political ferment—there emerged such special fields of study as social stratification, bureaucracy, political sociology, social movements, and social change. Moreover, for mem-

---

* Attention to this admonition might have modified Alvin Gouldner's frequently criticized treatment of the alleged interconnections between Talcott Parsons's biography, particularly his long-time affiliation with ivy schools Amherst and Harvard, and his theoretical work, as presented in part two of *The Coming Crisis of Western Sociology* (New York: Basic Books, 1970).

† Three distinguished, and conspicuously contrasting, examples are Reinhold Bendix, originally from Germany, with undergraduate and graduate degrees from Chicago; C. Wright Mills, out of Texas with a doctorate from Wisconsin; and Norman Birnbaum, a New Yorker with degrees from Williams and Harvard.

bers of that generation and for many of their students (and with
a scholarly assist from refugee sociologists)* the European master
builders, Karl Marx, Max Weber, and Emile Durkheim became
theoretical and methodological deities of American sociology. In
this country, then, beginning in the late 1940s, growing apace in
the following years, and continuing today in an era of "competing
paradigms," was a new kind of sociology which in its early development was in large measure the production of a generation of distinctive historical background.

This example of the impact of generational background on
scholarly production, sociological or otherwise, invokes a commonplace of intellectual and cultural history, but one that has been
insufficiently exploited in the sociology of American sociology.†
A more recent case that may warrant study is the emergence,
reaching large dimensions in the late 1960s and 1970s, of sociological preoccupation with everyday life, manifest in a variety of overlapping perspectives: symbolic interactionism, dramaturgy, ethnomethodology, "naturalism," sociology of the absurd, and so on.
The concern with the "construction of reality" at the grass-roots,
existential meaning, and with the tactics of face-to-face exchange,
together with the relative disregard of the structural and institutional features of society, it may be suggested, has affinities with
both the anarchistic individualism and the intimate communalism
of a generation of visible youth far different from their forerunners of the thirties and forties. The inconsistent but loudly
proclaimed values of the "turned-on" generation, from the pioneer
beats of the fifties to the widespread counterculture of the sixties
and later, were an important part of the educational background
of all students of this era and, to extend the present surmise, in
that generation are the chief exponents of the sociology of everyday life.

The suggested linkage between earlier cohort experience

* Personal experience with such assistance is reported in the section on "Beyond Fayerweather: Education from Abroad" in chap. 2.
† The relationship between generational background and the substance of
sociological work is one of several themes in Robert W. Friedrichs's excellent
study, *A Sociology of Sociology* (New York: The Free Press, 1970); and, with
specific reference to the work of Talcott Parsons, as noted above, is treated
rashly and at length by Alvin Gouldner in *The Coming Crisis of Western
Sociology*. A mammoth but in my view unsuccessful effort to bring out this
relationship, inter alia, is the neo-Marxist volume by Herman and Julia R.
Schwendinger, *The Sociologists of the Chair: A Radical Analysis of the
Formative Years of North American Sociology* (New York: Basic Books, 1974).

and later substantive preoccupations of sociologists stands as conjecture in this historical note—as do other asides in these recollections. To return to the generation of our present concern, however, it may be observed that it is hardly surprising that most of the graduates of the Depression and wartime years who became sociologists of note ignored phenomenological temptations; their theoretical masters were Marx, Weber, and Durkheim, the high priests of structural and institutional analysis. This observation holds of course for the scholars who began their study of sociology at City College.

Afterword: City College Revisited

City granted me a leave of absence in 1940–41 for work with the National Refugee Service and generously extended the leave for the following academic year to enable me to join the teaching faculty at Columbia. For four years, beginning early in 1942, I wore the uniform of an officer in the Air division of the United States Navy. As a rather weary veteran, I taught at CCNY for a single hectic semester in the spring of 1946, but surrendered my tenure at City (and, still viewing school administrators in somewhat jaundiced terms, declined an assistant deanship there) in favor of what I then assumed would be a short-lived stay at Smith College. This expectation soon dissolved midst the many attractions at Smith—students, faculty, the physical beauty and cultural cornucopia of the "Valley"—but nostalgic memories of my first academic love, and indeed of the cosmopolitan life of New York, were sufficiently strong to lead me to accept in 1952 an invitation to move to City as chairman of the Department of Sociology and Anthropology.

To return to the scene of my prolonged apprenticeship as a lowly instructor in this exalted post was a personal tribute, or so I assumed. But the circumstances surrounding the invitation were less than felicitous—and challenged my firm conviction that collegial bodies should themselves select their officers with minimal participation by the higher administration. In this unusual case, the department and its chairman, the anthropologist Burt Aginsky, had been under intensive investigation for several years by a special faculty committee whose recommendations included the administrative appointment of an outsider as chair who was to be charged with the task of stabilizing what had long been a sorely troubled and irregularly governed department. Thus in the fall of 1952 I rejoined City College, not triumphantly, but in the role of a hatchet man, at least in the eyes of Aginsky and most of his faithful followers.

Burt Aginsky was in Europe on leave for the greater part of 1952–53, to my considerable benefit, for during his many years as chairman Aginsky had developed powerful control over all but a few of his colleagues, demonstrating both persuasive talent and manipulative skill. On the latter count, he had brought into the department a half dozen or more young men who had not completed the Ph.D. and who as lecturers without tenure-line status received decent salaries but were almost fully dependent on the chair for term-to-term or year-to-year reappointment. These modern-day retainers, moreover, with no legal voting rights, were enfranchised by Aginsky who proclaimed his support of collegial "democracy" while ruling his departmental realm with a firm hand. Personal domination of this order, as I learned soon after my return to City, was largely responsible for a dismal state of affairs: a group of generally able sociologists and anthropologists most of whom, nevertheless, not only were timid souls in the face of authority, but were far more preoccupied with currying the favor of a new chairman than with teaching and research.

There were of course members of the department who were neither timid nor sychophantic, among them the criminologist Harry Shulman whose own hope to become chairman became manifest shortly after my arrival, and John Collier, former United States Commissioner of Indian Affairs, a kindly elder statesman with no academic ambitions. But Aginsky's doughty enemy was Adolph Tomars. Tomars had taught at City since 1932 and for many years had been Samuel Joseph's close ally. Together they had supported Aginsky as Joseph's successor—only soon to face an entirely new pattern of departmental domination in the hands of a colleague whom they had sponsored. The subsequent open warfare between Tomars and Aginsky, with loudly voiced charges of infamy by both parties, instigated the prolonged investigation referred to above, resulting in a voluminous report* and culminating in my appointment as titular leader of this battle-scarred department.

---

* This report of a blue-ribbon faculty committee was a thousand or more pages in length, contained extensive testimony of many members of the department, including that of Aginsky and Tomars, and documented the most disgraceful state of departmental affairs I ever encountered in a long academic journey. I persuaded Buell Gallagher, the new and superb president of CCNY, to read the report, after which he remarked that he had been "wallowing in an academic sewer."

During the troubled years since the 1930s the Department of Sociology and Anthropology at City, like others throughout the country, had more than doubled in faculty size and student enrollment, without any noticeable gain in quality. There were a few excellent teachers, but much of the instruction was desultory; scholarly endeavor for most of the faculty appeared to rank far below concern with the chairman's proclivities and their job security. The Social Research Laboratory, once an effective training agency in field research, had greatly expanded its activities, but student participants were often poorly supervised, and for three or four Aginsky appointees the SRL was a conspicuous boondoggle.* Although by the 1950s academic standards had declined (and the alcoves had become relatively dormant), there were still many highly able students at City College, but few of them elected the major in sociology and anthropology, which was something less than demanding and thus quite popular with the rank and file. A happy exception to this depressing situation was David Matza, CCNY class of 1953.

In many ways Dave Matza was a throwback to the City College of the 1930s: he was a serious young intellectual of wide-ranging interests, a political activist of Marxist persuasion, a superior and critically minded student of the social sciences, and, like some of his predecessors of the Depression years, a frequent user of my (now expanded) personal library. Dave was the outstanding member of my upper-level courses in urban sociology and sociological theory, and I had the good luck to replace an uninterested colleague as his honors thesis adviser. Working with Dave—and with three or four other first-rate students—was splendid compensation for whatever tribulations I faced in the chair.

As a senior at City, Matza hoped to pursue graduate study in a department of sociology that was both strong in theory and open to interchange with the other social sciences. After lengthy discussions with Dave (remindful of the sessions with Morroe Berger in earlier years), I proposed Princeton's dual Department of Economics and Sociology with its theoretically powerful but diverse trio of Marion Levy, Wilbert Moore, and Melvin Tumin.

* Aginsky had introduced the Social Research Laboratory into the Evening Session under the "supervision" of two or three part-time fellows whose principal function, so far as I could ascertain, was to collect their bimonthly pay checks. One of these free-loaders was Lewis Yablonsky, a bright youngster who was completing the Ph.D. in sociology at New York University; I moved him to a position in the day session where he proved to be an able teacher— Yablonsky's subsequent record as author of several volumes is well known.

Thus, with a fellowship in hand, Dave went to Princeton in 1953 with the aspiration of writing a doctoral dissertation of broad theoretical scope—and with little knowledge of what he then viewed as the mundane field of criminology. Two unforseen events, however, upset this ambitious plan: Dave's theoretical interests found no outlet, and even were denigrated, in the seminar taught by the then-Parsonian Marion Levy; and, on the positive side and partly in reaction to this discouraging experience, Dave developed a close relationship with Gresham Sykes, the outstanding young criminologist under whose tutelage Levy's rejectee thrived. "Grex" Sykes, clearly, has good reason to be proud of David Matza's later-day and widely proclaimed accomplishments: distinguished pieces in leading scholarly journals; the provocative and award-winning volume, *Delinquency and Drift* (1964); the unique, naturalistic study, *Becoming Deviant* (1969); a Guggenheim Fellowship; early promotion to senior rank in Berkeley's excellent Department of Sociology.

At City College in 1952–53, there may have been other youngsters in sociology of Dave Matza's ability and promise, but my contacts with students were limited by what I took to be the responsibilities of an administratively appointed chairman. The two most difficult and most time-consuming tasks were closely related: the effort to rid a large number of faculty of the ingrained attitudes of vassalage in order to enable them frankly to express their views on all matters of departmental concern; and the attempt to convince them, by demonstration not "democratic" rhetoric, of both the importance of collegial norms in academic affairs and the nonauthoritarian aspirations of the present chairman. That these endeavors were appreciated in some degree was suggested by an unexpected departmental gesture. Notwithstanding a shaky start when I faced the suspicion of most and the open hostility of a few of my colleagues, toward the end of the first semester following the announcement of my forthcoming departure from City, all but two of them (Aginsky and Shulman) signed a petition urging me to stay on in the chair—an expression of confidence that buoyed my spirits.

There were other rewards of this year at CCNY, by no means the least of which was the proximity of Columbia and of old friends there and elsewhere in New York. A related dividend was our Columbia-owned apartment on Morningside Drive, which placed us a short block from the residence of the university's President Eisenhower, whom I glimpsed from time to time, and across the street from the Faculty Club, where gossip and speculation about the next president of the nation were in good supply. Of some importance in my future professional undertakings, far more so than I realized at the time, was my acceptance of an advisory editorship with Doubleday and my initiation into the strange world of commercial publishing. But the greatest satisfaction during this hectic year was the selection, both the procedure and the outcome, of my successor. For following my recommendation and in contrast with the method used in the preceding year, when the appointment of the chairman was made without formal participation by the faculty, the department conducted its own canvass and submitted the names of three candidates. Robert Bierstedt was the first choice of both the department and the administration. Without imposition from above, then, an old fellow student, long-time friend, and fine scholar went to City College in the fall of 1953.* At the same time my own shift of academic scene was the return to Smith College where I was to remain for another seven years.

---

* Bierstedt had joined other members of the faculty at the University of Illinois in strongly protesting the dismissal of the university's outstanding president, George D. Stoddard, a disgraceful action engineered by the reactionary chairman of the board of trustees, my Illinois classmate Park Livingston, and assisted by his fellow trustee, the "immortal" Harold "Red" Grange; hence Bob was attracted by the City College post. His rival candidates were the distinguished scholars, anthropologist Cora Du Bois and Leo Lowenthal of the Frankfurt group, who shortly were to join the faculties, respectively, of Harvard and Berkeley.

4

Sociology and the Ivy Tradition:
Smith College, 1946–1960

As a "NEW YORKER for life" in the 1930s and as a teacher at CCNY during most of the decade, I would have considered a move to New England's Northampton and to Smith College as impossible or, if not, as a stroke of evil fortune. At the time, I thought of Smith as an ivy-clad school attended by daughters of the affluent and by some graduates of Birch Wathen, as a curious academic home for such well-known leftists as Granville Hicks and Newton Arvin, as a conventional institution headed by the reputedly unconventional and nationally acclaimed educator William Allen Neilson, and as an attractive community which I visited occasionally in 1934 and '35 in pursuit of my then-intended, Donna Lindsay.* That this limited and distorted view would be greatly changed by my longest academic affiliation was inconceivable in those years. This firm conviction was shattered by a conspiracy of circumstances and the happy play of chance.

Changing Academic Scenes: A Contemplated Sojourn

In the fall of 1945, following my return from the Far East and still in uniform on terminal leave, I decided to visit old haunts in New England for a week or so, as part of "readjustment"

---

* A graduate of Birch Wathen, brilliant student and a shining light at Smith, Donna Lindsay, as noted in chap. 3, married the City College alumnus Jonas Salk (in 1939). I have not seen Donna since about 1940, but my great admiration for this remarkable woman has remained over these many years.

to civilian life.* After several days on Cape Cod, our summer home for many prewar years, my mother's veteran car carried me to Boston's North Shore for a night of renewed jolliment with a former fellow officer and then was coaxed westward to Northampton where I had frolicked years before. In my memory of that brief stay only two events remain. One was an altogether unexpected dinner in Wiggins Tavern with the recently retired president of Smith, William Allen Neilson, whose warm hospitality was laced with tales of his protection of sociologists whose investigations of students' sexual experiences had offended parental sensitivities. The other was a stimulating, but also unanticipated, two-hour session with Smith's distinguished sociologist, Gladys Bryson.

Even in this first encounter, "Miss" Bryson—"Professor" or "Doctor" offended the inverse snobbery of ivy schools—gave ample evidence of her keen intelligence, sharp wit, and open candor. Her manifest knowledge of sociological literature, to my surprise, included close familiarity with *Class and American Sociology:* her appraisal embodied both a degree of approval of my dissertational effort and acute criticism of the book's shortcomings. More surprising, after an hour or more of shoptalk, Miss Bryson suggested that I become a candidate for a position in her department which was expected following the retirement of Frank Hankins in 1946. This suggestion was largely based, I suspect, on her admiration of my mentor Robert MacIver, for clearly she was not impressed by my naval uniform, ribbons and all, nor by my laudation of New York's public City College and my unhidden bias against private, unisexual schools. Moreover, my low-pitched and slow-paced conversational voice invoked her skepticism as to my ability to lecture effectively in the large introductory course, long a departmental showpiece taught by Hankins and a sure assignment for his successor. But these discouraging reactions were not distressing for at the time I had no serious intention of applying for a position at Smith.

Within a few months after the visit to Northampton, however, full-fledged return to civilian status brought with it a reassessment of both the residential and occupational components of life in New York. In keeping perhaps with the restlessness of other veterans, the notion of changing my prewar scene had increasing

* With the stream of returning veterans, this theme was pursued by a good many psychologists, sociologists, and others, including Willard Waller in *The Veteran Strikes Back* (New York: Dryden, 1944). My own readjustment, so it seemed, required no more than a few hours.

appeal as the weeks went by—in my case as a vacation from the pressures and pleasures of the big city. The idea of such a move was strengthened by the large demands of my post at City College, a tenured position protected during military service to which I returned in the spring of 1946. But far outweighing these considerations was an event I judged (correctly, as the future was to show) as of great importance: Robert MacIver's proposal that we collaborate on a textbook based upon his masterly treatise *Society*. This surprising invitation was accepted without hesitation, but with mixed reactions: pleasure and pride, of course, stemming from the prospect of working in association with my distinguished mentor, trepidation in view of my questionable qualifications for the enterprise, and an uneasy conviction that the combination of a heavy teaching schedule at CCNY and the diversions of the city would seriously handicap this large-scale project. This conviction triggered an inquiry to Gladys Bryson as to the availability of the job in her department.

The upshot, following another and more formal visit to Northampton, was the offer of an assistant professorship at Smith College (the rank was advanced a step a few months later) for a three-year term. Before accepting the invitation, I explained that the book with MacIver might be completed earlier than scheduled and, in such an unlikely event, that as a confirmed urbanite I might wish to return to New York before the expiration of the appointment. But this precaution seemed to be of little concern to my future colleagues or to President Herbert Davis whose confidence in the compelling attractions at Smith and the Connecticut Valley was far greater than my own. That good judgment was on their side is suggested by the duration of what I then assumed would be a short-lived academic sojourn: including leaves of absence, I remained a member of the Smith College faculty for fourteen years.

It was evident in 1946 that the move from City College to Smith would bring with it a new mode of occupational life. Whereas CCNY was a large, public, nontuition school for men with an almost exclusively male faculty and administration, Smith was a relatively small (2,000 plus students), private and expensive, residential women's college, with a mixed faculty, a corps of female deans, and a male president. Beyond these obvious contrasts, it was quite apparent that my classroom performance in Smith's more intimate "community" would be on fuller display than at City, subject to the scrutiny of not only students but their bill-paying parents, old-girl alumnae, and both departmental and collegewide faculty. Of greater concern was the student body I would be facing: middle- and upper-class young women from all regions of the country rather than young men, fellow New Yorkers, largely from working-class families. Here then was a far different academic scene, one that I approached with limited knowledge, considerable diffidence, and indeed with some distorted or mistaken notions about the working world of Smith.

Smith's Sociological Tradition:
Frank Hankins and Company

In earlier years I had little inkling that among the Seven Sisters, Smith College was unique in several respects, one of which was its lengthy tradition of harboring leading sociologists. The low repute of sociology in ivy schools, female and male, was widely known. In the thirties I was aware of only three of the field's notables on the faculties of women's colleges: Willard Waller at Barnard, Joseph Folsom at Vassar, and Frank Hankins at Smith. Hankins had been chairman at Smith from 1922 until his retirement in 1946. One of his predecessors was F. Stuart Chapin whose eight-year tenure (1912–1920) was briefly interrupted by World War I. Among the several outstanding sociologists Hankins brought to Smith were Harry Elmer Barnes (1923–1930),* Howard Becker (1931–1935), and, fresh from Harvard, Kingsley Davis (1934–1936). The nationwide prestige of these scholars is signaled by the fact that Chapin, Hankins, Becker, and Davis were each elected president of the American Sociological Society, an office held by Hankins while at Smith following his term as the first editor of the *American Sociological Review*.

Frank Hankins was an eminent sociologist and demographer, both an ardent proponent of a strictly scientific sociology and a concerned humanist, a distinguished author and skillful lecturer, a provocative and influential teacher. At Clark Univer-

---

* The bombastic Barnes, who had been a colleague of Hankins at Clark University, was a member of the Departments of Economics and Sociology. A historian and jack of all social science trades, publicist, and prodigious author, one of Barnes's propensities at Smith was said to be that of a gadfly among younger faculty members, encouraging their deviation from academic conventions (he held traditional history to be "mostly bunk"); one of his protégés in this respect, so the story goes, was the youthful Granville Hicks. The move of Hicks into the Communist party may have been encouraged by Barnes's penchant, but Barnes himself, an independent intellectual and social critic, belonged to no political party.

sity, then an important center of research, graduate study, and scholarly controversy (highlighted by the famous visits of Sigmund Freud and Havelock Ellis), Hankins headed the Department of Political and Social Science for fourteen years (1908–1922) where he encouraged such future scholars as E. Franklin Frazier, Clifford Kirkpatrick, and Howard Odum to pursue careers as sociologists. Although there were no male students at the school to which he moved when Clark encountered grave financial problems, Hankins continued to teach men—at Amherst, where he subversively introduced sociology under the cloak of "economics," and as a visiting professor at Columbia, the New School, Berkeley, and, following his retirement from Smith, for two years (1946–1948) at the University of Pennsylvania. At Smith, however, as Hankins soon learned, first-rate students were in large supply.

And so were stimulating faculty colleagues of both sexes. At various times in the 1920s and '30s Hankins's fellow scholars in history and the social sciences included Ray Billington, G. A. Borgese, Merle Curti, Harold Faulkner, Elisabeth Koffka, Hans Kohn, and Will Orton, as well as Barnes, Becker, Bryson, and Davis in his own department. Together with equally talented men and women in the humanities and arts, and under the powerful but permissive presidency of William Allen Neilson, Smith, like the earlier Clark University, was a noncloistered and exciting center where Hankins came into his own as a social activist, a leader of his profession, and a prolific author. He contributed widely to learned journals, anthologies, and the original *Encyclopaedia of the Social Sciences* (seventeen articles, among them excellent pieces on Charles Darwin, birth control, divorce, and social discrimination), and his several books included the controversial study, *The Racial Basis of Civilization: A Critique of the Nordic Doctrine* (1926). When Frank died in his ninety-second year, the following paragraphs from his obituary represent my effort to summarize the sociological character of his work and to suggest the outstanding character of the man:

> Hankins was a scientific determinist, but he remained skeptical of the capacity of social science to rival the theoretical and applied achievements of the natural sciences because of the complexity and changing nature of social causation. In a recent private document, he expressed his general orientation by rejecting the "robot" notion "that the stream of culture is a wholly independent variable and mankind wholly depen-

dent thereon, because the human mind is the catalytic agent in culture change and scientific knowledge the basic progressive factor therein." His writings show an abiding and powerful interest in the role of biological factors in social life and history and, conversely, in the roles of such selective processes as urbanization, education, persecution, and war in the determination of population quantity and quality. He argued strongly that differential fertility between classes is dysfunctional for society and that this problem should be met by birth control: more for the lower strata and less for the privileged.

Hankins was critical of the egalitarian assumption of political democracy, but he condemned authoritarian institutions and practices and advocated maximization of opportunity for all. In *The Racial Basis of Civilization* and elsewhere, he questioned the view that members of different racial stocks are equally capable of individual and cultural achievement, but emphasized the fact that the populations of all large societies are mixed, maintained that such mixture is physically and socially beneficial, and denounced racist policies. Hankins' work, then, wears the three traditional faces of sociology: scientific, humanistic, and reformistic.

In the circles of both town and gown, and among both cosmopolitans and locals, Frank Hankins enjoyed wide esteem and deep affection. Tough-minded, at times viewed as stubborn, a doughty opponent in debate, he persistently sought new knowledge and ideas, had little use for conventional or fashionable wisdom as such, and welcomed the challenge of intellectual dispute. He was a sensitive and generous friend, a chairman guided by collegial norms, and a wise counselor who encouraged students and younger colleagues to pursue their own interests. He was a delightful companion, splendid host, skillful gardener, enthusiastic philatelist, and became in recent decades an investment expert—and, of course, he was much more.*

Under Hankins's leadership during his twenty-four years at Smith, sociology became firmly established as a legitimate, if not fully reputable, field of study, at the time an infrequent de-

* Charles H. Page, "Frank Hamilton Hankins, 1887–1970," *American Sociologist* 5, no. 3 (August 1970): 288–89. There are slight changes in the wording in the second paragraph of this quotation which correspond with the original manuscript.

velopment in the unfriendly academic environment of ivy schools.* Hankins's own scholarly and professional accomplishments, as well as his prowess as a teacher, were of considerable help on this score—clearly, he was one of the faculty stars. And his recruitment of such sociologists as Howard Becker, Gladys Bryson, Neal DeNood, and Margaret Marsh gave the department strength and diversity then rarely found in colleges of liberal arts. Other circumstances, to be sure, helped to account for the prestige of the department, for example, a college president who supported unconventional innovations, an eminent and cooperative Smith School of Social Work, a vigorous and longstanding feminism. But the creation of a sturdy sociological tradition at Smith was largely the achievement of Frank Hankins and his colleagues.

"GB": Sociologist and Latter-day Moral Philosopher

A peer of Frank Hankins in the development of sociology as a successful academic enterprise at Smith was Gladys Eugenia Bryson, widely known as "GB." A native Kentuckian of Scottish background, GB earned graduate degrees at Berkeley and for several years she was national secretary of the YWCA. She renewed her formal studies as a postdoctoral Sterling Fellow at Yale, and in 1931 at the age of thirty-seven joined the Smith faculty, where she gained senior rank in 1940 and succeeded Hankins as chair of the Department of Sociology and Anthropology. From the midforties until a few months before her death in 1952, GB was the department's dominant voice in a small but markedly diverse and frequently vociferous group of teaching sociologists.

As teacher and counselor, as head of her department, and as an esteemed member of both the larger faculty and her profession, GB's forceful personality was highlighted by a delightful and sometimes disturbing candor, a limited tolerance of foolishness signaled by occasional thrusts of acerbity, a no-nonsense demeanor that only faintly obscured her zest for life, an uncompromising intellectual honesty, and a great gift for friendship. A powerful feminist, she addressed her younger male colleagues as

---

* In "Sociology as an Educational Enterprise," pp. 10–12, I have commented on the "challenge of adversity" faced by sociologists in such schools; Hankins and his colleagues met this challenge successfully.

"Bud," a term that carried both comradely affection and keen awareness of our masculine weaknesses. GB was a tough-minded liberal who had no patience with bigotry of any kind, as well as a warm-hearted humanist in her various academic and professional roles.

She was chairperson for many years, but she no doubt would have scoffed at the use of this graceless term—as a feminist she was concerned with mightier discriminations faced by women. As a senior member of the faculty, GB was a champion of high academic standards, scholarly excellence, and, especially, devoted teaching—in a college of liberal arts, she firmly believed, the first order of an instructor's business should be the student's intellectual growth. In the chair, she was a stickler for collegial norms, so much so that departmental meetings often continued beyond a tolerable duration: all of us were allowed seemingly endless time to air our views—a bonanza for many academics.* GB's attractive apartment in Lawrence House, where she was faculty resident for many years, was not only an overly personalized setting for these extended and frequently disputatious sessions, but also provided the chair with a first-hand supply of student gossip that served at times as disconcerting "evaluation" of our teaching follies and triumphs. These departures from academic conventions, however, were far outweighed by GB's effective leadership, her first allegiance to the welfare of the department, her wise counsel freely given, and her strong support of our professional and scholarly pursuits.

GB's own major scholarly interest was the history of social theory, which she had developed as a student and one-time colleague of Berkeley's luminary Frederick J. Teggert. In the 1930s she wrote a series of first-rate papers on "prediscoveries" of modern-day sociological conceptions, and in 1945 she published her widely acclaimed *Man and Society: The Scottish Inquiry of the Eighteenth Century*. This meticulous work on the ideas of a remarkable group of academic and nonacademic moral philosophers about the nature of man, society, and social institutions opened up an important area of historical scholarship: the study of the formulations of these Scotsmen as "generalized ancestors"

---

* Some of us, notably Neal DeNood and myself, indecently exploited this opportunity. Implications of such proclivity among males in a mixed faculty are suggested below.

of twentieth-century sociology.* GB's continuing interest in this largely unexplored path of intellectual history is evident in the opening chapters of her book on the foundations of sociology in the United States, a work-in-progress at the time of her final illness, in which the influence of the Scottish moralists on both French and American pioneers (for example, Auguste Comte, Albion W. Small, and Franklin H. Giddings) is brought out clearly. The completion of this highly promising volume surely would have enhanced Gladys Bryson's already established reputation as a scholar of note.

To refer to GB as a "latter-day moral philosopher" may be stretching essayist license beyond tolerable limits—and surely, as a modern and modest sociologist, she would have rejected out-of-hand such an ancient and lofty designation. But in several respects GB shared with the subjects of her major work qualities of mind and temperament consistent with her Scottish heritage. As in the case of the moral philosophers, she belonged to the school of both common and moral sense.† She was a powerful proponent of intellectual and political liberality. Like Francis Hutcheson and his successors, she was convinced that effective teaching unhampered by convention or dogma greatly benefits society. Her trained skepticism made her a partial ally of the exceptional David Hume. And, most important, she firmly believed that ethical considerations should be the "final arbiter in matters of social organization and behavior."‡

This strongly principled woman, outspoken in her convictions, was less than beloved by a few of her colleagues, but GB was held in great affection and admiration by most. An indication of her wider esteem in professional circles was her election to the presidency of the Eastern Sociological Society in 1945—the first

---

* The academics, in Scottish universities, included Francis Hutcheson, Adam Smith, Thomas Reid, Adam Ferguson, and Dugald Stewart; outside the universities were David Hume, Lord Kames, and Lord Monboddo. Bryson's volume was a predecessor of later studies of these "prediscoverers," notably Louis Schneider's *The Scottish Moralists* (Chicago: University of Chicago Press, 1967).
† The Scottish moral philosophers were often called the "Common-Sense School" and at times the "Moral-Sense School." See *Man and Society*, pp. 10–11.
‡ Ibid., p. 25.

woman to hold this office.* Had she survived the 1950s, as a scholar-teacher of distinction, a proven leader, and a veteran feminist, surely Gladys Bryson would have joined the ranks of the eminent women who in recent years have become stars of their own professions.

Academic Women and Men:
A Two-Sex Professoriate

At Smith, GB was more skillful in dealing with men than with women and, when called for, in keeping us in line. The large number of men on the faculty, including some alleged sexists, gave her ample opportunity to exercise this talent. Such a state of academic affairs was new to me, for City College had been almost exclusively a male enterprise; relations with the other sex were very largely extracurricular. Thus, as a member of a mixed faculty in an ivy-clad college, I had much to learn about both academic women and their male coworkers.

When I arrived at Smith in 1946, women made up two-thirds of the faculty; by 1960 the sexes were equally divided. During my first year all but a dozen of the some 75 men were married, in contrast with the single status of 114 of the 132 women; in the expanded faculty of fourteen years later the proportions of married women and single men had grown somewhat, but spinsterhood on the one side and domestic bondage on the other remained dominant in the college's instructional staff. Each of these demographic and social categories warrants comment.

At Smith and other sister colleges of the ivy tradition, faculty women were involved in a mode of occupational life that was both rewarding and frustrating. As teachers in an excellent school that maintained high educational standards, they enjoyed well-prepared and generally able students, they garnered a measure of status conferred by daughters of affluent parents, and they held jobs in a prestigious college where women far outnumbered and frequently outranked men. And in those years (seemingly more so than today) they, together with men on the faculty, were members of an academic community in which civility and other social graces were in large supply.

* Jessie Bernard, Mirra Komarovsky, Alice Rossi, Renee Fox, Matilda Riley, Helen MacGill Hughes, and Cynthia Epstein were presidents of the Eastern Sociological Society in later years.

At the same time, the recipients of these benefits were severely disadvantaged in their scholarly and professional careers, by the pervasive sexism of the academic world. For however meritorious their accomplishments, only a very few received invitations from major universities with extensive research facilities, developed graduate programs, and direct contact with leaders in their fields.* This traditional exclusivism meant that Smith, along with two or three of the other Seven Sisters, stood at the occupational apex for almost all women scholars.

Of the small contingent of married women on the Smith faculty, several were in the same departments as their husbands—at the time something of an anomaly in academia. According to local gossip, these pairings were largely a product of former President Neilson's money-saving practice based on the principle that two can live as cheaply as one. However ungrounded this charge, it appeared that almost all of these working wives suffered lower salaries and slower promotions than their husbands, and not necessarily because of differences in age or merit.† In at least some of these cases sexual discrimination was at work, but this seemed to be of less concern to both women and men on the faculty than the alleged undue influence of married couples in departmental affairs. Thus during my years at Smith, unsubstantiated but widespread accusations of breakfast-table chicanery or even attempted power grabs were leveled at married professors in the Departments of Art, French, Philosophy, and Psychology. Innuendos of this order (giving support to antinepotistic conviction) helped to shape my long-held bias against the appointment of married academics in the same department.‡

* One of the "very few" was the eminent Marjorie Nicholson who went to Columbia University. Another was political scientist Gwendolyn Carter who, after twenty years at Smith, became Director of African Studies at Northwestern University in 1964. In subsequent years, there were two or three equally distinguished women scholars who moved from Smith to major universities, but such cases have been rare.

† Alice and Morris Lazerowitz, both logicians of wide repute, were exceptions: Alice rose through the professorial ranks and became chair of the Department of Philosophy a year or two in advance of Morris—a rare case of "ladies first."

‡ This bias, seemingly held by many members of the professoriate, at least in my own generation, would work against the departmental appointment of such notable sociological couples as Everett and Helen Hughes, Kingsley Davis and Judith Blake, Lewis and Rose Coser, and Peter and Alice Rossi; currently (1981) the Cosers and Rossis are members of the same departments, at SUNY, Stony Brook, and the University of Massachusetts, respectively.

Most of the faculty women at Smith, however, were unmarried, singletons who differed widely in age, educational background, scholarly and personal disposition, professional attainment, and academic rank. But this diversified assemblage included a group of senior scholar-teachers whose similarities in certain respects were impressive: they were devoted and first-rate students of their respective subjects, their courses were demanding but well elected, they seemed to thrive on intellectual disputation, and most of them were sturdy feminists who brooked no sexist nonsense from the men around them. In those years there were some thirty or forty of these tough-minded spinsters at Smith, among them some remarkable women who were colorful and powerful figures in a variety of fields, one of whom was Gladys Bryson in sociology. Others whom I had the good fortune to know were GB's close friend Virginia Corwin, popular teacher and outstanding student of world religions (whose spinsterhood ended following her retirement); the philosopher Mary Evelyn Clarke, adventuresome and fearless world traveler (who thus emulated other unmarried Englishwomen of an earlier generation); Mary Ellen Chase, popular publicist, Biblical scholar, and campus prima donna (whose soft beauty only slightly masked her iron will); Chase's housemate Eleanor Duckett, famed classicist and medievalist (who remained an entrancing lecturer and hard-working scholar into her nineties); Jean Wilson, a fine historian and director of Smith's superior honors program. These women were representatives of a wonderful academic breed which is now vanishing. But their one-time students and younger colleagues of an earlier era remain in their debt—they enriched our lives in many ways.

Veteran spinsters of this select breed, however, along with other faculty women, were susceptible to an institutional disability especially prevalent in small colleges of liberal arts, which in my earlier teaching years had been a relatively minor part of academic life at City College and Columbia. In contrast, at Smith an intense and never-ending preoccupation with educational tactics consumed a great deal of time and energy of the faculty. Both excellent scholar-teachers and other academics, both many women and a smaller number of men, were deeply concerned with course requirements, departmental jurisdictions, prerequisites, proposals for new course offerings, "breadth" requirements, and curricular "reform." These were matters of some importance in an undergraduate school, but for those few of us who leaned toward a Mark Hopkinesque view of education this preoccupation was likely to be a dreary, if not a fruitless, exercise. More important, for women on the faculty, victims of academic sexist discrimination and thus for whom a teaching post at Smith was very apt to represent top professional achievement, heavy involvement with curricular niceties frequently far outweighed concern with research and writing.

This imbalance, as I have suggested, was by no means a female monopoly, for a good many men at Smith also succumbed to what I have called an institutional disability. Yet it was evident that more women than men were affected by this situation. In large part this differential was due to contrasting expectations concerning careers. Unlike most faculty women, many men, at least with respect to their aspirations, viewed a few years at Smith as a stage of professional advancement. For such men, with an eye on the possibility of moving to a major university, as quite a few did in fact do,* there was good reason to limit their role in college busy-work in favor of credential-producing scholarly research. These ambitious careerists, while often highly esteemed and in some cases members of Smith's show-case elite, contributed less to the day-to-day operations of the college, and indeed to its long-range stability, than did their female colleagues.

Faculty men, clearly, enjoyed advantages at Smith, including those associated with their greater occupational mobility. An altogether different kind of asset, not attributable to institutional discrimination, derived from a combination of biological and cultural circumstances that was rarely if ever recognized by members of either sex: the nature of the male voice. As a newcomer to a women's college, I was often struck and sometimes puzzled by the attention afforded male colleagues in meetings of the faculty, committees, or the department—even when their, or my own, contributions to discussion or debate were far less cogent and less skillfully phrased than those of women in such gatherings. Within a year or so, however, I came to believe firmly (but with little support for this "outrageous" view, as some fellow teachers put it) that the attention-getting facility of many men was simply a product of their genetic equipment, as reinforced by a cultural tradition that unfortunately gives special value to "masculine" timbre,

* Beginning in the 1930s, Smith College has been a stepping stone for such distinguished scholars as Merle Curti and Hans Kohn in history, Robert Gorham Davis and Daniel Aaron in American literature, Fritz Heider and James Gibson in psychology, and Howard Becker, Kingsley Davis, and Bernard Barber in sociology. It should be noted, however, that several male luminaries were on the Smith faculty for many years and remained until retirement—for example, Harold Faulkner in history, Newton Arvin in American literature, Oliver Larkin in art, Howard Parshley in zoology, and Frank Hankins in sociology.

pitch, and volume. In the world of musical artistry, there may be no such sexist discrimination, but in academic faculties and other such assemblies these unwon vocal attributes of men work in their favor.*

An altogether unrelated and, for a few intolerant people, a more significant part of life at Smith was the gossip about homosexuality. It was no doubt inevitable at the time, before the days of opened closet doors and gay liberation, that some of the many single faculty women (as well as a number of students) would be the subject of wagging tongues. Their victims included two or three conspicuous lesbians, a larger social circle of women on the faculty and nonteaching staff, and several "Boston friendships," female couples who lived together, often for many years. But for most of us, these cases were taken in stride: they were viewed as a normal situation in a unisexual, female-oriented institution—and of no relevance to Smith's educational pursuits.

The handful of Smith's male, bachelor homosexuals (it was generally—and unrealistically—assumed that all married men were exclusively heterosexual) faced more visible difficulties than did their female counterparts—in keeping with an Anglo-American tradition that sanctioned close attachments between women but not between men. Although the well-known sexual proclivities of two of the most eminent senior members of the faculty elicited little more than casual comment, younger and less prominent men were exposed to a variety of discomforts: snide palaver among safely married males, admonishments to marry from unperceptive colleagues (single young women were in large supply), and even attempts of sexual entrapment by adventuresome and aggressive students. During my fourteen years at Smith, however, there were no public scandals concerning either male or female homosexuality and no member of either sex, to my knowledge, was penalized professionally because of his or her sexual disposition.†

* My own successes in the Smith faculty, such as they were, were greatly aided, surely, by what many people have termed a "good voice"—another instance of the play of sheer luck in a career.
† Shortly after we left Smith in 1960, this putative record came to an end when the distinguished scholar and esteemed teacher (and dear friend of my wife and me), Newton Arvin, together with two of his junior colleagues were involved in a widely publicized homosexual episode that resulted in Arvin's early retirement and the dismissal of his two colleagues. Had this public exposure occurred a few years later, it may be surmised, no such consequences would have followed because by then the sexual "revolution" and gay liberation were in ascendency.

Homosexuals on the Smith faculty, as reputedly was the case elsewhere, were most likely to be members of the "aesthetic" departments of literature and the arts, although they were also represented in the more mundane fields. For unknown reasons, however, individuals of gay inclination very rarely appeared in the social sciences. During my many years at Smith there was only a single case in the Department of Sociology and Anthropology.

Sociology as a Teaching Enterprise

In 1946–47, my first year at Smith, the department's teaching staff consisted of the chair and our one senior professor, Gladys Bryson, associate professors Margaret Alexander Marsh and Neal DeNood, a newly appointed assistant professor, instructors Adelaide Cromwell Hill and Helen Sullivan Mims, and the director of the School for Social Work, Florence Day as a part-time auxiliary. With the exception of GB, whose professional and scholarly credentials were well established, our curricula vitae gave no indication of special merit: Marsh held early degrees from Smith (A.B. 1914; A.M. 1916) and as a sociologist-anthropologist was known elsewhere primarily as author of several articles on Latin America. DeNood was a Harvard Ph.D., but had published almost nothing. My own Columbia degree had required the publication of my dissertation. Both Hill and Mims, appointed the preceding year with doctorates not yet in hand, were then beginners in the academic climb. Moreover, the department's title was misleading, for, at that time, there were no certified anthropologists among us, although GB and Margaret Marsh taught courses in the subject. But this skimpy inventory of formal scholarly accomplishments is deceptive—it tells little about the department as an educational and teaching agency.

GB herself, as I have recorded, was an excellent scholar-teacher. And her strong leadership was marked, on the one hand, by warm encouragement of whatever capabilities the rest of us possessed and, on the other, by candid criticism of our academic follies. On both counts our activities kept her rather busy.

The eldest in years but young in spirit, and least troublesome among us, was one of Smith's finest teachers, Margaret Marsh, admired and held in affection by students and colleagues alike. Margaret's widely elected courses on "The Expansion of Western Culture," showpieces in the college's curriculum, were a successful synthesis of the anthropology of cultural change, the sociology of what was later called "modernization," and the eco-

nomics of imperialism. Lacking the doctorate and the author of
no full-scale volume,* but an outstanding teacher and highly
valued member of the faculty, Margaret not only obtained senior
rank in 1953 (indicating the good sense of her department and the
administration), but was twice appointed class dean, a demanding—and, in my view, an ill-conceived—office which she graced
with rare distinction.

My single male companion in sociology, Neal DeNood,
had been a member of Talcott Parsons's "first generation" of
graduate students at Harvard where he had allegedly held his own
with such brilliant tyros as Kingsley Davis, Robert Merton, and
Wilbert Moore. During his first year at Smith (1937–38) he
startled both his colleagues and a good many undergraduates by
using Parsons's recently published *Structure of Social Action* as
the text in a course in theory. This pedagogical blunder was soon
forgiven, however, for shortly DeNood became an enormously
popular teacher of courses in social maladjustment and social disorganization, widely elected by young women attracted by the
study of crime and delinquency, mental disorders, suicide, and
other "deviant" phenomena.† A good many students were also attracted by DeNood's prowess as a lecturer, his unorthodox views,
his penchant for the sensational, and his psychotherapeutic coun-
seling of troubled individuals. The latter propensities were condemned at times by some of us, as was his seemingly permanent
inattention to scholarly "production." But these putative academic
delinquencies were outweighed by Neal DeNood's contributions
to the sociological education of the thousands of women who
passed through his classes between 1937 and 1968.‡

Of those women, one of the many notables was Adelaide
Cromwell (class of 1940—cum laude, Phi Beta Kappa, and so on).
After graduate study at the University of Pennsylvania and Bryn
Mawr, some teaching at Hunter College, and marriage to Henry
Hill, "Addie" returned to her alma mater as an instructor in

* Marsh's most influential publication was the first-rate article, "Monoculture
and the Level of Living," *Inter-American Economic Affairs* 1, no. 1 (June
1947).
† "Social Disorganization" was a widely used title for courses that a short
time earlier had often carried the misnomer "Social Pathology" and years
later the misleading designation of "Deviance." At the time, many students
at Smith and elsewhere preferred "Sex, Sin, and Sewers" or "Nuts and Sluts."
‡ Ill health brought about Neal DeNood's early retirement from Smith in
1968; he died in 1972.

1945—the first black to hold a full-time faculty position in a female ivy school. In keeping with her earlier triumphs, Addie Hill's two-year stay in the Department of Sociology and Anthropology was marked by distinction, enhanced by a happy combination of disarming candor and uninhibited spontaneity that delighted her students and most of her colleagues. Together with Margaret Marsh and Helen Mims, Addie carried discussion sections in the introductory course in which I lectured; these three contributed greatly to the course's alleged success during my Smith initiation. With a brilliant husband in Boston and prompted by higher aims than were realizable in a junior faculty job, Addie left us in 1947 to pursue the doctorate at Harvard and thereafter to embark on what was to be a splendid and continuing professional career.* But to have been her working colleague for a brief time and since then to have enjoyed Addie's warm friendship are among my blessings.

I have lost track of Addie's sister-instructor Helen Mims in recent decades, but her unique departmental role during my first and her final year at Smith stands out in my memories. Helen, the widow of an able but short-lived political scientist,† was an excellent and unconventional sociologist. Her interests ranged widely over the humanities and social sciences, and she brought to her teaching and scholarship extensive knowledge, stimulating unorthodoxies, and well-exercised critical acumen—qualities that had strong appeal for the more able students and like-minded members of the faculty. Within the department, however, except for her close friend Margaret Marsh, she received little support from her senior colleagues, toward two of whom she was openly hostile. In 1947, Helen Mims, with my strong backing and perhaps with a sigh of relief, left Smith to join David Riesman and his assemblage of brilliant young social scientists at the University of Chicago.‡

Thus during my first year at Smith these four women and two men—Bryson, DeNood, Hill, Marsh, Mims, and Page—were

* Professor of sociology and director of Afro-American Studies at Boston University, Adelaide Cromwell Gulliver (she married Philip Gulliver in 1973) is a luminary in educational circles and community affairs, member of numerous prestigious organizations, recipient of honorary degrees, and mother of a highly talented son, Anthony C. Hill.

† Edwin Mims, Jr., author of *The Majority of the People* (New York: Modern Age Books, 1941), among other works.

‡ Riesman's teaching staff included, among others, Daniel Bell, Morris Janowitz, Philip Rieff, and Edward Shils.

responsible for the formal sociological education of two to three hundred young females in a school of the ivy tradition. The staff was to expand in the following years, its male contingent was to grow, and several first-rate young scholars were to join its ranks. Throughout my tenure (and continuing today), however, the department retained not only an inevitable array of contrasting and sometimes clashing personalities, but a striking intellectual and pedagogical diversity—a large asset, I am convinced, for sociology as a teaching and scholarly enterprise.* At Smith, as at all or most colleges of liberal arts, certain advantages and difficulties faced by such an enterprise may warrant comment.

One advantage enjoyed by all departments in a small college is the extensive contact with representatives of related disciplines. At Smith, unlike the departmental isolation and consequent provincialism prevailing in many large universities, close relations with members of other fields were an important feature of the educational as well as the informal activities of the college. Students in sociology regularly were enrolled, usually as part of their major, in excellent and relevant courses or seminars taught, for example, by Daniel Aaron in American culture, David Donald in American history, Donald Matthews and William Leuchtenberg in American politics, Virginia Corwin in world religions, and Elsa Siipola in the psychology of personality.† These curricular interconnections greatly strengthened the students' sociological education, of course, and they had intellectual rewards for the faculty as well. But in Smith's *gemeinschaftliche* setting they were also intermixed with a kind of interdepartmental warfare.

The competitive struggle for majors was especially intense in the social sciences and psychology. (The latter's preoccupation with experimentation provided a rationale for psychology's curricular designation as a natural science—a bone of contention in

* My convictions on this score were strongly influenced by experience in the contrasting schools of CCNY and Smith College, and were codified in the essay "Sociology as a Teaching Enterprise," which provides the title to the present section of these recollections.

† These six cases of distinguished scholar-teachers illustrate a point made above, i.e., the sexual contrast in academic mobility: Aaron moved from Smith to Harvard, Donald to Columbia (and then to Princeton, Johns Hopkins, and Harvard), Matthews to North Carolina (and then to the universities of Michigan and Washington), and Leuchtenberg to Columbia; whereas Corwin and Siipola remained at Smith until retirement.

certain quarters.)* The departments of history, literature, and the arts, with a roster of able scholars teaching in cultural areas traditionally presumed to be appropriate for young women, had large enrollments, while physics, chemistry, and mathematics attracted relatively few students. But education, government, psychology, and sociology were involved in confrontation, only thinly shrouded by public decorum, which at times reached internecine proportions. In this competitive arena, as the smallest department in the social science division of the faculty and viewed by many as the least reputable of its disciplines, sociology faced some difficulties. It was therefore a major departmental victory and a boost to my own ego when our introductory course, from which majors were recruited, more than doubled in size my second year at Smith (1947–48)—when some silly students were heard to proclaim "maje with Page." And it was a shock to many members of the faculty (one of whom called it a "scandal") when by 1948–49 about forty juniors and seniors were majoring in sociology, when that year nine or ten of our students graduated with honors, and when two of these equaled a college record for any department by garnering summa cum laude degrees. This accomplishment required a good measure of luck, of course, but during the following years sociology became firmly established locally (as it did in numerous schools at the time, to be sure) as a generally acknowledged academic field of decent repute.

This departmental drive for student clients helped to give a special emphasis to competent teaching, a skill that usually is more highly valued in colleges of liberal arts than in "production" oriented multiversities. Smith had (and has) a large number of excellent teachers and some of them—for instance, Daniel Aaron in American studies, Elsa Siipola in psychology, Leo Weinstein in political science—were exemplars of superior pedagogical performance. Thus competition was tough for sociology, but during my tenure (and later) its ranks included several classroom experts who kept our teaching enterprise afloat. Moreover, our accomplishments in this respect, as in other departments—and in contrast with the lip service given to teaching ability in many or most multiversities—received appropriate institutional recognition.†

* Modern psychology's problematic status as a natural science stands in contrast with its one-time designation as "the philosophy of the mind."

† My own move to senior rank took place after a mere three years at Smith. This promotion came as a complete surprise—surely a rare instance of what, ideally, should be common practice in academia. I had received some feelers

Once more, in contrast with the faculties of specialists in large universities, Smith's small contingent of sociologists was perforce composed of "generalists" (in recent decades an anathematic term in certain circles), for each of us taught an array of courses among the several offered by the department. Thus, over the years, in addition to introductory sociology, my assignments included the directorship of an interdisciplinary course in modern American society,* social stratification, race and ethnic relations, both European and American theory, and, far afield from my training, the family, as well as seminars in theoretical perspectives, social change, organizational analysis, social movements, popular culture, and Soviet Russia (the last together with George Gibian, Helen Muchnic, and Klemens von Klemperer—who, unlike their sociological colleague, had strong credentials for this senior offering). This wide assortment of instructional responsibilities may have discouraged or even precluded the kind of specialized scholarship that so often pays dividends in the academic marketplace. However, it required familiarity with a large and diverse social science literature which turned out to be a valuable asset in both my work as editor and my later teaching of sociological theory to graduate students at Princeton and Massachusetts. This undergraduate smorgasbord also kept me busy at what was always my foremost and fondest academic role: schoolteacher.

---

and two or three firm invitations from other schools, but these were uninvolved in any negotiations with my department or the college administration. For, contrary to my earlier expectations, I had found academic life at Smith richly rewarding and Leonora and I, although veteran New Yorkers, had fallen in love with Northampton. These sentiments were reinforced when, with no prewarning, the news of my promotion to a full professorship appeared in the local newspaper. During the evening of that spring day in 1950 nonprofessorial celebration ensued.

* This course was introduced in 1947–48, when scholars in this country and England were writing or contemplating general assessments of contemporary American society, illustrated by Margaret Mead's (earlier) *And Keep Your Powder Dry* (New York: Morrow, 1942), Geoffrey Gorer's *The American People* (New York: Norton, 1948), and the "reader" *Modern American Society,* ed. Kingsley Davis, Harry C. Bredemeir, and Marion J. Levy, Jr. A few years later appeared the first edition of the impressive "sociological interpretation," *American Society* by Robin M. Williams, Jr. (New York: Knopf, 1951), and still later the comprehensive work by the scholar-journalist Max Lerner, *America as a Civilization* (New York: Simon and Schuster, 1957). Our course ("Social Science 192") was a curricular effort consistent with the thrust of such volumes.

Students and Sociologists in a Woman's College of the Fifties

If teaching at City College in the thirties had been an exciting and unrepeatable experience, the job at Smith in the postwar years had its own rewards—far different in several respects, but not without one important similarity. The differences in social and institutional setting were conspicuous: in the family and ethnic background, degree of affluence, political disposition, life expectations, and the sex of the students; in the glaring contrast between the overly crowded, spartan facilities of a public free-tuition school and the many appurtenances of an ivy-clad residential college located in a lovely New England town; and, by no means least, in the historical divergence between the tumultuous Depression decade and a period marked by the quietism of Eisenhower, the rigidities of the Cold War, the devil-hunting by Joe McCarthy. On another level, the publication of such interpretive volumes as David Riesman's *The Lonely Crowd* (1950), David M. Potter's *People of Plenty* (1954), William H. Whyte's *The Organization Man* (1956), and Daniel Bell's *The End of Ideology* (1960) indicated that new sociological themes were in ascendancy. The principal similarity between teaching at CCNY and Smith was the presence in each school of a sizable minority of highly able, intellectually engaged students.

Many people at the time (as they do today) held stereotypical conceptions of Smith students. Thus certain of my former colleagues in New York took me to task for deserting the disadvantaged and aspiring young men of City College for a swanky "finishing school" serving "daughters of the rich." As with most stereotypes, such views were anchored in a modicum of reality, but they were large distortions of what in fact comprised, respectively, the institutional earmarks of Smith itself and the social characteristics of its student body. A goodly majority of Smithies did come from upper middle-class families and a few from America's elite. But extensive scholarships and student aid programs helped to support a sizable number of the less affluent and occasionally a student or two of working-class parentage. Ethnically, while a fairly large majority of the students (and a somewhat smaller percentage of the faculty) were Wasps, minorities included a heavy representation of Jews, probably fewer Catholics, and, in contrast with its large increase in recent years, only a tiny number of token blacks.*

* As in other schools of the ivy tradition, notably Harvard and Williams, a few black students had attended Smith for many decades—among them Otelia Cromwell, class of 1900, aunt of the sociologist Adelaide Cromwell Hill.

Most of these young women, it seemed, were husband-seekers, as one might expect. A good many, however, were also job-hunters whose B.A. degrees from a superior school carried far too little weight, even when supplemented by the secretarial training then widely demanded in a male-dominated and sexist working world. Nevertheless, quite a few Smith graduates moved directly into a variety of occupations, while a smaller number undertook graduate study with a view to professional careers—in teaching, social work, and, in exceptional cases, law, medicine, and academic scholarship. The foremost goals of most students, however, were those that loomed large among all college women in the fifties: happy and presumably permanent marriage, carefully planned and Spockian reared children, and companionable familialism in split-level homes. Thus a kind of enlightened domesticity, combined with political conservatism, a mild liberalism, or both, permeated student life at Smith, as elsewhere.* But this widespread and *generally* accurate portrayal of the college generation of the fifties is a limited, indeed a one-sided, depiction of the interests and aspirations of Smith College undergraduates.

Of the students who majored in sociology there were few exemplars of the stereotypical image of their generation. Some of these women became social workers, with or without professional training, others joined community service agencies as volunteers or salaried employees, while a handful of scholarly bent enrolled in graduate departments of sociology with a view to academic careers in this expanding and increasingly respectable field.† Almost all of these sociologists-to-be, together with a good many others, were participants in Smith's excellent honors program, in which—as departmental director of honors for more than a de-

---

* Survey data on the occupational and familial aspirations of college women and men in the late 1940s and early '50s are presented and ably analyzed in Ernest Havemann and Patricia Salter West, *They Went to College* (New York: Harcourt Brace, 1952); see esp. part three on "Portrait of the Ex-Coed." A somewhat later study is the excellent volume, Rose K. Goldsen et al., *What College Students Think* (Princeton, N.J.: D. Van Nostrand, 1960); see esp. chaps. 1, 2, and 4.

† Among these were Renee Fox and Dorothy Strang Bordes, class of 1949, whose accomplishments at Smith and thereafter are sketched below; Alice Taylor, class of 1950, who as the wife and professional partner of Lincoln H. Day became a widely known demographer; and Martha Richmond, class of 1961, who as Martha Fowlkes reappears in chap. 7 as an outstanding graduate student at the University of Massachusetts and who later became a dean at Smith College.

cade—I not only worked closely with highly talented undergraduates but, inadvertently, received considerable preparation for
teaching later graduate courses at Princeton and Massachusetts.
In these universities, however, none of the many recipients of the
Ph.D. was superior in intellect and sociological percipience to the
top honors students at Smith—among them three extraordinary
young scholars: Renee Fox, Dorothy Strang Bordes, and Lorre
Dinkelspiel.

My first encounter with Renee Fox took place in the fall
of 1947 when she began her junior year. A victim of very severe
poliomyelitis, Renee had been hospitalized during most of 1945–
46, as a sophomore had continued her academic studies at Whittier
College with the same distinction that had marked her work as a
Smith freshman. Upon returning to the college she visited my
office to discuss her eligibility (*sic*) to enter the honors program.
In the years that followed, until my departure from Smith in
1960, no student in sociology, or probably in any field, rivaled
Renee in combining intellectual brilliance and humane concern—
qualities that have never left her.

During her last two years at Smith, Renee was an impressive leader of the department's honors students: her superior
intellect and scholarly accomplishments went hand in hand with
a mature social sensitivity infrequently seen in youthful circles.
In seminars and less formal sessions she was the group's most effective teacher, and both her oral presentations and papers were
graced by an artistry extremely rare among sociologists, young or
old. This amply demonstrated talent prompted me, as her adviser, and in disregard for future benefit to my own profession,
to downplay Renee's emerging aspiration to become an academic
sociologist and to encourage her to consider less constraining fields.
Her artistic and creative bent, I thought, should be given freer
play than graduate training in sociology generally permits.

This view, however, ran counter to Renee's inclinations,
which were supported* by Bernard Barber who, fresh from graduate study at Harvard, had accepted a position at Smith in 1948.
At my suggestion and with Renee's approval, he had become director of her honors thesis—in keeping with my belief that junior
faculty members should participate in the department's most rewarding teaching assignment.† Barber not only fulfilled this role

---

* "Supported," but somewhat reluctantly, Renee has recently told me.
† Renee's honors thesis, an excellent study of the values of American literary
artists who became Communists in the 1920s and '30s, was completed shortly

with expertise, but soon became Renee's principal mentor, close friend, and a sponsor of her pursuit of the doctorate at his alma mater. Thus this remarkable young woman, after graduating from Smith with highest honors in 1949, later that year joined Talcott Parsons and company to seek certification as a professional sociologist.

From the beginning, Renee's career in the academy and in her profession has been spectacular. Her Harvard dissertation resulted in the volume *Experiment Perilous* (1959), a sensitive and revealing study of "physicians and patients facing the unknown," and in subsequent years she brought her creative and literary talents to *The Emerging Physician* (1968) and *The Courage to Fail* (1974). These books, together with numerous papers published here and abroad, are major and altogether unique contributions to the sociology of medicine, the professions, and science which put on display not only Renee's scholarly and research skills, but her long-standing concern with human tribulation and fortitude. Renee has decorated the faculties of Barnard College, Harvard, and most recently the University of Pennsylvania where, as professor of sociology, psychiatry, and medicine, she chaired her department for several years. She has taught and conducted research in Belgium and Africa, served as director and vice president of the Social Science Research Council and president of the Eastern Sociological Society, she is on the board of directors of the National Academy of Arts and Sciences and an elected member of the council of the AAAS's Institute of Medicine. Recipient of various awards and honorary degrees, at the age of forty-seven Renee Fox was made a doctor of humane letters by Smith College in 1975.

A quarter of a century earlier, Renee's running mate for highest honors in sociology was Dorothy Strang who, with a yearling husband in tow, graduated from Smith as Dorothy Bordes. While both of these members of the class of 1949 won top academic awards (junior Phi Beta Kappa, the summa degree) and both were young intellectuals of great scholarly promise, they differed strikingly in other respects. In contrast with Renee's in-

---

before the publication of the testimonial volume, *The God That Failed,* ed. Richard Grossman (New York: Harper, 1949) and, in some measure, anticipated Daniel Aaron's superb *Writers on the Left,* published in 1961. The thesis also was an early illustration of Renee's continuing talent in bridging the social sciences and the humanities; among her teachers at Smith were the men of letters, Aaron, Robert Gorham Davis, and Newton Arvin.

grained modesty, impeccable decorum, and social sensitivity, Dorothy displayed her talents boldly, at times rode roughshod over others, and had little use for "middle-class" conventions—on this count she would have been at home among the "turned-on" youth of the 1960s. Dorothy's aggressive and bohemian propensities, however, were outweighed by her enthusiasm for the world of ideas, her devotion to learning, and her scholastic accomplishments.

Among Dorothy's achievements was a prize-winning honors thesis on what was then an unlikely subject for an undergraduate undertaking: the influence of Freudian theory on cultural anthropology. This subject was closely related to her keen interest in the study of personality (and related no doubt to her own experience with psychotherapy, noted below), and the thesis itself showed the beneficial influence of the personality psychologist Elsa Siipola, one of Dorothy's principal mentors. Written under the direction of Gladys Bryson, this undergraduate work in intellectual history and the sociology of social science was far more impressive than most master's theses and compared favorably with a good many doctoral dissertations—it was a large first step, we on the faculty believed at the time, toward what probably would be a highly successful academic career. The thesis also carried considerable weight at Harvard and Columbia where its author was offered major fellowships for graduate study in sociology.

Dorothy's election of Columbia was at least partly a result of her marriage in her junior year to Peter Bordes, an undergraduate at Yale. Bordes also had been accepted by Columbia's Department of Sociology, and these newlyweds wished to face together both the excitements of New York and the challenges of Morningside Heights. The latter were met successfully during their first year of study in Fayerweather Hall, but in different measure: Dorothy lived up to her superior record at Smith by producing top-level papers for Robert Merton and others, while Peter, although an able student, trailed his spouse by several lengths. But this initial year (1949–50) at Columbia must have been a time of troubles for Dorothy, as well as one of academic victories, for her marriage became unstable and her emotional problems led to a subsequent period of institutionalization. Following her return to New York, Dorothy committed suicide on October 5, 1951.

Whatever may have been the triggering circumstances of this final act, its biographical roots no doubt were deep. For many years—as an undergraduate at Smith and earlier—Dorothy Strang had led a troubled inner life, hardly concealed by her intellectual prowess or by her spirited rebellion against convention; and her record of psychiatric care was longstanding. The death of this extraordinary woman, at the age of twenty-four, a tragic event for all who knew Dorothy, surely was a great loss for sociology itself.

A career in sociology, as I have noted, was a goal of few Smith undergraduates—no more than a dozen or so during my lengthy tenure in the college. Among the large majority of those for whom this goal had little or no appeal, however, there were some outstanding students of the field. One was Lorre Dinkelspiel (class of 1951), an intellectual peer of Renee Fox and Dorothy Bordes.

Lorre was seven when her family came to the United States in 1936, following migration from Germany and a period of time in England. Eleven years later she arrived at Smith with an excellent scholarship in hand. She lived in Lawrence House where Gladys Bryson was faculty resident, but during her first two years, when Lorre's scholastic and other achievements had already won attention, we had little hope that she would elect sociology as her major subject, for she seemed to have been captured by the rival Department of Government. Thus Lorre's decision to join our ranks in the spring of 1949 came as a happy surprise—and gave us reason to boast of another honors student of highest rank.

Lorre's superior academic record was a product of, whatever else, a keen analytical mind, an enormous capacity for sustained hard work, and a powerful drive to maximize her various undertakings.* This record was achieved while she carried a load of part-time jobs during the school year and full-time work throughout the "vacation" months. She possessed what more affluent Smithies may have viewed as severe disadvantages: minimal pocket money, a skimpy wardrobe, and few, if any, visits to the fleshpots of New York. But these were no great handicaps for Lorre, or so it seemed, for this engaging, oftentimes light-hearted, and far lovelier creature than most of her sister students was no confined "creature of the books." Her busy extracurricular life included high attainment in modern dance and, perhaps closest to her heart, what she held to be great success in Smith's most popular pastime, the acquisition of a husband.

Lorre's marriage to James Cochrane, a law student at Yale,

---

* Lorre's honors thesis of 250 or so pages, a comprehensive and critical study of industrial sociology, was a major illustration of this drive. As thesis director, I had to cut it short lest this undergraduate project was to become, say, a full-scale doctoral dissertation.

took place in the spring of her junior year in Smith's tiny chapel and, unlike most such affairs, according to a scenario that she herself had spelled out long before. Her graduation, as planned, corresponded with her husband's completion of his legal studies. Immediately thereafter this young lawyer and his wife confronted the task of making a living in New York. That they did well on this count was due in large part, I believe, to Lorre's hardly surprising success as a market analyst for Lever Brothers. She held this position until 1958 when, in a second, probably less-carefully plotted, and presumably permanent marriage she became, with her new husband and partner, an authority and dealer in the world of art.*

This career—from outstanding scholarly accomplishment as an undergraduate to successful breadwinning in a giant corporation to a nonbureaucratized and independent position in the cultural realm, with husbands along the way—is not altogether atypical of Smith College graduates in the 1950s. Lorre Dinkelspiel Stromberg attained a rewarding occupational and personal life some time ago. Had she chosen to follow the field of her undergraduate study, sociology, surely, would have been the gainer.

The three young women whose undergraduate feats and later careers are sketched above, a few others who perhaps should be ranked with that extraordinary trio, and the many rank-and-filers who passed through Smith's Department of Sociology and Anthropology between 1946 and 1960 confronted a faculty of frequently changing personnel. Five long-timers gave the department considerable stability: the veterans GB, Margaret Marsh, and Neal DeNood, myself, and (beginning in 1951) Ely Chinoy. Several sociologists and anthropologists, however, taught at the college relatively briefly, most of whom were moving upward in the academic procession of the 1950s. Among the dozen or more members of the faculty who were short-time departmental colleagues during my years at Smith were Bernard Barber, Michael Olmsted, and Allen Kassof.†

---

* The art gallery of Mr. and Mrs. Vernon A. Stromberg is located in Croton-on-the-Hudson, New York.
† A more comprehensive account would include, in addition to the earlier sketches of Helen Mims and Adelaide Hill, my vivid recollections of the following sojourners: Mary E. W. Goss whose later and continuing career as a well-known medical sociologist was preceded by a single year of effective teaching at Smith (1949–50); James McPherson (1952–1954), a gentle man of literary gifts and the husband of the able sociologist Gertrude McPherson; the brilliant but troubled Faye von Mehring with doctoral degrees in both

In the spring of 1948, in its search for a first-rate sociologist to fill a junior position, the department had narrowed the field to two promising youngsters from Columbia, Peter Blau and his friend and future wife, Zena Smith, both of whom had been impressive candidates during their visit to the college (in tandem on the same day—a departure from hiring conventions). The problem of selecting one of these two was avoided, however, when last-minute but powerful recommendations of Bernard Barber arrived from Columbia's Robert Merton and Harvard's Talcott Parsons. A few days later, this bright, handsome, and enthusiastic fellow spent a day or so with us at Smith. Then completing his dissertation for Harvard, Bernard joined the department in the fall of that year and, together with the historian-sociologist Elinor Barber, remained in Northampton through 1951–52.

This period must have been a rewarding one for the Barbers, professionally and personally, at least in some respects. They completed their Harvard dissertations: first, Bernard's unique study of public apathy and voluntarism and, later, Elinor's acclaimed work on class and social mobility in eighteenth-century France.* In his instructional role, Bernard supervised, in fine fashion, the theses of some of the department's most able honors students,† he played the major part in moving the introductory course in a functionalist direction, and he enriched the curriculum with a new offering in the area of his principal research at the time, the sociology of science. And, far more industrious than most of his colleagues, Bernard wrote *Science and the Social Order* (1952), the first volume of what expanded within a decade or so

---

sociology and anthropology whose tragic death occurred at the start of her second year at the college (1955–56); Hildred Geertz, splendid anthropologist, excellent teacher, and, as wife of Clifford Geertz, a commuter from Cambridge (1956–57); Alfred Harris, Africanist, anthropologist, and superb comic (1957–1959), who moved on to Brandeis and from there to Rochester; my one-time student Nathan Glazer, visitor for a term (in 1959), who in our midst found the lovely Sudochana Raghavan, his wife-to-be; the bright and irrepressible Henry Carsch whose antics alternatively amused and dismayed the outgoing chairman during the spring of 1960.

† These included Renee Fox, as noted above, and later Nancy Mazur and years, Bernard Barber's study has been published recently: *"Mass Apathy" and Voluntary Social Participation in the United States* (New York: Arno Press, 1980). Elinor Barber's dissertation led to *The Bourgeosie in 18th Century France* (Princeton, N.J.: Princeton University Press, 1955).

* These included Renee Fox, as noted above, and later Nancy Mazur and Lyle Lobel, both stars of the class of 1951.

into an impressive bibliography. These were no small accomplishments, managed while carrying a heavy teaching load and assuming new family responsibilities (Elinor Barber bore twin daughters during their second year in Northampton).

But there were frustrations for Barber, as well as high rewards, during his stay at Smith. Fresh from graduate study and teaching at Harvard where he had become a close student and strong advocate of the work of Talcott Parsons, he was understandably uneasy with the MacIverian perspective of the director of the introductory course, in which he had a leading role, and dissatisfied with its eclectic nature. More important, the increasingly deteriorating relationships between Bernard and his departmental colleagues reached a low point in his final year when he announced his disregard for all but one of us (the widely beloved Margaret Marsh) and openly crossed swords with the newcomer Ely Chinoy. Responsibility for this unhappy situation was by no means one-sided. Senior members of the department were less than fully supportive of Bernard's achievements and my own inattention to the responsibilities of collegiality and friendship was perhaps of greater significance. On that count, as well as sociological competence, Bernard found me lacking.

Some months before he left Smith Bernard and I discussed his future prospects at the college, which appeared to be very good indeed in view of his demonstrated capacities as a scholar and teacher. In the course of our exchange, however, I ventured the guess that he, like other ascending academics before him, would be moving to a major university in the near future. Shortly after this conversation he received at least two such invitations, one from Barnard College carrying a faculty affiliation with Columbia's powerful graduate department. Thus in 1952 Bernard Barber ended both a rewarding and frustrating four years at Smith and took a large step forward in his career as a sociologist of distinction.

Faced with Barber's forthcoming departure and my own leave of absence scheduled for 1952–53, during the preceding spring the department conducted what turned out to be a fruitful search for two sociologists: James McPherson from Columbia and Michael Olmsted from Harvard joined our ranks. Fairly soon after his arrival Mike Olmsted became a stalwart of the faculty whom we hoped would remain at Smith for many years; our hopes were shattered by his death in 1960.

Mike was only twenty-eight when he and his wife Patricia ("Pat") arrived in Northampton. But following his graduation from Harvard at the age of twenty his academic and professional attainments had been impressive: four years of successful teaching—social studies, history, English, and art—in secondary schools while earning graduate degrees in sociology and education; a laudable thesis on Catholicism and psychoanalysis at the University of Chicago; subsequently the doctorate from his alma mater where he demonstrated both sociological sophistication and skill as an experimentalist with a dissertation on small group interaction as a function of group norms and taught in a variety of Harvard's courses.

This rich background, together with Mike's several talents, his warm personality, and his devotion to students paid splendid dividends during his seven and a half years on the Smith faculty. He was an exacting but popular teacher of both departmental and interdisciplinary courses. Beyond the curriculum he brought erudition and critical acumen to lectures on diverse scholarly subjects; beyond the college he was a member of or counselor for various educational agencies. Along with his demanding instructional and extracurricular activities, Mike published frequently in professional journals and wrote *The Small Group*, which for many years was the most widely used text in the field.* Beginning in 1958, an additional achievement of Mike's was his superior editorial and artistic contribution to the *American Sociological Review*, a matter elaborated in chapter 6.

Mike Olmsted's feats during these years in Northampton clearly warrant fuller treatment than that presented in these recollections. Perhaps an inkling of the victories of Mike's foreshortened life and the strength of his character were reported long ago in the pages of the *ASR:*

On February 18, 1960, at a tragically young age, death ended the career of a superb student of sociology and other fields, a highly promising scholar, an exciting teacher, a talented member of the . . . academy, a beloved man. But Michael

* *The Small Group* (New York: Random House, 1959) was first published in the original paperback series, "Short Studies in Sociology." This edition remained in extensive use for more than fifteen years, until a revision, with only minor changes of substance and interpretation, very ably done by A. Paul Hare, was published in 1978. As editor of this series, I suggested that Mike undertake the book. I gave him a hard time while he was writing it, and following its publication I took great and everlasting pride in the altogether surprising dedication to "CHP." There is more about this series and other publishing matters in chap. 6.

Olmsted leaves a rich legacy to many of us: Patricia Crockett Olmsted, their sons Jeffrey and Michael, his former teachers and students and colleagues, his many friends within—and without—the collegiate community. Not least, he leaves affirmation of man's capacity for extraordinary courage: not until the final weeks of a year-long and inexorable illness, when there was no alternative, did he relinquish or reduce his many activities. Professor Olmsted's "vita" hardly reflects these activities, the wide range of his interests, his imaginative prowess, his sparkling wit. . . .

As a member of the *Review*'s editorial staff and as Book Review Editor, Michael Olmsted was a "promethean editorial colleague." . . . He was much more.*

During their years at Smith Bernard Barber and Michael Olmsted, each in a different style, enhanced both the college's and the wider sociological enterprise. And so did Allan Kassof, a third fine young scholar from Harvard's Department of Social Relations and, in his case, the Russian Research Center. Together with his lovely wife Arianne, Allen arrived in 1957 and remained in Northampton until his move to Princeton in 1961.

At Smith, from the outset, Allen's educational contributions were highlighted by the didactic expertise and social sensitivity he brought to the lecture hall, the smaller classroom, and to his relations with individual students, by his imaginative bent, and by a comprehension of the realities of academic culture frequently lacking among beginners. In and beyond the department, Allen was a splendid colleague and, for me, a wonderful companion. He was cooperative, understanding of his fellow teachers'—and his own—deficiencies, at once straightforward and considerate of others, and, not least, at times a tension-breaking comic. In his off-campus life, and with my full collaboration, he displayed great talent as a practical jokester.

But these foolish episodes were infrequent, and Allen's vivaciousness imposed no restraint upon his professional pursuits. Sociological prowess and intellectual power, as well as superior pedagogic skill, marked his teaching. This included classroom colleagueship with the outstanding scholars George Gibian and Sidney Monas in the interdepartmental seminar on Russian society and culture. His own research in Soviet studies, the area of

* Charles H. Page, "Michael Seymour Olmsted, 1923–1960," *American Sociological Review* 25, no. 4 (August 1960): 575.

his Harvard dissertation, resulted in publications in scholarly journals and growing recognition in academia. Thus within a few years he traded the ivied walls of Smith for those of Princeton.

Only passing reference is made above to a sociologist who as a young scholar-teacher became our working colleague in 1951 and who, unlike others cited in the present section, remained at Smith until his death in 1975. The important contributions of Ely Chinoy to the college, to his profession, and to the sociological and humanistic education of thousands of students here and abroad warrant special comment.

Ely Chinoy

With the postwar expansion of sociology at Smith (as elsewhere), the department's search for an additional member in the spring of 1951 ended with the appointment of Dennis Wrong whom we judged, correctly, to be a future star. Late in May, however, Dennis was invited to become an assistant to George F. Kennan and, saddened by our loss, we wished him good fortune in his venture with the mighty. With last-minute desperation, we re-examined the credentials of candidates for the junior position, which had been assembled months before. The strongest dossier, in our view, belonged to one Ely Chinoy. Chinoy had studied for the doctorate at Columbia, was warmly recommended by Robert Lynd and Robert Merton, and had taught at several schools including the University of Toronto where he was then a member of the faculty. Telephone calls had happy results: the news of Chinoy's continuing wish to return to the States, a reluctant but generous release from Toronto, his acceptance of the tardily offered job, sight unseen on either side (a departure from sacred custom of the college), and the acquisition of a sociologist who for almost a quarter of a century would be a leading light at Smith.

From the outset, Ely's accomplishments, highlighted at Smith by his superior teaching, were impressive. His Columbia dissertation (following its completion, the study's formal defense was long delayed by Robert Lynd), slightly revised, was published as *Automobile Workers and the American Dream*, which became a minor sociological classic.* His other scholarly publications en-

---

* First published by Doubleday in 1955, a paperback edition was brought out ten years later by Beacon Press. Over the years, the study has been a frequently cited source in works in industrial and occupational sociology, social stratification, and American studies—a relatively rare destiny for a doctoral dissertation.

compass the diverse subjects of social mobility, urbanization, popular sociology, and sociological praxis; and for many years his *Society* was one of the few distinguished general textbooks in this heavily populated field.* Ely was an active and esteemed member of his profession and served on various committees of the ASA. He was a vigorous and respected leader in the college faculty, in 1960 he became chairman of the department, an office he held for six years, and later was named the Mary Huggins Gamble Professor of Sociology and Anthropology. In 1963–64 he was a visiting professor at the University of Leicester; and during his extensive travels he gave lectures in Britain, Western and Eastern Europe, Israel, and the Philippines.

This selective account of his professional achievements tells nothing about Ely as a rare and, for many of us, a beloved man, and little about our long-standing friendship. Two years after an automobile accident ended his life at the age of fifty-four, in the final session of a three-day symposium given in Ely's memory, I was asked to speak:

. . . Ely and I taught together, worked on books together, edited a scholarly journal together, plotted departmental strategy together, we fished together, sometimes we frolicked together—all of this for more than thirty years. So I have many, many memories of Ely and his accomplishments. What to single out today? I'll mention only two enormous talents of Ely's and a great gift that he has left us.

First and of special importance in the context of this symposium, Ely was a *master sociologist.* Our meetings here have given proper emphasis to his outstanding scholarship and great influence in the study of work and workers, but Ely was also a splendid "general sociologist" (to use an old-fashioned term), brought out in his teaching here and abroad, in his far-ranging lectures and conference papers, in the critical assessment of his many book reviews, and perhaps most notably in one of the very few first-rate general textbooks that sociology can boast. Many years ago, in the Foreword to the first edition of Ely's *Society,* I spelled out what seemed to me to be the severe and seldom-met criteria of a good text, and then wrote: "These proposed requirements of the meritorious . . .

---

* *Society: An Introduction to Sociology* (New York: Random House, 1961, rev. 1967); my own estimate of this text appears in the foreword, from which a quotation is presented below.

textbook are large demands. They suggest that the author of such a work must be, at once, a devoted and critical student of his field, a wise and experienced scholar-teacher, and a concerned member of the human community. That these are realistic goals, however, is amply reaffirmed by Ely Chinoy's *Society*." Only a master-sociologist could have written this splendid volume. . . .

Second, and this is related to his superior sociology, Ely was what I'll call a *humane realist*. This is to say that he saw things whole, in perspective, and always with reference to the norms of both human decency and objective analysis. Ely was a fine sociologist, *but* he was sharply critical of a field too often marked by pretension, intellectual provincialism, and shoddy goods—he would have none of these. Ely was a great and enthusiastic teacher, *but* he was keenly aware of the educational delinquencies and trained incapacities of academic men and women—including his own shortcomings. Ely gave huge amounts of energy and time and talent to the well-being of Smith College, *but* he had little patience for her institutional stodginess, silly departmental rivalries, her discriminations and prejudices, and the other sore spots that becolor any school. Ely was a warm and wonderful friend, *but* he was what a good friend should be: he was capable of raising hell when our follies called for candor. Ely was a hard-working and serious man—about his scholarship, his profession, his family, himself, *but* his humane realism, his perspective, gave him an almost ever-present light-heartedness and a marvelous sense of the comic and absurd that color all of our activities. Ely, as he might have said of one he loved, was a *mensch*.

Finally, Ely left us all with a precious treasure—in the form of three magnificent people. . . . To Helen and Michael and Claire we give our love.*

Smith, Politics, and Joe McCarthy

Ely Chinoy and I were among the political semiactivists at Smith throughout the 1950s. In the more immediate postwar years, American leftists and many sympathetic liberals had enjoyed a short-lived renaissance, reaching its peak in 1948 when they rallied behind Henry Wallace in his run for the presidency. Their political efforts, like those of their forerunners in the 1930s,

* Charles H. Page, "Ely Chinoy," presented at the "Smith College Symposium on Humanizing Work," April 2, 1977.

extended to the campus and at Smith, as at other schools, there was a small contingent of Wallacites. But in the less turbulent fifties most academics of liberal persuasion, among them ex-radicals of earlier days, were disenchanted with the Stalinists. They voted for Adlai Stevenson, among their leading spokesmen was Arthur Schlesinger, and they joined Americans for Democratic Action and similar organizations of the liberal, anti-communist front. Although a self-proclaimed socialist of long standing (as I remain today), I shared this respectable political position with many others, including a large contingent of the Smith faculty.

But on one important count our generally moderate political life carried considerable excitement and, for at least some among us, considerable trepidation. For during the early fifties Joe McCarthy, the senator from Wisconsin, was on the rampage, leading with a frightening bellicosity a far-flung search for Communists and fellow subversives who allegedly were ensconced in colleges and universities, as well as in government, the performing arts, and elsewhere. In the nationwide witch-hunting atmosphere of the times, exacerbated by the Cold War, academics of radical or merely unconventional bent faced severe pressure toward conformity and, in many cases, real or threatened dismissal from their teaching jobs. This pressure was far stronger, the sanctions more prevalent, and administrative support of faculty "deviants" much weaker in public and lower quality schools than in well endowed, prestigious, and private institutions such as Smith.* In some measure, however, McCarthyism invaded all of academia, provoked anxiety among many teachers, and presented presidents and boards of trustees with the task of protecting academic freedom—a task performed splendidly by some and ignored by others. On this score, Smith's faculty was served very well indeed.

The administration's important role in safeguarding the rights of teachers and in shielding the college from Red-hunting attacks is illustrated by the first of three events sketched below.

* Extensive confirmation of this contrast is presented in Paul H. Lazarsfeld and Wagner Thielens, Jr., *The Academic Mind: Social Scientists in a Time of Crisis* (Glencoe, Ill.: The Free Press, 1958), esp. chaps. 2 and 7. The "witch-hunting atmosphere of the times" is depicted in the survey study, Samuel A. Stouffer, *Communism, Conformity, and Civil Liberties* (New York: Doubleday, 1955). An excellent analysis of the "climate of opinion" in the nation and the state of affairs in the postwar academic world is Robert M. MacIver, *Academic Freedom in Our Time* (New York: Columbia University Press, 1955).

The second episode involved a countermove on the part of aroused men and women on the faculty itself, while the third brought Joe McCarthy face-to-face with most of us at Smith together with many nonacademic residents of Northampton and the surrounding community. These events were something less than earth-shaking nationally, but locally they provided political drama and instruction with regard to political reality. The following report reverses their chronology:

Early in 1954 several thousand of her sister alumnae received a letter from Aloise B. Heath, graduate of Smith and sister of William F. Buckley, the precocious and severe critic of *his* college in the widely read volume *God and Man at Yale* (1951). Mrs. Heath wrote as the secretary of a "Committee for Discrimination in Giving" (other members of the committee, if any, were unidentified); her message began: "All of us, of course, realize that a contribution to a cause or an institution implies, on the part of the contributor, not merely a gesture of loyalty, but an active assumption of moral responsibility for that cause or institution."* This eye opener was followed by the suggestion that certain men and women teaching at Smith "may be influencing young minds in a direction contrary to the philosophical principles in which most of us believe," and named five teachers "and other members of the Smith College faculty," unnamed, who presumably rejected such principles by virtue of their past or present association with organizations "cited as Communist or Communist-fronts by the Attorney General of the United States and the Committee on Un-American Activities." Mrs. Heath's provocative letter ended on a virtuous and cautionary note: "Even with full knowledge of the political associations of the above-mentioned professors, some of us will choose to contribute to Smith College with money which helps make their employment possible. We suggest, however, that any alumna who cannot conscientiously, and with complete awareness of its implications, follow this course, withhold her donation until the Smith Administration explains its educational policy to her personal satisfaction." A few months later a pamphlet, which specified the proscribed organizational affiliations of the five putative faculty culprits, was mailed to all Smith Clubs, the alumnae's grass-roots, fund-raising agencies. This documented broadside, Mrs. Heath apparently hoped, not only would alert Smith graduates to grave dangers in their alma mater, but would

---

* Copies of this letter, dated February 23, 1954, and other materials cited below are contained in three fat files in the Smith College Archives.

also pressure the administration to constrain or weed out "subversives" in its midst. Mrs. Heath's efforts may have increased "discrimination in giving" on the part of a few alumnae (reportedly, donations mounted following her campaign), but otherwise they failed completely.

This failure may be attributed to a combination of circumstances characteristic of schools of the ivy tradition: a history of social, educational, and scholarly prestige that tolerated little interference with the college's affairs; a long-standing record of hospitality to intellectual and political diversity; alumnae who included stalwart defenders of civil rights, some of whom were of upper-class status; a strong distaste among students and graduates for the crudities and demagoguery of McCarthy who, irrespective of great differences in background, public style, and social grace, shared with Mrs. Heath a propensity for Red hunting; and, not least, an administration that defended the faculty with fortitude and alacrity. Thus President Benjamin F. Wright, aided by the political wisdom and moral strength of his assistant Helen Kirkpatrick,* responded firmly to Mrs. Heath and reaffirmed the principle of academic freedom as a governing policy of the college. Smith's attorney was placed at the disposal of the five accused members of the faculty. The latter met with a faculty-trustee committee, and without prolonged delay the board of trustees, chaired by the esteemed Smith loyalist Mrs. Amanda Bryan Kane, gave unanimous approval of the committee's unequivocal recommendation of full support of Professors Arvin, Dean, Faulkner, Jules, and Larkin.

Mrs. Heath's selection of this particular quintet raised some eyebrows. The literary scholar Newton Arvin, the painter Mervin Jules, and the art historian Oliver "Pete" Larkin were veteran stars of the faculty who, like many of us in earlier years, had belonged to organizations cited by the Committee on Un-American Activities as sympathetic to or controlled by the Communist party. But visiting professor Vera Micheles Dean, a political scientist of international stature, was barely tainted by questionable organizational ties and hardly a menace to the undergraduates. The most anomalous member of this distinguished group, however, was the prolific economic historian Harold U.

---

* Helen Kirkpatrick, Smith graduate in 1931 and later a well-known journalist, was a tower of political strength during her two or three years as assistant to President Wright. Subsequently she married Robbins Milbank, a Smith trustee from 1955 to 1961.

Faulkner. A member of the Smith faculty since 1925, he was the gentlest of men, held in affection by students and colleagues alike. The most radical act in his long career was his candidacy for Congress, long before, on the Socialist ticket—but in 1954 Harold's politics were considerably to the right of my own. How I, and several of my colleagues, escaped Aloise Buckley Heath's attention remains a mystery.

Looking back from today, this episode may seem to be a tempest in a teapot. But in those McCarthy-colored years it was a cause célèbre at Smith.

During the late fall of the preceding year the Smith chapter of the American Association of University Professors released a rather lengthy, anti-McCarthyite statement, all or parts of which appeared in several newspapers—and perhaps may have encouraged Mrs. Heath and her shadow committee to expose supposedly nefarious activities at the college.

The principal participants in this second episode of those Red-hunting years included the sociologists Ely Chinoy, secretary, and myself, president, of the local chapter of the AAUP. Together with other members of the group's executive committee, notably the liberal Daniel Aaron and the more conservative but equally staunch defender of individual liberty Vera Brown Holmes, we labored for a month or so to produce a document that would be, at once, a powerful indictment of ongoing threats to civil rights and freedom of inquiry by legislative committees, newspaper editors, and private citizens; an explication of the principles and obligations to which we as teachers subscribed in this time of troubles; and a statement that would receive the support of academics of diverse political and ideological preference. We were especially concerned with the extensive, high-handed activities of congressional and state committees, as the following excerpts from the almost thousand-word declaration illustrate:*

The actions of some committees and certain of their members have violated the very principles which we as teachers are seeking to communicate to our students: the careful search for facts, the objective appraisal of evidence, the avoidance of hasty conclusions. They have over-simplified complex problems and demonstrated little capacity for reasoned and pains-

* The AAUP statement of November 19, 1953, together with related documents, are filed in the Smith College Archives; the quotations below are taken from the statement itself.

taking judgment. They have questioned without justification the loyalty of American teachers as a whole and the integrity of distinguished universities. They have on occasion demonstrated ignorance of the law and of the constitution under which they have carried on their activities.

Their actions have frequently violated freedoms basic to the American way of life. They have subjected witnesses to what is in effect a public trial without granting them the protection and privileges guaranteed by law. They have ignored the fundamental rule of American law that men are presumed innocent until they are proven guilty. They have accepted the evil doctrine of guilt by association. Their behavior has led us to ask if they are searching for facts to be used as a basis for legislation or whether instead they are merely seeking personal publicity and political advantage. Their actions have given comfort to the enemies against whom they claim to be defending us. They have made us wonder whether we are not in greater danger from demagogues in our midst than we are from conspirators.

We were also alarmed by the "fear of new ideas, the confusion of dissent with treason, the increasing censorship of books," and "the pressure for conformity," and here we invoked what for us were the wise and apposite words of Justice Learned Hand:

Risk for risk, for myself I had rather take my chances that some traitors will escape detection than spread abroad a spirit of general suspicion and distrust, which accepts rumor and gossip in place of undismayed and unintimidated inquiry. I believe that community is already in process of decay where each man begins to eye his neighbor as a possible enemy, where nonconformity with the accepted creed, political as well as religious, is a mark of dissatisfaction; where denunciation, without specification or backing, takes the place of evidence; where faith in the eventual supremacy of reason has become so timid that we dare not enter our convictions in the open lists to win or lose.

Our statement was endorsed by the members of the local chapter of the AAUP, by a much larger number of the Smith faculty, and by several of the Association's chapters in other schools. Among the citizens of Northampton and nearby towns, however, there were strident voices of dissent from this alleged attempt to exculpate academic "Reds" and "Pinkos." In keeping with the McCarthyism of the times and with the senator's own inglorious numbers game, it was apparent, they proclaimed, that subversion of the nation and of its youth was widespread in colleges and universities—such as Smith. We were castigated severely. Some of these protectors of the common weal wrote angry letters to the *Daily Hampshire Gazette* or telephoned individuals on the AAUP executive committee, whose authorship of the group's declaration had been given in the press. One zealot, whose super-patriotism went hand in hand with blatant anti-Semitism (a frequent combination in this circle), but who remained anonymous, attacked Daniel Aaron and Ely Chinoy as "Communist Jews," and during an equally friendly call to me asked when I had changed my name to Page. Another fellow townsman and former army colonel, with greater courage, urged that he and I meet face to face; we did so—with results that he must have found displeasing. Incidents such as these, however trivial in retrospect, loomed large when Joe McCarthy was a national celebrity.

When Senator Joseph McCarthy himself was campaigning for re-election in 1952 and spoke at a number of colleges and universities including Smith, we were given the opportunity to observe this celebrity in action. On April 10 of that year the senator addressed an enormous audience in Northampton's largest auditorium, John M. Greene Hall where for many decades Smith students and faculty had assembled for such educational and cultural occasions as symphony concerts, weekly chapels, and faculty shows. McCarthy's appearance was theater of a sort, to be sure, but his performance was hardly representative of the traditional bill at John M. Greene.

He came to the college under the auspices of the Young Republican Club of Smith and at the instigation of a student who was the daughter of McCarthy's campaign manager. She had persuaded this moderate conservative group that all important viewpoints on controversial issues should be represented in local political activities, including the radical rightism then being espoused by many Americans. The wide appeal of this position and the popularity of McCarthy were illustrated by the turnout at John M. Greene: not by the attendance of a large percentage of Smith students and teachers, most of whom were highly critical of the demagoguery and unbridled Red baiting of McCarthy, but by many of the hundreds of townspeople from the Connecticut Valley who filled the hall to overflowing. With this mixed audience, however, the rabble-rousing senator could not have been at his best.

Upon arrival McCarthy was greeted by a lengthy but silent parade circling the auditorium in which some of the marchers carried signs "to protest what, it was well known, would be an indiscriminate attack by implication and innuendo upon his political opposites."* On this score, he fulfilled our expectations by reiterating the charge that "this country's policy is being shaped and directed from the Kremlin." In consideration of his hosts and the dangers they faced, he declared that "I see no reason why American fathers and mothers should hire communists to teach their sons and daughters" and "One way individuals can help to combat communism is by keeping a close watch on what is going on in every college in the nation." In addition to these all too familiar charges and admonitions, McCarthy invited *written* questions from the audience—and here he made his silliest mistake. After two or three of these blatant dice loadings, almost all of the spellbound listeners, including most of his supporters, recognized the ploy. Thus on a spring evening in 1952, Joe McCarthy seemed to us something less than the high-riding menace that clearly he was in fact.

Smith and Professional Socialization: Making Some of It

Apart from teaching, academic housekeeping, and a bit of politics, the fifties for me were a period of professional socialization, at least in some degree. In the thirties, as recorded earlier, I had been heavily involved in teaching, drawn-out study for the Ph.D., random leftist affairs, and recreational pursuits in New York City. In nonmetropolitan Northampton, however, and during these far different postwar years, both opportunity and a measure of motivation led to activities conventionally associated with the profession of sociology.

Early in this chapter I noted that an important reason for moving to Smith was the promise of surroundings less hectic than New York and more conducive to working on a book. I had begun the revision and expansion of MacIver's *Society* during the summer of 1946, and two years later delivered the completed manuscript to the publisher.† Co-authorship with an eminent

---

* Ellen Terry Lincoln, *Through the Grecourt Gates* (Northampton, Mass.: Smith College, 1978), p. 51. This account of "Distinguished Visitors to Smith College 1875–1975" includes a brief report of McCarthy's visit (pp. 51–52) from which the quotations in this paragraph are taken.
† The book was published as Robert M. MacIver and Charles H. Page, *So-*

scholar, as I was to learn subsequently, gave me entree to professional circles which, without this close association, would have been exceedingly difficult or impossible to enter—a case of conferred social visibility. Of far greater importance for my professional socialization were the lessons derived from the co-authorship itself. The chance to work intimately with MacIver's comprehensive textual treatise meant a great deal of reading in a good many areas and thereby enriched my sociological education. More, it was a challenging learning experience to produce a book that would not frighten off too many undergraduate students and at the same time maintain the intellectual and scholarly quality of a long-heralded work. My efforts to achieve a writing style that would not clash with MacIver's lucid and graceful exposition taught me much more than I then realized about an important part of sociological craftsmanship.*

From this rewarding collaboration I also learned some things about the world of publishing, especially the competitive textbook market. In the postwar years and into the 1950s the most successful introductory text commercially was an eclectic primer by William F. Ogburn and Meyer F. Nimkoff.† Until 1949 one of the very few intellectually challenging introductions to sociology was MacIver's *Society,* which some of us had used for many years. Most instructors, however, preferred elementary textbooks such as Ogburn and Nimkoff's, which, according to my biased view, helped to sustain the problematic academic status of sociology and performed a professional and educational disservice. In contrast with these primers, two theoretically sophisticated and highly analytical texts were published in 1949: MacIver and Page's *Society* and Kingsley Davis's *Human Society.*‡ Although each of

---

ciety: An Introductory Analysis (New York: Rinehart, 1949), an extensive revision and substantial enlargement of MacIver's *Society: Its Structure and Changes* (New York: Long and Smith, 1931) and *Society: A Textbook of Sociology* (New York: Rinehart, 1937). The theoretical perspective is the same and the conceptual system remains almost unchanged in these three editions of *Society.*

* That I succeeded on this score in some measure was noted in reviews and personal letters. One generous commentator wrote: "Page's contributions are so effectively blended as to produce a seamless fabric of exposition" (*American Sociological Review* 14, no. 6 [December 1949]: 824).

† *Sociology* (New York: Houghton Mifflin, 1940); other editions followed.

‡ New York: Macmillan, 1949. Much of Davis's fine book is written from a functionalist perspective, and thirty years later remains an excellent intro-

these volumes elicited favorable, even enthusiastic, reviews and was adopted in a good many schools, in the increasingly massive textbook market neither enjoyed a great commercial success. The new *Society,* however, was widely used in Britain for several years and, in ten or more translations, was read by students and teachers in many countries throughout the world. Thus the name of *Society*'s junior author, notwithstanding his meager record of scholarly publications, came to be known in sociological circles at home and abroad.

In this country, both my visibility and professional socialization were given boosts by the publication of a substantial number of book reviews, beginning in 1950 and continuing through most of my years at Smith. The large majority of these appeared in the *American Sociological Review* and the *American Journal of Sociology,* but now and then they were seen in publications as diverse as *Isis* and *The New Republic.* Editors defined my principal areas of "expertise" as social stratification, sociological theory, and leisure and sport; and I had the good luck to be assigned volumes by such worthies as Peter Blau, Kingsley Davis, Marion Levy, Robert Merton, Arnold Rose, W. L. Warner, and Robin Williams—as well as books and at least a few nonbooks by lesser fry. Reviewing, like my earlier collaboration on *Society,* not only put my name before the profession, but—of greater educational significance—required close reading and careful evaluation of different types of sociological work.

Beginning in 1952, my education was widened and my visibility was increased by a new and challenging professional role: advisory editor in sociology for commercial publishers. Advantages and disadvantages of this marginal position—between the academic world and the marts of trade—are discussed at some length in chapter 6. It should be noted here, however, that association with Doubleday and later Random House during the fifties kept me in close touch with a variety of sociological subject areas and with many working sociologists and enabled me to gain a reputation within the field as an editor of competence.

During the fifties participation in the sociological guild was also educational, but in a rather different way. In 1955 I was elected vice president of the Eastern Sociological Society, a year

---

duction to that theoretical orientation. *Human Society* also shows the influence of nonfunctionalist Robert MacIver, notably in chap. 3 on social norms, chap. 11 on primary and secondary groups, and chap. 22 on social change.

or two later to the executive committee of the Society for the Study of Social Problems, and in 1957 to the Council of the American Sociological Society. During my half-dozen years on the Council I rubbed elbows, and sometimes crossed swords, with prominent sociologists—and added to my knowledge of leadership and conflict in formal organizations. My professional maturation was also benefited no doubt by such set-backs as the failure in 1952 to win a Guggenheim Fellowship for a study of sport, the loss of the presidency of the ESS to my teacher and close friend Ted Abel in 1956, two defeats for the vice presidency of the ASS(A), and in 1957 a reluctant but inescapable declination of a Fulbright award to teach at the London School of Economics because of having accepted a surprising invitation.

Sometime in the spring of that year Donald Young, then secretary of the ASS, telephoned the news of an invitation from the society to become editor of the *American Sociological Review* for the three-year term, 1958–1960. Although I had well-grounded doubts about my qualifications for this important job, after a day or two of "careful consideration" in keeping with academic protocol, I agreed to take on this challenging assignment—and entered into a new kind of editorial work a few months later.

From the beginning in 1946, my professional life at Smith had been blessed with good fortune: a steady supply of excellent students, the emergence of warm friendships with faculty colleagues (and townspeople), strong support by my department and the college. And my wife and I, ex-New Yorkers, had become, if not New Englanders, dedicated Northamptonites. These occupational and residential riches were a major reason why I was not interested by offers from other schools, which came with some frequency during an era when both sociology and the larger academy were booming. But the powerful attractions of Smith and Northampton gave way in the spring of 1959 with a call (as was once said) from Princeton University.

5

Sociology and the Ivy Tradition:

Princeton University, 1960–1965

NOTWITHSTANDING THE powerful attractions of Smith and Northampton, in the mid-fifties I began to question certain features of what on many counts was a rewarding and even exciting academic job. It was quite easy, if not unavoidable, to be a big frog in Smith's educational pond, but this role demanded a preoccupation with the ever-changing curriculum and other niceties of the college's educational enterprise for which I had limited capacity. Of greater significance, as I became more and more involved in the scholarly and professional concerns of sociology, increasingly I regretted the absence of graduate students at Smith, and would recollect with nostalgia my brief association with the Columbia faculty in 1941–42. On the positive side, among the many advantages of Smith was its modest size: it encouraged facultywide collegiality, which I prized, and discouraged departmental provincialism, which I decried; this was an important reason for my having declined two or three invitations from large state universities. If I were ever to leave Smith, I would say at times, the move would have to be to a small university with excellent programs of both undergraduate and graduate study. Almost the only school meeting these desiderata, to my knowledge, was far beyond my reach—ivied Princeton.

This was my assumption when, a few days before the annual meeting of the Eastern Sociological Society in the spring of 1959, I received an overseas telephone call from Wilbert Moore—his message was brief but puzzling. Wilbert suggested that we meet during the ESS weekend session, when he would have returned from Paris, to discuss an unspecified but "important matter," and we set a time and place. Thus in the Moores' hotel room, fortified with their generous hospitality, I first heard the startling news of a probable offer from Princeton—in the event, as Wilbert tactfully put it, that I "might be interested." I was.

During the following month or so the preliminaries were pursued: a visit to Princeton to meet with the sociologists, President Robert Goheen, and Dean Douglas Brown; compilation of a vita and supporting documents that might pass muster with the administration and board of trustees; and, on June 17, 1959, my letter of acceptance to the formal invitation extended by Richard Lester of the Department of Economics and Sociology. As professor of sociology, I was slated to become the first chairman of an independent department in September 1960.

Sociology without Portfolio

The postponement of the Princeton appointment until 1960 gave me an additional year at Smith which was needed to complete the term as editor of the *American Sociological Review*. I had agreed, however, to visit Princeton periodically throughout that year and to meet with my future colleagues and with the university's administrative officers in preparation for the ensuing departmental autonomy. During those visits I learned a few things about the traditions and operations of the school that would be, I then assumed, my final academic home—and a good deal about Princeton's ongoing sociological enterprise.

Until 1960, the organizational location of sociology at Princeton was a throwback to an arrangement that had disappeared long ago in most American universities. In the early decades of the century, representatives of this new and often suspect social science, as it moved toward independent status, frequently found a temporary home in an established department—in economics, political science, or even philosophy. But sociology at Princeton was laggard,* emerging only after World War II as a curricular component. During its first fifteen years, however, sociology enjoyed sturdy growth as a division of the powerful Department of Economics.

The senior members of the sociology group during this

---

* "Laggard," but less so than the ivy-clad colleges of Williams and Amherst where sociology was not introduced until the 1960s.

predepartmental period were the eminent scholar and policy-shaper Frank Notestein who had joined Princeton's Office of Population Research (OPR) in 1936, had become its director in 1941, and as professor of demography cast his lot with the sociologists shortly before his retirement in 1959; and Frederick Stephan, a leading social statistician and for many years a mainstay in the graduate program. Beginning in 1942, the scholarly prowess of Kingsley Davis strengthened both the OPR and Princeton's program in sociology until this future luminary moved to Columbia in 1948; in 1943 Wilbert Moore moved to Princeton as a research associate in the OPR and soon thereafter became a member of the teaching faculty. During the next dozen years Wilbert was joined by several young men who, like Davis and Moore, were destined to become sociologists of note: Marion Levy and Melvin Tumin in 1947, Gerald Breese in 1949, Morroe Berger and Gresham Sykes in 1952, Edward Tiryakian (along with the fine anthropologist-sociologist Paul Bohannan) in 1956. When I arrived in Princeton in 1960 all of these notables except Notestein, Davis, Sykes, and Bohannan, together with a protégé of Moore's, Heinz Hartmann, and the young anthropologist Peter Kunstadter, were on hand.

As a division of the Department of Economics and Sociology, this group had functioned quite independently for some time—almost as a department "without portfolio," in which undergraduates could pursue a major and graduate students could earn the Ph.D. in sociology.* Thus during 1959–60, when I met with the Princeton sociologists every six or seven weeks in preparation for departmental autonomy, our discussions generally involved issues that were less than momentous. Whether the new department should be named "Sociology" or "Sociology and Anthropology" stimulated some debate, in which I won a very minor victory. But in a meeting with the full professors (Breese, Levy, Moore, and Stephan) my not-so-innocent inquiry about Mel Tumin's nonpromotion provoked a prolonged and heated exchange—my initiation into what I soon came to realize was a ticklish subject among, and beyond, Princeton's sociologists. For the most part, however, departmental matters of concern—the undergraduate curriculum, the graduate program, recruitment of

---

* Among the sociology majors at Princeton in earlier years was Edward Tiryakian, B.A. summa cum laude, 1952; the first Princeton doctorate in sociology was S. M. ("Mike") Miller, Ph.D., 1951.

faculty, and so on—had been on the sociologists' working agenda for some time. Upon arrival, my designation as Princeton's "first chairman of sociology" obscured what was merely a de jure status.

For the next five years (and thereafter), however, as the new Department of Sociology and Anthropology expanded and took on the privileges and obligations of independence, we faced substantial problems of curriculum and personnel. Our efforts, successful and unsuccessful, to cope with some of these are, in themselves, of some sociological interest.

Princeton Sociologists: A Star-Studded Faculty

For a man of middle age who had spent most of his youthful teaching years at City College followed later by a prolonged tenure at Smith, the move to Princeton was a "great leap forward": whatever my career ambitions, they were realized in full measure. My self-congratulation, however, was mixed with trepidation, stemming in only small part from the university's prestige. In contrast with the circumstances of my earlier jobs, the anxieties of the new position were largely those of a sociologist of limited scholarly attainment facing close colleagueship, and from the chair no less, with an array of sociological stars. The Princeton department was a small one, but its nine members in 1960 included both established leaders in their respective fields (Berger, Breese, Levy, Moore, Stephan, Tumin) and leaders-soon-to-be (Hartmann, Tiryakian). These eight sociologists, together with the six newcomers who joined the department during my five years as chairman (Marvin Bressler, Richard Hamilton, Allen Kassof, William Michelson, Charles Westoff, Maurice Zeitlin) warrant far more extensive comment than that presented in the following sketches.

This caveat holds especially for Wilbert E. Moore who for many years, long before and indeed throughout my chairmanship, was the mainstay of the Princeton sociologists. Wil, as some of his many friends called him, came from the Northwest, earned his first degree and studied the Book at fundamentalist Linfield College (his later writings are graced with Biblical allusions). After receiving an M.A. from the University of Oregon, he arrived at Harvard in time to join Talcott Parsons's remarkable "first generation" of Ph.D.'s. Since 1940, when he received the doctorate, Wilbert Moore's scholarly and professional contributions, like those of his Harvard fellow students Kingsley Davis, Robert Merton, and Robin Williams, to understate the case, have been impressive.*

Of Wilbert's several academic roles at Princeton, four stand out in my memory as of special significance for the development and well-being of the local sociological enterprise. His scholarly work, in quality and quantity, was surpassed by few social scientists, and on this score Wilbert was an exemplar for his colleagues. He was (and is) a fine teacher and, especially at the graduate level, an esteemed mentor whose important contributions to both the sociological and general education of his students have long been widely acknowledged. As a firmly committed sociologist who wished to see his own discipline strongly represented in a sometimes reluctant ivy school, Wilbert brought to the university a corps of unusually able young men (Levy, Tumin, Berger, Tiryakian, Hartmann) whose talents guaranteed the realization of this worthy ambition. Finally, although he avoided the chair himself in favor of less bureaucratic pursuits, as the most highly respected and warmly regarded member of the group, Wilbert was its functioning leader for many years. And during my own rocky voyage at Princeton he was the chairman's wise and generous tutor.

This task, however, occupied only a small segment of Wilbert Moore's professional life, a good deal of which was devoted to sociological scholarship. His contributions to several fields—industrial and occupational sociology, social economics, stratification, social change and economic development, social theory—are an honored and familiar part of the discipline's accomplishments. A special distinction of his numerous publications is their lucid, graceful, and economic expository style, a quality all too rarely found in scholarly work, sociological or otherwise. Like that of most superior sociologists, his writing displays an ironic bent and, as I have noted, it is colored by apposite Biblical references, an uncommon feature of modern sociological literature. These authorial virtues no doubt reflect a good supply of "natural talent," but they are also the product of Wilbert's extraordinary diligence

* Like Davis, Merton, and Williams, Moore has been president of the American Sociological Association (1966) and is a fellow member of the American Academy of Arts and Sciences and the American Philosophical Society. Among his numerous publications in a variety of fields are *Industrial Relations and the Social Order* (1951), *The Conduct of the Corporation* (1962), *Man, Time, and Society* (1963), *Social Change* (1963, rev. 1974), *The Professions* (1970), and *American Negro Slavery and Abolition* (1971)—this listing by no means exhausts Moore's formidable bibliography.

as a writer. His strictly disciplined and almost daily sessions at the desk are essential for the outstanding intellectual craftsmanship that marks his work.*

In 1964, to the great regret of his faculty colleagues, Wilbert Moore resigned from his professorship at Princeton to become Sociologist at the Russell Sage Foundation, but for several years he continued teaching at the university as a part-time lecturer. In 1970 he became Professor of Law and Sociology at the University of Denver.

At the time of my arrival at Princeton in 1960, Wilbert Moore's colleagues in sociology of longest standing were Marion J. Levy, Jr., and Melvin M. Tumin, both of whom had joined the faculty in 1947. The widely known and frequently lamented enmity between Levy and Tumin had begun early in their tenure, and remained a tense and sometimes troublesome situation for many years. Each of these brilliant men, however, played a major role in the development of sociology as an important field of study at the university and both of them, although with highly contrasting intellectual styles, became scholars of international repute.

Marion Levy's rise to scholarly prominence began soon after his arrival at Princeton. He brought strong credentials in both sociology and economics as well as the benefit of wartime training in Chinese and field experience in China.† Levy's *Family Revolution in Modern China,* an impressive doctoral dissertation, was published in 1949, and was followed by *The Structure of Society* (1952), a far more ambitious work—a Parsonian-oriented effort to explicate a conceptual scheme presented as a theoretical and methodological guide for the analysis of "any society" and therefore presumably of potential utility in comparative, macroscopic sociology.‡ The comparative study of social institutions,

---

* The phrase is from C. Wright Mills's essay "On Intellectual Craftsmanship" in *The Sociological Imagination* (New York: Oxford, 1959), pp. 195–226. Wilbert Moore's work habits correspond rather closely with Mills's desiderata for the intellectual craftsman. My appreciation of Moore's fine craftsmanship was underscored by my editorial "work" on three of his many volumes (*Economy and Society,* 1955; *The Conduct of the Corporation,* 1962; and *Man, Time, and Society,* 1963); there was almost no work to be done.

† Levy's degrees include A.B., Harvard (economics), 1939; A.M., University of Texas (economics), 1940; and Ph.D., Harvard (sociology), 1947. He served in the U.S. Navy from 1942 to 1946.

‡ The controversial nature of *Family Revolution in China* is illustrated by Maurice T. Price's review in the *American Sociological Review* 16, no. 3 (June 1951): 408–9. My own assessment of *The Structure of Society* is to be

with special emphasis on "modernization" and Chinese and Japanese societies, has long been Levy's forte in sociology, in the Program in East Asian Studies, and in the Woodrow Wilson School of Public and International Affairs, in all of which over the years he has continued to be a leading figure. During my own stay at Princeton, and in pursuit of his abiding theoretical and substantive interests, he produced a typescript of some 1,800 pages, a large part of which was published subsequently as the two-volume tome, *Modernization and the Structure of Societies: A Setting for International Affairs* (1966). This partial list of publications represents the work of a devoted, energetic, and highly able scholar whose accomplishments and aims surpass those of all but a few academic sociologists.

As a Princeton sociologist, Marion Levy played several roles, and some of them won no kudos from either his colleagues or students. As a scholar-teacher he was a unique kind of Parsonian functionalist whose theoretical and analytical prowess impressed most of us, whatever our own orientations. He was the department's unrelenting "standard bearer" who frequently and in no uncertain terms took his fellow sociologists to task for what he considered their scholarly and educational deficiencies. He was an ardent defender of the scientific faith who admonished some of us for a lack of interest in what he called the "science game." One of Princeton's eccentrics, he affected overalls with bib (thus garbed, he even startled candidates at oral examinations, several years before the sartorial revolution of the later 1960s), he skillfully whittled an ever-shrinking stick, and, in the company of one of his splendid dogs, he toured the campus. In his striking, arboreal home, he was a gracious host, and for newcomers in the department the donor of both warmly encouraging words and thoughtful gifts. In those years at least, Marion Levy was a colorful and

---

found in the same journal (18, no. 2 [April 1953]: 206–7), and includes the following comment: "This volume . . . is a bold and impressive intellectual performance, highlighted especially by the author's logical skill, meticulous exegesis, familiarity with the natural sciences, conspicuous effort to match the latters' theoretical sophistication, and wise insistence on the non-causal nature of his formulations. But the performance is dimmed, I believe, by definitional preoccupation beyond the demands of conceptual precision and explicitness; by monotony of exposition . . . , defended as essential in a *general* study, though occasionally relieved by flights of bright wit; by reliance on Parsons for even many of the detailed illustrations, painfully remindful of students who play back teacher's examples on examinations."

contradictory character: bright, witty, warm-hearted, but cantankerous, caustically critical, and arrogant, or so I saw him in
my no doubt biased view.

In some measure, this view was shared by others, both faculty and students. Yet, however difficult he could be at times,
Levy's outstanding talents were honored by his colleagues in the
department, the Woodrow Wilson School, and elsewhere: he attained senior rank in 1959 and a few years later, when he received
highly tempting invitations from the universities of Chicago and
Michigan, all but one of his fellow professors in sociology (including the biased chairman) supported what turned out to be a successful effort to keep him on the local faculty. In more recent
years, Levy's honors from Princeton have continued to mount.*

Levy was acclaimed by some of his students; damned by
others. However impressive his analytical prowess and however
scintilating his classroom performances (as they were reported to
be), his courses were feared by some of the more timid souls and,
especially among graduate students, were a popular topic of ungentle critical assessment. But all students of Marion Levy's, I am
sure (and as I once told him), underwent an indelible educational
experience: they would long remember this extraordinary teacher
and appreciate his mastery of his subject.

In some respects, Melvin Tumin and Marion Levy were
rather alike. Both were dynamic, energetic, and articulate men
with a propensity for verbal combat. Both were highly able, professionally ambitious, and hard-working scholars, and both were
authors of impressive publications. And each of these veteran
Princetonians was an effective, and at times a controversial, activist
in both departmental affairs and other programs of the university.
These similarities, however, were overshadowed by conspicuous
contrasts—in sociological perspective, substantive interests, and
personal style. Levy's scholarly preoccupations, as I have indicated,
were systemic theory of the Parsonian genre, the comparative
analysis of "modernization," and the time-worn quest to move
sociology in a rigorous scientific direction. Tumin, far more concerned with the humanistic and reformistic dimensions of the
discipline, was also a first-rate student of theory, but in both teach-

* In 1965 Levy was appointed Professor of Sociology and International Affairs as a member of the permanent faculties of both the department and
the Woodrow Wilson School; in 1971 he became director of the Program in
East Asian Studies, and in the same year was named the Richard A. Musgrove
Professor of Sociology and International Affairs.

ing and research he focused his attention on the concrete and problem-laden fields of social stratification, race and ethnicity, crime and delinquency, and education.* Levy, out of Texas, Harvardian, and trained in hard economics, often seemed to be indifferent to or to stand above ideological and political conflicts. Tumin, from Newark, a graduate of non-ivy schools, and with degrees in "soft" sociology and anthropology,† was an ardent exponent of egalitarian and democratic values, an outspoken social critic, and a vigorous opponent of ethnic and racial discrimination.

The antagonism between these two sociologists, I am sure, was exacerbated by striking differences in social and individual styles. Each was a devoted husband, father, and homemaker, but beyond these domestic roles Levy and Tumin appeared to have little in common. Whereas most of Levy's extrafamilial activities seemed to be closely associated with his scholarly and professional undertakings, the circles in which Tumin moved included activists in politics and social reform, artists and writers (among his close friends were Saul Bellow, Harold Rosenberg, and Philip Roth), and members of New York's "family" of Jewish intellectuals. Their shared identity as Jews, moreover, was expressed in far different ways: Levy, at least ostensibly, gave little heed to his ethnic background, while Tumin, son of a rabbi, proudly proclaimed his status as a *landsman.* On this score, manifestations of their "marginality" were worlds apart. And in academic and professional matters, Levy's outwardly cool and often sardonic manner sometimes would clash with Tumin's marked intensity and seemingly deeper involvement in educational affairs.

Mel Tumin was a popular and superior teacher, in part because of his wide range of interests and his many-sided life

---

* Tumin's numerous publications include, among other books, the following volumes: *Caste in a Peasant Society* (1952), *Desegregation: Resistance and Readiness* (1958), *Social Class and Social Change in Puerto Rico* (with Arnold S. Feldman, 1961), *Intergroup Attitudes of Youth and Adults in England, France, and Germany* (1965), *Quality and Equality in Education* (1966), *Social Stratification* (1967), *Crimes of Violence: Causes and Prevention* (1969), and *Patterns of Society* (1973).

† Like Ely Chinoy and others who became prominent academics, Tumin was strongly influenced by the philosopher and remarkable teacher Ralph Ross, then at Newark College; Ross's impact on American sociologists warrants study. Following his years at Newark, Tumin received the B.A. and M.A. degrees from the University of Wisconsin and, in 1944, the Ph.D. from Northwestern University.

(for five years he was the elected Coroner of Mercer County): students were fully aware that he was no cloistered academic. Moreover, Mel was, and remains, a brilliant, articulate, and dynamic individual whose performance in the classroom rarely, if ever, bored even the most blasé Princetonians, although his strongly stated views may have put off or bypassed some of the more conservative undergraduates. His instructional expertise, together with his widely acclaimed scholarly accomplishments and his extradepartmental contributions to the university, in my opinion, should have guaranteed Tumin's promotion to the full professorship before I arrived at Princeton in 1960. But others had thought otherwise, for Mel Tumin and his published work were a controversial subject, among Princeton's sociologists and elsewhere.

I became keenly aware of criticisms of Mel and his alleged scholarly shortcomings when, in my first formal meeting with the senior sociologists, his putative professional deficiencies were discussed at length and when, following a determined defense of what I judged to be an outstanding record, Mel was supported by all but one of us for advancement to senior rank. This recommendation, however, was disapproved for two successive years by the top-level "Committee of Three," elected by the faculty, and by President Robert Goheen. A major responsibility of the new departmental chairman, in my view of the job, was the rectification of what appeared to have been a miscarriage of academic justice. Mel Tumin's promotion was finally approved by the administration in 1963.

No such postponement of earned award had marked the career of Gerald Breese who as an assistant professor joined Princeton sociologists in 1949 and ten years later attained senior rank. With a doctorate from the University of Chicago* and two years of experience in housing studies with the Social Science Research Council, Gerry was well qualified for his position as director of Princeton's Bureau of Urban Research, a position he held from 1950 to 1966. During several of these years he was closely associated with the Delhi Regional Master Plan, taught in Cairo

* Breese's Ph.D. was awarded in 1947 and his dissertation, a unique contribution to ecological literature, was published in 1949 as *Daytime Population of the Central Business District of Chicago.* Earlier he had received a B.D. from Yale (1938) and had served as sociologist and dean of men at Pacific University (1938–1941). In later years his extensive experience abroad was ably exploited in *Urbanization in Old and New Countries* (1964) and *Urbanization in Newly Developing Countries* (1966).

as a Fulbright Professor in 1954–55, and lectured in South Africa and Australia—activities that benefited, surely, both the Bureau and Gerry's students. He was a quiet and attractive man of no pretensions, but neither in the classroom nor in his scholarly work did Gerry Breese win the stardom of his dynamic and sometimes bombastic colleagues Marion Levy and Mel Tumin.

Nonetheless, Gerry brought to the department and to the university qualities of great importance in collegial organizations: unquestioned personal and professional integrity, respect for the undertakings of others, institutional loyalty, and cooperative generosity (which I indecently exploited by persuading Gerry to become departmental secretary—hardly a chore for a senior professor). Numerous demonstrations of these virtues received less acclaim than the scholarly and teaching accomplishments of other Princeton sociologists, but they were highly valued, not least by Gerry's chairman.

In the chair and as a newcomer, I enjoyed similar support from our eldest colleague, Frederick Stephan, who, as professor of social statistics, had been a member of the Princeton faculty since 1952. Like Gerry Breese, although many years earlier, Fred had studied for the Ph.D. at Chicago, but without completing the degree.* Lack of the union card, however, apparently had been no handicap in Stephan's professional career: he had taught at the University of Pittsburgh (1927–1934) and Cornell (1940–1947), held important posts in the American Statistical Association, Social Science Research Council, and the Bureau of Social Research. He was a scholar whose knowledge, wisdom, and technical expertise were frequently called upon by institutions and individuals engaged in social research in this country and abroad.

During the 1950s and in keeping with expectations at the time of his appointment, Fred had directed a large-scale, strongly financed, and well-publicized study of the undergraduate educational process at Princeton which, to the disappointment of many educators (and at least some of the student subjects), never reached the publication stage. The failure to carry this highly promising investigation to fruition seemed to rankle Fred himself throughout his remaining years at the university.

For the rest of us it was evident that this abortive research venture was far outweighed by Fred's important contributions to

---

* That the Ph.D., however useful, is not a requirement for eminence in sociology (or in other fields) is illustrated by the careers of George Homans, David Riesman, and Edward Shils—to name an otherwise motley threesome.

his profession, the university, and sociology at Princeton. As a leading authority on the methods and both the merits and limitations of empirical research and as a superior social statistician, Fred was a very busy consultant to governmental and private agencies and, locally, his expertise informed research projects ranging from modest studies by undergraduates to large-scale investigations in the social sciences (including demography—he was a long-time and esteemed Associate of the Office of Population Research). In sociology, he was not known as a classroom virtuoso, but as the department's senior statistician Fred almost single-handedly, and often in time-consuming tutorial sessions, played a major role as a teacher of quantitative methods—on this score, a good many able sociologists, former graduate students at Princeton, are in his debt. Fred Stephan, although a less colorful figure than some of his more controversial colleagues, during the 1950s and '60s was one of its sociological stars.*

Morroe Berger, years younger than Fred Stephan, also joined the Princeton faculty in 1952. Morroe's earlier feats as an undergraduate at City College, as well as some of his subsequent scholarly achievements, were sketched earlier and need no elaboration here. But his diverse activities at Princeton and his rise to international prominence warrant comment.

Before becoming a fully committed academic Morroe had worked in New York as a free-lance journalist, as a part-time teacher, and in social research—with a Columbia Ph.D. in hand and with a background of wartime study of Arabic and military service in the Middle East.† This unique combination of credentials, together with his demonstrated intellectual and scholarly ability, prompted at least two of his former teachers, Robert Mac-Iver and me, to recommend him enthusiastically for a newly created position at Princeton; no sociologist in our opinion was as well qualified as Morroe Berger for a junior faculty post that called for both excellence as an all-round sociologist and strong promise as a specialist in Near Eastern studies.

This promise was soon fulfilled. During his first year at Princeton Morroe became closely associated with the eminent

---

* Fred Stephan remained an active member of the faculty until 1971, the year of his death.

† Military experience during World War II in various parts of the world played an important role in the subsequent careers of several American social scientists; among the sociologists at Princeton, Morroe Berger (Near East) and Marion Levy (Far East) are cases in point.

scholar Philip K. Hitti and resumed his study of Arabic. In 1953–54 he traveled in the Near East and interviewed, among others, some 250 higher civil servants, research that led to the pioneer study, *Bureaucracy and Society in Modern Egypt* (1957). Subsequently his numerous publications included the widely acclaimed *The Arab World Today* (1962), which firmly established Morroe as sociology's leading authority on the societies and cultures of the Middle East, a status that over the years meant his heavy involvement in programs of private and public research agencies.* Along with these responsibilities were Morroe's administrative duties at Princeton: in the footsteps of Hitti, as director of the Program in Near Eastern Studies for a decade, for almost as long as chairman of the university's Council on International and Regional Studies, and as chairman of the Department of Sociology for a three-year term. Somehow this City College alumnus also managed major undertakings in Egypt frequently enough to earn from his colleagues the accolade of "our commuter to Cairo."

Yet, from his undergraduate years, Morroe transcended specialization, even with so gigantic a subject as the modern Middle East. He did this successfully but with a measure of disregard for academic convention, notably in his studies in the history and sociology of the arts. His scholarly publications include *Madame de Stael on Politics, Literature, and National Character* (1964), a volume that Morroe translated, edited, and introduced with a lengthy essay on that extraordinary Frenchwoman's life and social thought; and his more recent *Real and Imagined Worlds: The Novel and the Social Sciences* (1977). Morroe's contributions to jazz music are matched by those of few, if any, sociologists: they extend from a prize-winning M.A. thesis on "Jazz: Resistance to the Diffusion of a Culture Pattern," published in the *Journal of Negro History* in 1951, to a biography of that remarkable artist Benny Carter, with discography by Edward Berger, Morroe's eldest son. This was Morroe's final work—he died in 1981 at the early age of sixty-three.

Throughout his Princeton years Morroe's principal scholarly interests were the Middle East, the arts, and politics and

* In 1960 Berger organized and directed the Cairo Conference on "The New Metropolis in the Arab World"; as an expert on the Near East, he held important committee assignments in the Social Science Research Council, the American Council of Learned Societies, the Twentieth-Century Fund, the Ford Foundation, and the U.S. Department of State; in 1967 he was president of the Middle East Studies Association.

race,* and in each of these fields, he shined as a sociologist. But Morroe was far less interested in the changing theoretical and methodological fashions, the conceptual niceties, and the intra-disciplinary battles of sociology than in developing an under-standing of important areas of social and cultural life with the aid of a broad sociological perspective. That this perspective was inspired by the works of Ignazio Silone, John Dos Passos, and Morris Raphael Cohen, as well as those of Thorstein Veblen and Robert MacIver, is in keeping with the humanistic tradition of sociology—all too often forgotten or ignored in our age of scien-tistic ascendancy.

If natural science was no model for Morroe Berger's soci-ology, neither was it for Edward Tiryakian's. Ed, whose Princeton B.A. had won highest honors and whose Harvard Ph.D. had re-ceived high marks from his mentors Sorokin and Parsons, had returned to his alma mater in 1956 as a member of the faculty. He soon became widely known as an exciting lecturer (by the time of my arrival in 1960 his undergraduate classes were among the most popular in sociology), and he was held in high esteem by his students and fellow sociologists. Two years later we lost a splendid scholar-teacher when Ed joined Harvard's Department of Social Relations.

This unexpected move, in response to a belated invitation from Harvard in the late spring of 1962, might have been pre-vented by an exercise of better judgment on the part of Prince-ton's sociologists, including their unforeseeing chairman. But at the time only one of us, our foremost advocate of a rigorous sci-ence of sociology, Marion Levy, was sufficiently percipient to view Ed's first major work, then in press, as a significant contribu-tion to what might well become an important theoretical per-spective in American sociology. That work, with the graceless Durkheimian title *Sociologism and Existentialism* (1962), proved to be an early landmark in the upsurge of phenomenological soci-ology in this country. And during his post-Princeton years, first at Harvard and since 1965 at Duke University, Ed Tiryakian's credentials as a major sociologist have been firmly established— with expertise in social theory, social change, and the sociology of religion, as well as existential phenomenology.†

* Illustrated by *Equality by Statute* (1952, extensively revised in 1967) and the UNESCO study "Racial Equality and the Law" (1965).
† Among his other publications, Tiryakian has been editor of and contributor to the following volumes: *Sociological Theory, Values, and Sociocultural*

These worthies—Moore, Levy, Tumin, Breese, Stephan, Berger, and Tiryakian—manned Princeton's newly instituted Department of Sociology and Anthropology in 1960, together with a pair of younger colleagues, Heinz Hartmann and Peter Kunstadter, and an all-too-apprehensive chairman fresh from a women's college. Hartmann, a protégé of Wilbert Moore, had been an outstanding graduate student and following the completion of the doctorate taught in the department briefly, but with success, before returning to his native West Germany. Kunstadter, with a Ph.D. from Michigan, had joined the Princeton faculty in 1959, served ably for three or four years as its only full-time anthropologist, and survived this disciplinary loneliness until anthropology became decently staffed and achieved departmental status. Of these ten men, between 1960 and 1965 three—Tiryakian, Hartmann, and our anchorman Moore—left Princeton. Several newcomers, however, both stars and potential stars, ‘joined the university's sociological ranks.

The first of these was Allen Kassof whose exploits at Smith College were noted earlier. Allen, rather reluctant to forsake the various pleasures of Smith and Northampton, was lured to Princeton in 1961; he was the department's leading candidate for a newly created position earmarked for a young scholar with strong credentials in both sociology and Russian studies.* Allen's tenure at Princeton was marked by an unusual mixture of academic and administrative roles—and, in keeping with his personal proclivities, by brief but spirit-lifting intervals of hijinks.

During one of the three years of his initial appointment, a generously financed leave of absence enabled the Kassof family to live in Switzerland while Allen made periodic trips eastward pursuing his research on Soviet society. Following this productive period and with the strong support of the Director of Princeton's

---

Change (1963), *Theoretical Sociology: Perspectives and Developments* (with John C. McKinney, 1970), *The Phenomena of Sociology* (1971), and *On The Margin of the Visible: Sociology, the Esoteric, and the Occult* (1974).

* In 1961 the university received a substantial grant from the Ford Foundation which financed several junior posts in the social sciences with a view to strengthening Princeton's Program in Russian Studies. Kassof's training at Harvard's Russian Research Center, his ongoing research and superior teaching record at Smith, his evident scholarly potential, and his impressive personal qualities led to his appointment as a William Paterson Bicentennial Preceptor, the most prestigious—and lucrative—assistant professorship at Princeton.

Program in Russian Studies, in 1965 Allen won promotion and tenure, and for the next dozen years displayed his talents in a variety of positions.

From the outset, and in keeping with his earlier classroom triumphs at Smith, Allen was hailed as a first-rate teacher both by the many Princetonians who elected his undergraduate courses and by the handful of graduate students who braved the demanding subject of Russian studies as a major field for the doctorate. Among the latter, at least two of Kassof's protégés have achieved scholarly distinction: Paul Hollander, whose works include the widely praised *Soviet and American Society* (1973, revised in 1978) and *Political Pilgrims* (1981); and Walter D. Connor, whose accomplishments as sociologist and Sovietologist are highlighted by the volumes *Deviance and Soviet Society* (1972) and *Socialism, Politics, and Equality* (1978). The length of Allen's own bibliography has been limited by the administrative preoccupations noted below and, no doubt, by his long-standing preference for programmatic rather than strictly academic pursuits, but the high quality of his scholarship is attested to by such publications as *The Soviet Youth Program: Regimentation and Rebellion* (1965) and *Prospects for Soviet Society* (1968) which he edited and co-authored.

Allen's administrative skills were first revealed when, following my own departure from Princeton in 1965, he became an assistant dean of the College for a three-year term, a post that also required a talent for coping with diversity. Among the several and dissimilar duties of this temporary assignment, for example, was the administration of the Critical Language Program which broke sacred precedent by bringing female undergraduates to Princeton as students in residence. Thus Allen became a kind of housemother and the university's first "dean of women," positions for which he seemed to have still another talent. More consistent with his professional credentials, periodically Allen served as acting director of the Program in Russian Studies and as an associate professor he taught part time in the Department of Sociology. He gave up his tenure in 1972, but as a lecturer for another five years he continued to offer courses on Soviet society. He resigned from Princeton in 1977.

Allen's step-by-step reduction of academic responsibilities had been initiated in 1968 when he accepted a major administrative position with the International Research and Exchanges Board (IREX), the agency that finances and superintends visiting stints for American scholars and students in the USSR and other "curtain" countries in Eastern Europe. This demanding assignment became more than a full-time job in 1972 and since then, as both the executive director of IREX and a frequent visitor to Communist nations, Allen has achieved a prominence consistent with his long-standing capabilities. His move to IREX brought substantial losses to Princeton and to academic sociology. But Allen Kassof's present-day position as scholar-administrator in a highly important and increasingly difficult office is a splendid professional achievement which might well serve as a model for many of today's young scholars.*

Charles F. Westoff joined Princeton's sociologists in 1962. *Family Growth in Metropolitan America*, with Westoff as the senior author, had been published in the preceding year and was the first volume of what soon became a lengthy bibliography of distinguished demographic studies.† Westoff's rapid rise in his profession, initiated by degrees from Syracuse University and the University of Pennsylvania (he taught there, briefly, receiving the Ph.D. in 1952), had taken him to New York University where he was a chairman of one of NYU's sociology departments. Ansley Coale, the superb and foresighted director of Princeton's Office of Population Research, and I conspired to entice this budding luminary to bolster our ranks. Coale had first-hand knowledge of his research and scholarly skills, for Westoff had been a research associate of the OPR from 1955 to 1959. Three years later Charlie Westoff became its associate director and professor of sociology.

Charlie was named as the incoming departmental chairman in the spring of 1965, at a time when his predecessor was completing a five-year term of office in something less than glorious fashion.‡ This was a shaky period for the department, but short-

* Under Kassof's direction, among its other important contributions, IREX has sponsored the training of a sizable cadré of Soviet and Eastern European specialists. Kassof's stature in this field is suggested by his appointment in 1978 to the President's Commission on Foreign Language and International Studies.

† In addition to *Family Growth* and numerous articles in scholarly journals, Westoff is the co-author of *The Third Child* (1963), *College Women and Fertility Values* (1967), *The Later Years of Childbearing* (1969), *From Now to Zero* (1971), *Reproduction in the United States* (1965, 1971), *Toward the End of Growth: Population in America* (1973), *The Contraceptive Revolution* (1976), *Demographic Dynamics in America* (1977), and, since this note was written (in 1979), no doubt other books—all sturdy volumes, not the product of an academic sausage machine.

‡ My failures as the chair (as well as some claimed accomplishments) are reported in the final section of the present chapter.

lived: Charlie's astuteness and strong leadership were largely responsible for bringing unprecedented strength and stability to sociology at Princeton. His successful tenure in the chair continued until 1970, a year later he succeeded Ansley Coale as director of the OPR, and in 1972 he became the Maurice P. During Professor of Demographic Studies and Sociology. Charlie Westoff's achievements, matched by few American demographers, multiply today.*

Marvin Bressler, who arrived at Princeton in 1963, and Charlie Westoff had been fellow graduate students, recipients of Ph.D.'s and teaching colleagues at Pennsylvania; subsequently they had become fellow chairmen at New York University where Marvin headed the Department of Educational Sociology. At Princeton, the linkages between their lives continued: Marvin's appointment followed Charlie's by a year, later he succeeded Charlie in the chair. Both are men of striking comeliness, athletic skill, and, from time to time, adventurous inclination. They are also academics of distinction and each of these *Wunderkinder,* in his own distinctive way, brought scholarly and educational wealth to Princeton.

In 1961 Princeton received a generous grant from the Roger William Strauss Foundation for the support of a "Council on Human Relations"—and, as it turned out, this led to the appointment of Marvin Bressler. The foundation had given the council its name, something of a misnomer for the principal function of this interdisciplinary body (with representatives from the Departments of Economics, History, Politics, Psychology, and Sociology) was the sponsorship of research of presumptive relevance for the understanding of public issues and the formation of public policy. Its initial activity, however, was the search for a senior social scientist with strong credentials to lead the council and to bring needed strength to the relatively small Department of Sociology. Thus as the titular head of both groups, I spent considerable time arranging visits to Princeton by several possible candidates. Something of a dark horse in a year-long parade of established luminaries, but with the strong backing of the council, the department, and the administration, Marvin received an invitation to become chairman of the Roger William Strauss

* Among other high offices Westoff has been the executive director of the Commission on Population Growth and the American Future (1970–1972), president of the Population Association of America (1974–75), and vice chairman of the Alan Guttmacher Institute (1977–).

Council on Human Relations and professor of sociology. To our delight, he accepted this dual position.

Marvin's rare combination of gifts enhanced this post and indeed the larger life of Princeton. Author of a modest list of publications (in contrast with his prolific colleagues, Berger, Tumin, and Westoff), Marvin's writings are distinguished by fine scholarly workmanship, ironic thrust, and graceful style, but they only faintly suggest his wide erudition and critical skill.* These capacities came into full flower in the classroom—Marvin is a spectacular teacher. These same qualities, together with both managerial talent and a sensitive consideration for others, have also helped to account for his administrative triumphs: as leader of the Council on Human Relations, as the continuing chairman of the Department of Sociology, and, atop a Princeton summit for a time, as the chairman of the Commission on the Future of the College (1970–1972).

The large responsibilities of high office have never seemed to interfere significantly with another, in this case self-appointed, role: as surely the funniest man in sociology, if not in the whole academy, Marvin is a renowned humorist. In the lecture hall, at what otherwise might be dreary departmental and other faculty meetings, and in less formal gatherings at Princeton and elsewhere Marvin's anecdotes and sallies are great entertainment. But they are also sharp reminders of life's ever-present absurdities—there is educational method, I suspect, in this comical madness. Marvin's free-wheeling humor, moreover, is mixed with keen and sometimes deadly wit.

Both wit and humor, I should add, were by no means lacking among some other Princeton sociologists of the 1960s—a happy fact that helped us to survive troublesome situations. Both Marion Levy and Morroe Berger, for example, although far different personalities in most respects, possessed a sophisticated wit

---

* Before coming to Princeton in 1963, Bressler published the volumes *Indian Students on the American Campus* (with Richard D. Lambert, 1956) and *Tax-Supported Medical Institutional Care for the Needy and Medically Needy* (1957); more revelatory of his erudition and critical acumen is "Some Selected Aspects of American Sociology, September, 1959 to December, 1960," *Annals of the American Academy of Political and Social Science*, vol. 337, pp. 146–59. Soon after his arrival appeared the seminal essay, "The Conventional Wisdom of Education and Sociology" (chap. 4 in Page, *Sociology and Contemporary Education*). Indicative of his leadership role at Princeton and as an educator is the later *Report of the Commission on the Future of the College* (1973).

which enlivened departmental sessions, at times with Marion himself the victim of Morroe's devastating gibes. On a nonagonistic and much lighter side, certain members of the group—notably Allen Kassof, Charlie Westoff, and Marvin Bressler, with their chairman feebly following suit—periodically indulged in clownery entirely out of keeping with the dignity popularly associated with serious scholar-teachers. But tomfoolery of this order, I am convinced, is a needed change, and hardly a liability, in what is oftentimes the sober-sided lives of academics.

During my chairmanship at Princeton (1960–1965) three other sociologists (and two anthropologists) joined the department for relatively brief periods in junior positions—Maurice Zeitlin, Richard Hamilton, and William Michelson, each of whom thereafter was to win scholarly distinction. Maurice had pursued the doctorate at Berkeley and done dissertational research in Cuba, and he arrived at Princeton with strong credentials. His two-year stay,* however, although marked by considerable success in the ivy setting, was an uneasy time for Maurice and, in some measure, for others of us. He seemed to view Princeton undergraduates as generally conservative "sons of the rich" of limited intellectual capacity and often addressed them in keeping with this stereotypical misconception—hardly an effective pedagogical practice. More dramatically, and consistent with his admiration of the Castro regime buttressed by his Marxist perspective, Maurice appeared on television at the time of the missile crisis in 1962 to deliver what was reported to be a blistering critique of American policy and practice in Cuba. He thereby alarmed at least a few Princeton alumni who voiced their indignation to the university's president and senior dean and, through them, to the chairman of Zeitlin's department; this episode kept me busy for a time. But Old Nassau survived. Following his rather rocky years at Princeton he moved to the University of Wisconsin where his scholarly accomplishments, first at Madison and later at UCLA, have established Maurice Zeitlin among this country's leading Marxist sociologists.

Zeitlin's successor, Richard Hamilton, was also a leftist, but the academic decorum of this soft-spoken, diffident but engaging young scholar stands in sharp contrast with Maurice's fiery

---

* Maurice Zeitlin came to Princeton as an instructor in the fall of 1961, to be followed a year later by the arrival of his older brother Irving as a graduate student. Irving Zeitlin's achievements at Princeton and later on are sketched below.

disposition. As a Columbia-trained political sociologist skilled in the analysis of survey data, in both his research and teaching he challenged the work of S. M. Lipset and others which stressed the conservatism and "authoritarianism" of the American working class and, more generally, he emphasized the utilities of a Marxist or neo-Marxist sociology. This perspective probably encouraged Dick to follow Maurice to Wisconsin in 1966, where his rapid rise to senior rank did not prevent his move to McGill University within a few years. Like Zeitlin's, Dick Hamilton's excellent research publications gave scholarly substance, as distinct from ideological proclamation, to the sociological left.

A different brand of sociology was represented by William Michelson who became a member of the department in 1964. Bill had graduated from Princeton with high honors three years earlier and had almost completed the Ph.D. at Harvard when he returned to his alma mater at the age of twenty-four. Already a keen student of urbanism and human ecology, Bill brought expertise and a fresh viewpoint to the Bureau of Urban Research where he joined forces with its director, Gerry Breese; and as a dedicated and able teacher he brought needed strength to Princeton's undergraduate program in sociology. By the time he moved to the University of Toronto in 1967 Bill Michelson was well on his way to distinguished achievement in the study of the sociological and psychological dimensions of the human environment.

These fourteen men brightened Princeton's sociological endeavors during my five years in the chair. Their marked diversity of substantive interest, theoretical perspective, ideological stance, and personal style, together with their individual skills as scholar-teachers, paid rich educational dividends for sociology, especially in the graduate program. These differences also worked against a strong departmental solidarity and now and then caused trouble in our ranks. "Stewardship" in this mixed coterie of talent was not always easy going. Whatever the difficulties, however, the chance to work closely with such colleagues, if only for a few years, was a matter of lasting pride and brought high rewards, professional and personal.

Princeton's Undergraduate Program

While still part of a joint department the Princeton sociologists had developed a strong program of graduate study. In keeping with a widespread pattern in ivy schools, however, they had been less successful in promoting sociology among undergraduate students. Thus an announced reason for the appointment of a Smith professor to head an independent department in 1960 was my reputed success as teacher and chairman in another ivy-clad institution. Whatever the justification of this reputation, my accomplishments with the undergraduate program at Princeton were all too meager.

There were some gains, to be sure, the most important of which were the appointments of Allen Kassof, Charlie Westoff, and Marvin Bressler, each of whom brought classroom expertise to his undergraduate courses; but we lost the able and popular lecturer Ed Tiryakian. My own teaching contributions were minimal: I took over the sophomore-level course required for the major, which for some time had been passed from hand to hand, and managed to give introductory sociology a measure of reputability; but, insensitive to our enrollment problem, I initiated a course on family and kinship in contemporary society, hardly a subject of wide appeal among Princetonians. As chairman, I tried to persuade the department to overhaul and enliven the undergraduate curriculum, but with almost no success—some of my distinguished colleagues seemed to view these bread-and-butter courses as a secondary matter.*

This shortcoming, personal and departmental, was particularly unfortunate in an institution where an ancient heritage identified "Princetonians" as undergraduates and "Princeton" as primarily a college of liberal arts. No such imagery clung to the graduate school, which was only weakly tied to the ivy tradition. However, almost all members of the faculty (Fred Stephan in sociology was a rare exception), whatever their other instructional duties, taught undergraduate courses and their accomplishments in this role were an important measure of the rating of their departments. Thus one reason for the rather shaky status of sociology, notwithstanding its excellent reputation at the graduate level, was the low enrollment in some of the undergraduate courses. Another was the small number of sociology majors, especially in comparison with the other social sciences.

* The undergraduate program was quite strong in a few areas, for example, social disorganization and criminology (Tumin) and industrial and occupational sociology (Moore). But there were no courses in race and ethnic relations, social change and social movements, political sociology (until 1969), and other socially significant subjects of wide appeal. This curricular backwardness continued until after my departure from Princeton in 1965, a situation commented upon in the final section of the present chapter.

Our instructional strength was also reduced by the substantial contributions of sociology's most able teachers to extra-departmental programs: Morroe Berger in Near Eastern Studies, Marvin Bressler in the Council on Human Relations, Allen Kassof in Russian Studies, Mel Tumin in American Civilization and the Woodrow Wilson School, Charlie Westoff in the Office of Population Research. These superior scholar-teachers, like Marion Levy in East Eastern Studies and the Woodrow Wilson School, brought sociological knowledge to Princeton students in various fields of study, but this important educational activity (criticized at times by President Goheen as an unwise "scattering" of talent) took place beyond the purview of the undergraduate program in sociology.

Two atypical components of this program, both strongly featured at Princeton and prescribed for all departments in the humanities and social sciences, were the "preceptorial conference" and the requirement of independent study for all undergraduates. The latter was by no means perfunctory: it included a year of individual research preceding the writing of a senior thesis and a final comprehensive examination in two broad fields of sociology.[*] These heavy demands and the generally laudable performances of Princetonians justified, I believe, the catalogue's boast of "an honors program for all."

The preceptorial conference, initiated in 1905 by Woodrow Wilson who thereby sought "to *animate* the pursuit of knowledge" (my emphasis), was a sacred Princeton institution, but something less than the powerful educational method depicted in the catalogue. The preceptorial, a weekly discussion group of ten or fewer participants, supplementing course lectures, was described as "an exploratory undertaking for both student and instructor. The exchange and testing of ideas under the guidance of a preceptor provides stimulation, opportunity for independent thought and the exercise of judgment on critical issues"[†]—desiderata, one might surmise, neglected elsewhere. In practice, of course, preceptorials varied widely in style and effectiveness, and some of these unstructured sessions no doubt offered more friendly relaxation than intellectual challenge. They were led by faculty of all

[*] During my years at Princeton, students elected two of the following fields: comparative cultures and social institutions, modern industrial society, social differentiation and stratification, social organization and disorganization.
[†] *Official Register of Princeton University, The Undergraduate Announcement* 1963–1964, p. 32.

ranks, often irrespective of qualification for a particular subject, and this practice not only guaranteed wide diversity, but served a latent function unforeseen by President Wilson. For preceptors (at least in sociology) usually "prepared" for the informal meetings by attending the lectures and thus were auditors of both their colleagues' didactic efforts and the undergraduates' frequently unrestrained comments on courses and teachers. Under such circumstances "everybody" was alert to curricular and pedagogical strengths and weaknesses in a given department—there was little need for either a problem-laden system of "student evaluation" or the abominable practice of classroom visitations by senior faculty.

Most members of the faculty of whatever rank conducted preceptorials, and a variety of such assignments was apt to be highly educational. In this way, my own schooling in sociology was strengthened by auditing excellent lectures given by Morroe Berger on cultural trends in American society, Marvin Bressler on social science methodology, Mel Tumin on crime and delinquency, and Dick Hamilton on political behavior. During one year my education was served by a bold venture as preceptor in an extradepartmental, experimental course in the natural sciences. As a "generalist," a role markedly out-of-fashion in an age of specialization, my preceptorial duties may have been too widely scattered. But, like many others, I learned important lessons, sociological and otherwise, by participating in this hoary Wilsonian enterprise—lessons taught both by my colleagues' lectures and in the far less formal sessions by Princeton undergraduates themselves.

The Graduate Program

Whatever the shortcomings of the undergraduate program, at the graduate level Princeton's Department of Sociology could claim considerable success. A combination of happy circumstances undergirded this achievement: a graduate faculty that included outstanding scholar-teachers; a dedicated director of graduate study, Tumin, who managed this demanding job with both administrative efficiency and sensitivity to the problems and potentialities of students; a group of talented doctoral candidates; strong support by the Princeton administration, especially from a friendly physicist, the late Donald R. Hamilton, the highly able graduate dean; and, perhaps most important, certain features of the graduate program itself.

This was an unusual, probably a unique, program among American institutions in the education of doctors of philosophy. In contrast with large state universities and, say, my own Columbia, Princeton's total graduate enrollment was limited to a thousand students, with each department assigned a strict arithmetical quota based upon an annual assessment of local faculty strength and current trends in the academic disciplines; sociology's quota in the 1960s (and later) rarely exceeded ten new students a year. This restriction meant that there were never more than about thirty departmental Ph.D. candidates in residence, which facilitated both camaraderie in the student group and the student-faculty interaction that plays a highly important role in graduate study. These carefully selected men and women (there were only two or three women in sociology—more, however, than in any other department) were strongly financed: if, as in many cases, they were not supported by "outside" awards, they usually received fellowships from Princeton's ample supply. This meant that almost all students could give their full time to their studies without the burden of either the ubiquitous teaching assistantships of other schools or other lowly paid employment. This advantage, in turn, greatly helped to accelerate the completion of the Ph.D. The Princeton norm of three years must have been the shortest in American schools, and a few able and fast-paced students in sociology lowered this time substantially. In several respects, then, here was an elite graduate program.

It was also a program in "higher education," to use this generally misleading phrase with some degree of accuracy. The *formal* provisions for the Princeton doctorate were minimal: a single year in residence, no indicated number or specified course requirements (from time to time a boldly independent student, as in the legendary case of Jack Douglas, would avoid all or most courses), written and oral general examinations, a dissertation. However, the three-day examinations were a genuinely rugged exercise and the standards for dissertations were high—publication, unlike the old Columbia days, was not required, but a good many met public appraisal as full-scale volumes.* This com-

* The several published books originally written as dissertations during my years at Princeton include the following: Jack D. Douglas, *The Social Meanings of Suicide* (Princeton, N.J.: Princeton University Press, 1967); John P. Hewitt, *Social Stratification and Deviant Behavior* (New York: Random House, 1970); Arthur B. Shostak, *America's Forgotten Labor Organization* (Princeton, N.J.: Industrial Relations Section, Princeton University, 1962); and Ian Weinberg, *The English Public Schools* (New York: Atherton, 1967).

bination of official permissiveness and carefully judged demonstration of scholarly competence, on the one hand, threw students largely on their own and, on the other, helped to instill in them a professional confidence oftentimes missing among academic tyros—the maturity of young Princeton Ph.D.'s was frequently remarked in sociological circles. This admirable quality, of course, was only partly a product of a nurturing graduate program in which self-education overshadowed "training": it also reflected the individual propensities of the students themselves.

Graduate students at Princeton, as at other major universities, were a mixed lot—in class and ethnic origin, educational background, political and ideological stance, and, for a few, in nationality. On these counts, and in life style they bore very little resemblance to popular stereotypes of ivy-school undergraduates, a contrast vividly illustrated by the incoming group in sociology in the fall of 1960. As a fellow newcomer, an untried occupant of the departmental chair, and, in an effort to enrich my indoctrination, as acting director of graduate study (during Mel Tumin's leave of absence), I met with the new arrivals and found myself confronting a conspicuously heterogenous group.*

Some Princeton "Products"

Among the hundred or more graduate students who, at one time or another, were in residence during my own years at Princeton, many warrant special billing in any historical account of the period.† The following sketches therefore reflect a high

* The group included Robert Cook, Harvey Choldin, Muhammed Gessous, Paul Hollander, Michael Lewis, and Harry Webb; exploits of Cook, Hollander, and Lewis receive attention below. Harvey Choldin disliked Princeton's graduate program, after a year's frustration transferred to the University of Chicago where he received the Ph.D., and teaches at the University of Illinois. Muhammed Gessous, author of a widely acclaimed Princeton dissertation that indicated great scholarly promise returned to his native Morocco some years ago where he is the country's leading sociologist. Harry Webb, no stickler for academic convention, joined the faculty of Michigan State University before completing the doctorate, subsequently taught elsewhere in Michigan, for a time made important contributions to the sociology of sport, but for long stretches has seemed to disappear from sight.

† This comment also holds for several earlier doctoral students who became prominent sociological scholars, for example, S. M. Miller, Princeton's first Ph.D. in sociology (1951); Stanley Udy (Ph.D., 1958); David Matza (Ph.D., 1959), whose accomplishments are noted in chap. 3; Harrison White, whose

degree of selectivity, largely based upon personal consideration: my generally close relations with these stalwarts when they were doctoral candidates at Princeton, and the happy circumstance of continuing friendships with all of them* until the present day.

During my initial Princeton years the revered leader of the graduate students was Bernard (Bernie) Beck, whose conspicuous youth obscured neither his intellectual strength nor his sophistication concerning academic culture. Bernie was no more than twenty when, as a graduate of Brooklyn College, he arrived at Princeton in 1958; two years later, following brilliant performances in both courses and the Ph.D. examinations, he became an expert tutor for more recent arrivals in the peculiarities of Princeton sociology and Princeton sociologists, as well as something of a model for his less-experienced fellow students. Bernie's youth probably encouraged him to remain with us beyond the three-year norm, and unanticipated difficulties with his dissertation (on religion in primitive societies) helped to delay completion of the doctorate until 1963.

But Bernie's achievements have been, and continue to be, impressive. Among his accomplishments at Princeton, he won the powerful support of his principal mentor Marion Levy, who held Bernie in great esteem irrespective of their conflicting views on sociological and social issues. With the Ph.D. in hand and financed by the National Science Foundation, he spent a year (1963–64) in Denmark where, after trans-Atlantic telephone conversations with some of us concerning the relative merits of Columbia and Stanford, he accepted a faculty position at Stanford. There he was less than enthusiastic about the heavy emphasis on quantitative analysis, found a congenial fellow newcomer in Howard S. Becker, and after a single year (1964–65) he and Becker moved to Northwestern where both of them have long been teachers of renown. Bernie is an outstanding scholar-teacher in at least four fields— sociological theory, comparative institutions, religion, and social welfare. As a leader in his academic profession he has been elected (in 1975) to the presidency of the Society for the Study of Social

---

doctorate in physics from M.I.T. was followed by a Princeton Ph.D. in sociology in 1960; and Jack Douglas (Ph.D., 1965), who had completed his residence at Princeton immediately preceding my arrival in 1960. The contrasting perspectives of these five, ranging from mathematical sociology to phenomenology, is illustrative of the long-standing theoretical and methodological diversity of Princeton sociologists themselves.

* Except Juan Marsal, who died in 1979, as noted below.

Problems. But his bibliography, consisting largely of a handful of learned and provocative articles, is modest—his interests go far beyond the world of scholarly "production." Foremost among these in recent years is the living theater: Bernie Beck may be the only distinguished professional actor among American sociologists.

Recently there have been rumors that Bernie Beck may soon leave academia so as to give full reign to his thespianic talent. Bob Cook, a member of "my" class at Princeton, definitely left the ivy halls many years ago, to move into quite different fields. Since 1969 Bob has been an activist in the International Association of Bridge, Structural, and Ornamental Iron Workers, and his periodic jobs in this highly skilled and rugged occupation have been combined, since 1973, with the equally demanding task of maintaining a hundred-acre timberland where the Cooks are an esteemed family in Worthington, Massachusetts, producing what may be the finest maple syrup in this New England region. Bob's busy life today, anchored in nonacademic pursuits, stands in sharp contrast with his earlier years in Princeton and New Haven.

At Princeton, Bob's personal attributes and unusual background—on the one hand, a comely man of powerful physique, keen intelligence, and quiet dignity; on the other, an engineer from Rensselaer Polytechnic Institute, ex-marine, and untutored newcomer to sociology—gave him a unique position among the graduate students. Within a few months after his arrival he had demonstrated an aptitude for scholarly work, full eligibility for strong fellowship support, and a marked capacity for leadership. During the next four years Bob, with a first-rate dissertation on ideological trends among American businessmen,* completed the Princeton Ph.D., broadened his graduate education with advanced study at Columbia (underwritten by the Social Science Research Council), and, in 1964, after considering alternative invitations, accepted a faculty post at Yale.

Bob's five years at Yale must have been both rewarding and frustrating; clearly, they were exciting, at least in some respects. From the outset, he was a highly successful and popular teacher, although his outspoken political views may have exasperated conservatives among his students. His radicalization, which had been underway at Princeton or before, ripened in association with such

---

* "The Theory of Democratic Leadership in American Business Enterprise," written under the direction of Wilbert Moore, Bob Cook's principal mentor. Subsequently Moore and Cook became co-editors of the volume *Readings in Social Change* (Englewood Cliffs, N.J.: Prentice Hall, 1967).

nonconformist colleagues as his friend Staughton Lynd.* In 1966, as an Independent and vigorous opponent of the miserable misadventure in Vietnam, Bob ran for Congress—sufficiently strongly to defeat his Republican, though not his Democratic, opponent; and two years later, as a proven vote getter, he tried once more. These extramural excursions brought him to public attention as a man of unswerving moral principle and great integrity, and they may have played a role in Bob Cook's departure from Yale and the ivy cloister in 1969.

Paul Hollander and Mike Lewis, both of whom were also members of the graduate group entering Princeton in 1960, were to become my working colleagues in later years. Their scholarly and sociological deeds at the University of Massachusetts are reported in chapter 7.

As the group's "oldster" at twenty-eight, Paul arrived at Princeton with the advantages of intellectual maturity, strong undergraduate and graduate degrees in sociology and earlier training (in a Budapest high school of Communist Hungary) in the Russian language. These assets, together with a keen analytical mind and powerful motivation, enabled Paul to move through the doctoral program speedily and with distinction: following a certified triumph in the general examinations he completed the dissertation as a Ford Foundation Foreign Area Training Fellow in 1962.† This lucrative fellowship financed a year's study of Soviet society in Europe and at Harvard's Russian Research Center; having firmly established his bona fides at the center, as well as at Princeton, he was appointed to Harvard's faculty in 1963. After five years in the now-defunct Department of Social Relations, Paul Hollander joined company with the expanding group of sociologists—and with a former fellow Princetonian—at Massachusetts.

Mike Lewis followed Paul to Massachusetts in 1969, moving from the University of Illinois. Mike had spent five years in his first full-time faculty post in Champaign-Urbana as an associate of the Bureau of Educational Research and as a teaching colleague

---

* Staughton Lynd is the son of Robert S. Lynd.

† Hollander's Ph.D. dissertation, "The New Man and His Enemies: A Study of the Stalinist Conceptions of Good and Evil Personified," was directed by Allen Kassof; Morroe Berger and I also served on the dissertation committee. Unfortunately, this excellent study was not published, but part of it forms the basis of "Models of Behavior in Stalinist Literature: A Case Study of Totalitarian Values and Controls," *American Sociological Review* 31, no. 3 (June 1963): 352–64.

of such sociologists as Bernard Farber, the late Louis Schneider, and Rita Simon. (Earlier he had taught briefly at Rutgers.) This tour, combining intensive field investigation and close contact with highly able scholars, was excellent preparation for Mike's successful career at Massachusetts.

Mike's residence at Princeton (1960–1962), preceded by an undergraduate degree and brief encounter with graduate study at Brooklyn College, was marked by both academic and extracurricular success. A major part of Mike's academic study was pursued with Mel Tumin and Wilbert Moore, and his dissertation, largely based upon field research in Harlem, challenged conventional sociological views concerning the effects of matrifocalism among black families.* Perhaps Princeton's strongest influence on Mike Lewis, resulting from both his formal and informal activities as a graduate student, was the implantation of the conviction that few, if any, occupations are as rewarding as that of academic men and women.

Myron (Mickey) Glazer joined the graduate group in 1961 following a year as research assistant in Princeton's Industrial Relations Section while completing a master's degree at Rutgers. Earlier Mickey had studied sociology at New York's City College (A.B., 1956) and, like many graduates of that non-ivy school, had elected social work as his profession. After two years of preparatory study for this quasi-academic field, however, the career of scholar-teacher became his foremost goal—as it turned out, a goal consistent with his talents.

These were amply demonstrated at Princeton and, in larger measure, in the years thereafter. At Princeton, Mickey chose Latin American Studies as a field of specialization, hurdled the Ph.D. examinations in this area and others in commendable fashion, and, supported by the Doherty Foundation, in 1963–64 conducted field research in Chile among that country's politically active university students. This adventuresome exploration, undertaken with his wife, Penina, led to a doctoral dissertation, the basis of publications that firmly established Mickey's scholarly credentials.†

---

* Lewis's dissertation "Competence and the American Racial Dichotomy: A Study in the Dynamics of Victimization," was directed by Tumin; I also served on the dissertation committee.

† A large part of Glazer's dissertation ("The Professional and Political Attitudes of Chilean University Students") appears in Frank Bonilla and Myron Glazer, *Student Politics in Chile* (New York: Basic Books, 1970); a related

The Glazers moved to Northampton in 1965 where their domestic life is combined with continuing professional accomplishment—Penina in the classroom and as dean of faculty at Hampshire College and Mickey as sociologist at Smith. Mickey's rise from junior rank to the full professorship was managed in a decade, he served for six years (1974–1980) as departmental chairman, and he is esteemed and held in affection by both his students and colleagues. His most widely known published work, *The Research Adventure* (1972), is an excellent introduction to the methodological, strategic, and ethical problems of field investigation—and gives ample evidence on the printed page of Mickey Glazer's status as a fine scholar-teacher.*

Following Glazer by a year, among the new arrivals at Princeton in 1962 were Juan (Pancho) Marsal, Irving (Irv) Zeitlin, and Howard Boughey.

Juan Marsal, "Pancho," wonderfully young in heart, was the oldest of the group and, in contrast with his fellow students, came to Princeton with solid professional credentials in hand. He had taught in both European and Argentinian institutions, had won a doctor of law degree at the University of Barcelona, and, in sociology, had studied for three years with the eminent Gino Germani and other scholars at the University of Buenos Aires—it was not surprising that he tackled the Princeton doctoral program with confidence. Pancho's personal assets, moreover, included keen intelligence, critical acumen, a happy capacity for both demanding work and pace-changing play, and, not least, a large supply of self-assurance. With these advantages, attainment of the Ph.D. was managed with little difficulty, culminated by a first-rate dissertation on sociology in Latin America. By the time he left Princeton in 1965, Pancho was well launched on what was to be a distinguished, but all too brief, career.

During the decade following his Princeton years, Pancho's professional program was jam-packed, diversified, and peripatetic.

---

essay is included in Arthur Liebman, Kenneth N. Walker, and Myron Glazer, *Latin American University Students: A Six-Nation Study* (Cambridge: Harvard University Press, 1972).

* This characterization holds equally for Penina Glazer, an able historian and Mickey's long-time collaborator. Illustrations of their *formal* collaboration include the elementary textbook *Sociology: Understanding Society* (Englewood Cliffs, N.J.: Prentice Hall, 1978) by Peter I. Rose, Penina M. Glazer, and Myron Glazer; and the Glazers' unique study of Israeli "War Resisters in the Land of Battle," *Dissent,* Summer 1977.

He taught and conducted research in Argentina, Mexico, the United States, and Spain; he gave lectures and symposia in many of the universities in these countries and in Chile, England, and Germany; he edited the *Revista Latin-Americana de Sociologia* (1968–1970), as well as several anthologies; and his own publications included numerous articles in scholarly journals and a larger number of books than most sociologists manage in a lifetime.* By 1975 Pancho's home base, Argentina, had become untenable for a scholar of outspoken, left-liberal convictions, prompting him to return to his native Catalonia where he became senior professor and chairman of the Department of Sociology at the Universidad Autonoma de Barcelona. Here, for a few years, he maintained a breath-taking pace in his various professional activities. This energetic, vital, at times officious and cantankerous, but lovable man was killed in a highway accident on March 5, 1979.†

There were similarities between Irving Zeitlin and Pancho Marsal when they descended on Princeton in 1962. Both were older (Irv was almost thirty-four) and had survived more of life's battles than other newcomers; both were married to lovely, talented women and the fathers of three young children; and both, although from far different backgrounds, were of radical disposition. Irv's political and ideological views had been nurtured in the organized labor circles of Detroit, especially the Marxist-Zionists, and had been further shaped by six years (1950–1956) of rugged work in an Israeli kibbutz. Apparently this experience helped to arouse his interest in an academic career, for following his return from abroad Irv completed a B.A. and a master's degree in sociology at Wayne State University and thereafter applied for admission to Princeton's graduate program.

Irv completed the Ph.D. in two years, notwithstanding a time-consuming (and family-supporting) job as principal of the

---

* Preceded by the volume *La Sociologia en la Argentina* (Buenos Aires: Fabril, 1963), these books include *Cambio Social in America Latina* (Buenos Aires: Solar-Hachette, 1967), *Hacer la America* (Buenos Aires: Editorial de Instituto, 1969), *Revoluciones y Contrarevoluciones* (Barcelona: Peninsula, 1975), *La Sombra del Poder: Intellectuales y Politica en Espana, Argentina, y Mexico* (Madrid: Cuadernos para el dialogo, 1975), and *La Sociologia* (Barcelona: Salvat, 1975). As Wilbert Moore reminds me in personal correspondence, "At Barcelona he founded the intermittent journal, *Papers*, reflecting his constant but good-humored complaints at Princeton that he was everlastingly involved in writing course papers."

† A few months before his death, my wife, Leonora, and I spent a joyous day with Pancho Marsal in his beautiful Barcelona.

Hebrew school in the local Jewish Center—an extraordinary performance requiring organizational skills, self-discipline, and enormous energy. (He attributed this feat to a need to "catch up" with his younger colleagues and, so I guessed at the time, with his younger brother Maurice.) Toward the end of his first year he sailed smoothly through the general examinations and, with almost no break, devoted the following months to his dissertation, an expertly executed and generally favorable analysis of Marxist sociology, which he defended in the spring of 1964.* This demanding schedule limited Irv's extracurricular activities, but he somehow managed to keep his athlete's body in good trim and to lead a noncloistered social life.

A postdoctoral National Science Foundation fellowship took the Zeitlin family to Europe in 1964–65 in support of Irv's proposal to study with Maximilien Rubin, T. O. Bottomore, and other Marxist scholars—surely an atypical case of NSF patronage. This educational tour was followed by Irv's first faculty position at Indiana University, a year in England as visiting professor at Leicester, and in 1970 a move to Washington University in St. Louis, where Irv, now a full professor, joined forces with Alvin Gouldner, Helen Gouldner, and several younger colleagues who hoped to develop a center of Marxist studies. But these were difficult days for the Washington sociologists; after a brief and problem-filled year as chairman Irv accepted a senior post at the University of Toronto in 1972. There he headed a strong department for five years; he and his wife Esther, a sensitive and powerful painter, have seen their four splendid children become adults; and, as a scholar, Irv Zeitlin has continued the fast pace he had set for himself at Princeton.†

Howard Boughey, classmate and good friend of Irv Zeitlin,

---

* Zeitlin's dissertation, "Non-dogmatic Marxism: A Study in the Sociology of Karl Marx," in a slightly extended form, was published as *Marxism: A Re-Examination* (Princeton, N.J.: Van Nostrand, 1967).

† *Marxism: A Re-Examination* and *Ideology and the Development of Sociological Theory* (Englewood Cliffs, N.J.: Prentice Hall, 1968) were published during Zeitlin's years at Indiana University, and *Liberty, Equality, and Revolution in Alexis de Tocqueville* (Boston: Little, Brown, 1971) while he was in Washington. Since he has been at Toronto, the following volumes have appeared: *Capitalism and Imperialism: An Introduction to Neo-Marxist Concepts* (Chicago: Markham, 1972); *Rethinking Sociology: A Critique of Contemporary Theory* (New York: Appleton-Century-Crofts, 1973); and the comprehensive *The Social Condition of Humanity: An Introduction to Sociology* (New York: Oxford, 1980).

was also a student of great promise, but in background, intellectual orientation, and range of interests these two aspirants had little in common. As a middle-class youngster and undergraduate of Columbia Howard had been a disciple of the legendary Bill Casey. His exposure to Casey's brilliant iconoclasm, his subsequent eye-opening experience as a news reporter, and his own adventuresome disposition undergirded Howard's skeptical approach to sociological orthodoxies—scientistic, functionalist, or Marxist. And his keen interest in philosophy and the creative arts was closely related to his decision to pursue the humanistic rather than the scientific component of sociology itself. This choice, however, was no handicap in the many-sided Princeton department: Howard moved through the doctoral program in fine fashion and, except for the dissertation,* in the normal three-year period.

In 1965 Howard accepted an invitation from the University of California, Santa Barbara, where he spent four years as a full-time teacher of sociology (he had taught part time and in summer courses at Brooklyn College, Hunter College, and Rutgers). UCSB, like other California campuses, was then much more than an academic institution: this seaside community was a thriving center of both the turned-on generation and its middle-aged imitators, of heavy drug consumption and the new sexual "freedom," and generally of bohemian rejection of a "bourgeois" style of life. The Bougheys were activists in these countercultural shenanigans, no doubt at the expense of Howard's professional undertakings, as well as dismayed opponents of the American outrage in Vietnam. In 1969 Howard moved to the University of British Columbia to follow a rather different three-year program that included head-clearing fishing in the productive local waters, application for Canadian citizenship, and serious resumption of sociological scholarship.

While still at Princeton Howard had demonstrated a rare talent as a scholar-teacher which he continued to display in the classrooms of Santa Barbara and British Columbia. Since 1973 he has been a teaching luminary at the University of Toronto's Erindale College, and in recent years he also has been demonstrating his considerable writing skill. *The Insights of Sociology* (1978)

---

* Boughey's dissertation, "Blueprints for Behavior: Intentions of Architects to Influence Social Behavior Through Design," completed in 1967, brings together his interests in artistic enterprise and sociological analysis; this unique study was directed by Gerald Breese.

is a unique textbook that not only introduces students to the multisidedness of sociology in realistic terms (the field's several paradigmatic varieties are subsumed under the "three sociologies" of functionalism, activism, and naturalism), but gives ample evidence on the printed page of Howard's didactic expertise. His own theoretical orientation, acknowledged in this unusual volume, is the "naturalistic" branch of present-day phenomenology. As an exponent of this perspective, adopted only in his post-Princeton years, Howard Boughey is winning a respected place in present-day sociology.*

Whereas Howard Boughey's professional career has been colored and perhaps hampered by nonacademic involvements, Jack Hewitt's has followed a steady course—and continues to do so, as will be brought out in chapter 7 (Hewitt joined Paul Hollander, Mike Lewis, and me at the University of Massachusetts in 1970). Following undergraduate study at the State University of New York at Buffalo where his achievements included a major four-year scholarship, Phi Beta Kappa, a B.A. summa cum laude, and a coveted prize for excellence in sociology, Jack arrived at Princeton in 1963. At SUNY he had shown marked ability and, presumably, more than casual interest in statistics, a subject that we assumed he would accent in his graduate work and later as a "hard-fact" sociologist. But at Buffalo Jack had also explored various theoretical and methodological perspectives in sociology and anthropology and among them had become intrigued with Leslie White's controversial "culturology," especially White's view of the symbol as the basis of human behavior—here was the beginning of Hewitt's later role as a well-known symbolic interactionist. Jack's studies at Princeton, however, were not one sided, and they produced an unbroken continuation of his undergraduate record: he held major fellowships, sailed through the general examinations in his second year, and completed the Ph.D. with a strong dissertation in 1966.†

---

* Several years ago Boughey wrote "The Structure of Social Occasions," a lengthy research monograph and, in my opinion, an important contribution to phenomenological literature; it was not published at the time, but is now (1981) being revised with a view to publication. Currently he is also completing a textbook on deviance, *Casting Stones,* which reflects his theoretical perspective.

† Hewitt's dissertation, "Social Stratification and Social Productivity," written under the direction of Mel Tumin, in revised form was published as *Social Stratification and Deviant Behavior* (New York: Random House, 1970). In this study Hewitt's focus on self-esteem, as a causal mechanism linking social

While a graduate student at Princeton, Jack sometimes seemed to be the most conventional and sober minded of the nine talented young men, some of whose accomplishments have been reported above. His close attention to the job-at-hand and his serious demeanor, however, only faintly obscured an intellectual playfulness and a marked capacity to depart from established sociological paths, virtues that were to highlight his later scholarly work. The latter began on a modest scale while he taught at Oberlin College (1966–1968) and York University in Canada (1968–1970)—and grew apace following Jack Hewitt's arrival at Massachusetts in 1970.

Looking Backward: Rewards and Losses in an Ivy Setting

By far the largest reward of my own years at Princeton was fellowship with those faculty colleagues and graduate students whose sketchy portraits have filled so many of the preceding pages. Firm friendships were formed during this period which continue today, and less than a decade later three of those students, as I have noted, became my working companions at Massachusetts. There were other dividends of course accruing from this unexpectedly brief tour at Princeton, not the least of which was my own continued education in the vagaries of the sociological enterprise. But there were also disappointments and indeed some ego-shattering failures.

The latter include my largely unsuccessful efforts, recounted earlier, to strengthen the undergraduate program, especially at a time when sociology was booming elsewhere. Contributing to the shaky status of the program was the perhaps preventable loss of Ed Tiryakian, a splendid teacher, and the appointment of junior-level sociologists—Maurice Zeitlin, Dick Hamilton, Bill Michelson—who remained at Princeton only briefly. Here was a situation calling for stronger and more prescient leadership than I brought to the department between 1960 and 1965.

During those same years, however, several sociologists arrived at Princeton who excelled the rest of us as teachers, enriched an already excellent program, and, beyond sociology, brought their pedagogical, scholarly, and administrative skills to various

---

inequality and deviance, may be viewed as a forerunner of his later full-bodied work on "self and society."

interdisciplinary projects in the university—I took pride in the appointments of Charlie Westoff, Allen Kassof, and Marvin Bressler. And in my final year, as a lame-duck chairman, I had the additional satisfaction of successfully recruiting Suzanne Keller; shortly thereafter Suzanne became the first tenured woman professor at Princeton.

These gains for sociology and the larger university, in my own view, also were personal rewards, which were only partially offset by personal failures. Of the latter, an especially unhappy situation was a running battle of sorts with Marion Levy that began following my first few months at Princeton. We not only sharply disagreed about sociological and educational matters (the tough-minded "scientist" versus the soft-headed "humanist"), but I had no success in changing Levy's opinion of what he judged to be my scholarly and administrative incapacities. Whatever may have been my shortcomings (of which at least some were evident), this troubled relationship with Marion Levy was unique: I enjoyed collegial support and friendly ties with all other members of the department.*

In the wider faculty, I came to know as working colleagues and in some cases as good friends several distinguished Princetonians, a reward largely a dividend of my job as chairman, for this office carried with it membership in a number of interdepartmental agencies including the overseeing committee of the Woodrow Wilson School of Political and International Affairs, the Council on International and Regional Studies, the Office of Population Research, and the Council on Human Relations. Thus few weeks passed when I was not meeting with prominent scholars in the social sciences, history, and psychology.† These extradepart-

---

* I have seen very little of Marion Levy since 1965, but during a visit to Princeton in the spring of 1979, when I was gathering information for the present chapter, the only distracting note while chatting with Marion in his office was the (caged) presence of one of his present pets, a beady-eyed boa constrictor. Marion himself was altogether cordial and shrugged off as "old, forgotten history" my passing reference to the contentious nature of our earlier relationship.

† Among these were my fellow departmental chairmen Richard Lester (economics), Marver Bernstein (politics), and Jerome Blum (history); Gardner Patterson, economist and director of the Woodrow Wilson School, Klaus Knorr, economist and head of the school's Center of International Studies, and Joseph Strayer, the school's mainstay historian; the demographer Ansley Coale, director of the OPR; the psychologist Silvan Tompkins; the political scientists Harry Eckstein and the rising star Sidney Verba; the historians

mental sessions were multifunctional: they introduced me to a subculture of a professional elite, they served to protect me from an all-too-prevalent sociological provincialism, and they conferred upon an academic of modest accomplishment some degree of un-won status.

There were of course other rewarding features of life at Princeton, not the least of which was provided by what seemed to be a steady stream of visitors from abroad. Their two or three day stopovers, together with a large number of foreign graduate students in residence, brought a cosmopolitan flavor to the university which enriched the lives of all of us. Among the transients, moreover, were sociologists from Britain, Germany, Yugoslavia, Soviet Russia, Japan, and elsewhere. As departmental chairman and thus frequently their designated host, I learned a fair amount about the international impact of the mislabeled "American science" of sociology.

This lesson, taught by travelers from other lands, was expanded by still another reward of my five-year tenure at Princeton. It was during this period that I became for a time a marginal member of the sociological jet set, although in no way a rival of my globe-trotting colleagues Wilbert Moore, Mel Tumin, and Charlie Westoff.

Excursus: Ex-Innocent Abroad

In earlier years my travel abroad had been limited to three contrasting journeys: a uniformed tour in the Far East during World War II, a six-month prowl in Western Europe in 1955, and five years later a week or so in northern Italy attending the Fourth World Congress of the International Sociological Association. Brief comment may be in order concerning two of these pre-Princeton ventures, with special reference to sociology and sociologists.

My long-postponed *Wanderjahre* was made possible by Smith's President Wright's approval of my application for a sab-

---

Cyril Black, powerful chairman of the Council on International and Regional Studies, Eric Goldman who, on leave, became a frustrated White House scholar under President Lyndon Johnson, and John William Ward, chairman of the American Civilization Program who within a few years moved to the presidency of Amherst College; and the economist William Bowen who even as a youngster gave ample evidence of his destiny: in 1972 he became president of Princeton.

batical leave of absence (my first, although I had been teaching since 1931) and, especially, by Leonora's supportive sanction and encouragement (strongly disapproved by some folks who subscribed to the conventional view that spouses should always vacation together). Accordingly, early in February 1955 I sailed from New York and a few days later in LeHavre picked up a prepurchased midget "quatre chevaux" which, until July and following no premade plan, carried me safely through much of France, parts of Spain and Italy, and almost all of Britain. In keeping with the stated purpose of the sabbatical, specified in my formal application as "travel and relaxation," this half-year hegira of an adventure-seeking, forty-three-year-old academic was very largely a nonprofessional exercise. There were occasions, however, when I would be reminded of my sociological calling.

For example, in a Barcelona bookshop I was pleasantly surprised to learn that under-the-counter copies of a Spanish translation of MacIver and Page's *Society* were available—in disregard of the book's proscription by Franco's government (another translation of this subversive volume shortly was to be sold under similar conditions in Poland). And in Paris I paid some heed to my occupational role, not only by "discovering" the home of Auguste Comte almost next door to my Left Bank hotel, but in a bolder spirit by managing brief meetings with the eminent, but strikingly contrasting, Raymond Aron and Georges Gurvitch. But it was not until my six-week tour of Britain that I spent many enjoyable hours with fellow sociologists—in London with Norman Birnbaum, Tom Bottomore, David and Ruth Glass, and Donald McRae, and with Michael Banton and Tom Burns in Edinburgh. These fine scholars were warm and generous hosts of a traveler far from home, they taught me a great deal about soon-to-flourish British sociology, and in the years following 1955 I have been rewarded by their continuing friendship.*

The second pre-Princeton excursion abroad, taking me to the ISA Congress in 1959, was an unexpected dividend of the editorship of the *American Sociological Review*, permitting a

---

* Since 1955 I have spent considerable time with the seven sociologists named above, in both Britain and America. Norman Birnbaum, my initial and splendid guide in London, following thirteen years on the faculties of LSE (1953–1959) and Oxford (1959–1966), returned to his native country in 1966; two years later he became the first professor of sociology at Amherst College and thus a neighbor in the Valley. I last saw David Glass in his London home in 1978; he died in 1979.

week of elbow-rubbing with sociologists from many lands, among them a seemingly over-representation of my countrymen. Most of the meetings were held in Stresa on Lake Maggiore, the beauty of which remains in my memories more vividly than do the programmed sessions themselves, yet I recall my admiration of two or three of the formal papers.* As at most such gatherings, however, there were rewarding, nonscheduled activities, some of which stick with me.

One of these consisted of a stimulating day in Milan in company with C. Wright Mills. I chided my companion for the indexing of his "translations" of writings by Talcott Parsons in *The Sociological Imagination,* recently published and destined to be a very influential work in the 1960s.† But most of our time, happily, was given to the artistic wonders of a city neither of us had visited before, and, with no decent restraint, to the consumption of Italian pastries. Back in Stresa, among the numerous activities were informal sessions with scholars from the USSR. Although the Russian delegation, the first attending an ISA Congress, was strictly supervised by a "sociologist" who appeared to be a party hack, in the late evenings certain of its members, escaping temporarily from their ideological chaperon would share relaxing refreshment with some of their confreres from the West, resulting in at least a modicum of cultural exchange.

In the 1960s (and earlier), among the uncodified perquisites of a departmental chairmanship in an elite university were invitations to travel from time to time, in this country and abroad, with the academic jet set. However questionable one's credentials, these opportunities seemed to go with the job—a circumstance of

---

* One of these was an exploratory and provocative piece on personality disorders and social structure by Anne Parsons, daughter of Talcott; another was Robert Merton's "Social Conflict in Styles of Sociological Work," a characteristically learned and instructive essay in the sociology of sociology to which I sent students for many years. Merton's paper was originally published in Fourth World Congress, *Transactions* (Louvain: International Sociological Association, 1961) and is reprinted in Merton, *The Sociology of Science* (Chicago: University of Chicago Press, 1973) and elsewhere.

† The quotations from Parsons and their greatly condensed, lucid, and generally accurate reformulations by Mills appear on pp. 25–31 in *The Sociological Imagination* (New York: Oxford University Press, 1959); the index entry of the latter is "Parsons, Talcott . . . translated," p. 232. Mills denied responsibility for this entry, referring to a "professional indexer," but the entry is consistent with his well-known—and, in my unorthodox view, refreshing—talent for professional irreverencies.

which I took advantage during my years at Princeton. Recollections of two of these generously underwritten junkets, each of which took me to a foreign land hitherto unseen, complete the present excursus.

The first was a visit to Greece during the summer of 1962, engineered by Allen Kassof. Allen had been asked by a friend on the staff of the Athens Technological Institute to propose a "distinguished American sociologist" qualified to participate in an international conference on "human settlements" which was being organized by Constantinos Doxiadis, head of the institute and renowned, though controversial, city planner. In a spirit of friendship, but with highly questionable judgment, Allen put my name forward—a blatant example of cronyism at work in professional affairs. Thus I became one of a half-dozen Americans who, together with some thirty delegates from various other countries, gathered in Athens on a Sunday afternoon, embarked on a chartered ship the following morning, and spent a week midst the wonders of the Greek islands. The fact that I was out of my league in this assembly in no way decreased my enjoyment of the beauty of the eastern Mediterranean, the days with the marvels of antiquity (at night we sailed from island to island), the many luxuries of both ship and shore, the jolly evening hours supported by a well-stocked bar and a lively band, and by no means least the warm companionship.

My fellow Americans were a mixed quintet: Edmund Bacon, the eminent city planner, a quiet-voiced and sagacious Philadelphian; vivacious Leonard J. Duhl, noted psychiatrist with additional solid credentials as an urbanist; the bold-minded futurist R. Buckminster Fuller, an exemplar of gentle courtliness and humane sensibility; the Harvard economist Edward S. Mason, with a distinguished record in public and international affairs; and the seemingly ever-present, remarkable Margaret Mead. There were equally luminous delegates from other countries (France, Spain, Poland, Pakistan, India, and elsewhere), including among others the irrepressible Marshall McLuhan from Canada, the renowned biologist and wide-ranging intellectual C. H. Waddington from Scotland, and from England highly attractive Barbara Ward, keen economic analyst of developing societies. At the outset I was awed by this collection of celebrities. Soon, however, encouraged by their cordiality and willingness to exchange views with the only formally certified sociologist in the group, I became an active participant in its deliberations, even chairing a couple of our daily sessions.

These meetings, devoted to subjects of relevance to the central theme of "human settlements," were free-wheeling seminars in which discussion was guided only by such contributions as those assembled chose to make and, in some small degree, by the inclinations of the chair. They demanded little or nothing of the delegates and interrupted our sight-seeing and recreational preoccupations for merely an hour or so each day, conveniently scheduled in late morning. I remember very little of the substance of the sessions beyond the consensus that modern urban life leaves much to be desired, yet somehow we reached agreement on a statement of desiderata for the development of livable communities which received wide circulation in the world's press as "The Declaration of Delos."

This document was signed by the delegates on the final day of the conference in a ceremony skillfully staged by Doxiadis. In the ancient theater on the island of Delos, as the sun was setting over the Aegean, each of us walked to the *Logeion* and signed the declaration. Except for wide publicity given to the latter, to my knowledge this dramatic exercise had few if any consequences.

During this cultural excursion, however, there were events and individual performances that are unforgettable. One was an after-dinner talkathon by Buckminster Fuller that began about nine-thirty and ended an hour or so after I retired at 1 A.M.; the display of his awesome erudition, softened by Bucky's humane concern, was a spectacular, if fatiguing, exhibition.* Of a rather different order were private get-togethers with Marshall McLuhan. Late in the evenings we would meet on the captain's bridge where McLuhan, with a bottle of beer in hand, would try to enlighten me about what had been his pyrotechnic and all-too-confusing remarks in the morning seminars. He lacked Bucky's gentle patience, but these tutorials were generous and instructive. A third memorable event was the happy discovery that dignified Barbara Ward—an impressive social scientist, tough-minded social critic, and an altogether serious participant in the morning meetings—became in the evenings a comradely fun-lover who gave ample evidence of her dancing prowess. And at all hours, there was the brilliant, wonderfully outspoken, and exuberant Margaret Mead who, since I had last seen her several years before, had become a

---

* This was my first exposure to a Bucky Fuller "lecture," but in 1978 at the age of eighty-three, Fuller spent a week at the University of Massachusetts during which I heard another of his extraordinary presentations and had the good fortune to renew acquaintance with this remarkable man.

wiser and more tolerant woman of learning—although she had retained a jaundiced view of anthropology's sister discipline of sociology.

While my vocation was feebly represented at Doxiadis's extravaganza, sociology and sociologists moved onto center stage for a time during my second six-month visit to Europe in 1964. In contrast with the "bachelor" adventure of nine years earlier, Leonora and I traveled together on this delightful tour, a good deal of it following the path of my former journey in France, Spain, Italy, and Britain. But our travel plans were stretched far beyond their normal flexibility by an altogether surprising development, initiated on the final day of a month's stay on the Catalonian coast by a letter forwarded from Princeton: I had been invited as one of five American sociologists to visit West Germany and West Berlin. An exchange of letters between Bonn's Foreign Office and the traveling Pages led to several weeks of luxury, excitement, and, for me, education in the company of Joseph Maier, Carl Mayer, Robert Sutherland, Robert Winch, and, most important, Leonora. Irrespective of her nonacademic status, Leonora had been named a sixth "Professor of Sociology" with all the perquisites of the "Visitors' Program of the Federal Republic."

For a teacher of modest income and his wife, these perks were overwhelming: in addition to basic expenses, they included such surprises as opera and concert tickets, bridal suites in leading hotels, and two thousand marks for "cigarettes and other incidentals" (the large residue of which, after our departure from Germany, supported us through the Netherlands, across the Channel, and for a day or two in London). Our travels in Italy and Switzerland precluded the initial three days in Bonn and a trip on the Rhine, but we joined our compatriots in Heidelberg for the fifteenth Congress of the German Sociological Association, followed by a recreational weekend on Harz Mountain, thereafter visited a large part of West Germany, headquartered for a week in Kiel and another in Dusseldorf, and ended this lavish "study tour" with several days in Berlin. All along we enjoyed cordial hospitality, meeting with government officials, academics and students, politicians and journalists, industrial workers and farmers, and almost any others in whom we expressed interest. In keeping with my avocation, I even met with a manager of boxers. These diverse activities, however, were interspersed with generous allotments of unscheduled time and, moreover, our only formal responsibility was an hour's debriefing during the final day in Berlin.

The meetings in Heidelberg, in commemoration of the centenary of Max Weber's birth, were no more instructive than other activities during the tour. But for sociologists they carried special interest and, in addition, presented an extraordinary example of ideologically based assessments of a great scholar's work. Several of the participants gave papers consistent with the conventional appraisal of Weber as a giant figure in the development of modern sociology; these included an opening address by Talcott Parsons on "Evaluation and Objectivity in Social Science: An Interpretation of Max Weber's Contributions."* Laudation of Weber, however, was voiced by no means all of those attending the congress; much of Weber's work, at least by implication, was interpreted as contributing to the rise of Nazism in Germany, a position taken by many of the leftists on hand. Thus battle lines were drawn between defenders of Weber's commitment to rational dialogue and the pursuit of truth, probably a substantial majority of us, and Marxist or neo-Marxist critics, among them Herbert Marcuse. A large part of the frequently acerbic "scholarly" exchange, especially in the evening hours, was devoted to this issue.

Following the congress in Heidelberg, and under calmer conditions, there were meetings with sociologists in a number of German institutions including the already troubled Free University in West Berlin. On the sociological front, during the next six weeks in Britain there were reunions with old friends and fresh encounters with both senior and younger scholars who became friends in later years. On the latter score, we enjoyed the warm hospitality of T. H. and Nadine Marshall in Cambridge, who not long thereafter were our guests in Princeton, and whom we last saw in 1974 when six oldsters gathered for a grand dinner and evening in the Cambridge (Massachusetts) home of Everett and Helen Hughes. In cross-generational meetings, there were lively hours at the University of Leicester with Tony Giddens, who within a few years was to become England's most prolific theoretician, and with Eric Dunning, then beginning his career as a historian and sociologist of sport. At the time both were junior members of a department chaired by our gracious host, Ilya Neustadt,

---

* This impressive—and lucid, it should be stressed—essay, written in English but delivered by Parsons in a German translation, appears in the Proceedings of the German Sociological Association, the *Deutsche Gesselschaft fur Soziologie,* and was also published in the UNESCO *Journal of Social Sciences* 17, no. 1 (1965); it is reprinted in Parsons's *Sociological Theory and Modern Society* (New York: Free Press, 1967), chap. 3.

who had built a thriving sociological enterprise in the face of the traditional resistance of the British academy. And at Oxford's Nuffield College there was an all-too-brief exchange with a striking young woman recently arrived from Munich, Germany, Gertrud Lenzer, who was not only to become a noted American sociologist, but whose superior fishing skill was to put me to shame off Martha's Vineyard in 1977.

The European holiday in 1964, of course, was largely a nonsociological tour that had only feeble connection with my occupational pedigree. Throughout the trip, however, I assumed that return to Princeton would mean resumption of a teaching job that would carry through my remaining years in academic life; the circumstances that undermined this expectation are reported in chapter 7. But first, the chronology of these pages is interrupted by recollections of adventures and misadventures as editor.

6

Sociology and the Printed Page:

Journeys as an Editor, 1952–1980

IN THE PRECEDING pages on Smith and Princeton there is only passing reference to an undertaking that consumed much of my life at these two schools and that continued to do so later at Santa Cruz and Massachusetts. Even today, several years after retirement from teaching, editorial tasks occupy a bit of my working time. The span of the present chapter, then, is almost three decades—a period marked by the spectacular rise of "main-line" sociology in the 1950s and, later, by the discipline's fractionalization and by what appears to be evidence of sociology's recent decline. As another illustration of the importance of luck in personal history, the earlier expansion of the field corresponded with my initial years as editor of works in sociology.

My move into this role was sudden and altogether unexpected. With no previous experience, and certainly with too little trepidation, I became an editor in 1952. My only previous contacts with the world of publishing had been those of occasional authorship and, along with other exploitable academics, those resulting from publishers' requests to assess lengthy manuscripts for tiny fees. My surprise was understandable therefore when Frank Egner and Josephine Lees, two representatives of the giant firm of Doubleday, visited me at City College* in search of information about sociologists who might be qualified for an advisory position in a newly established division of their company; I offered the

---

* As noted in chap. 3, while on leave of absence from Smith in 1952–53 I served as chairman of the Department of Sociology and Anthropology at CCNY.

names of three or four scholars with seemingly strong credentials for the job. My surprise was much greater when, on the following day, I was invited to become Doubleday's Consulting Editor in Sociology and Anthropology.

Doubleday and Paperbacks: Beginner's Luck

In this case, "Consulting" in the title was misleading for, as I soon discovered, Frank Egner, the head of the department and a veteran editor of works in medicine, and Jo Lees, a former editor of books on sport, were even less familiar than I with publications for the "college trade" and knew very little about textual materials in the social sciences. This meant that the recommendations of a "seasoned" sociologist carried considerable weight and that my only major constraint was budgetary. But this limitation, at the outset, almost torpedoed what turned out to be a successful innovation in textbook publication.

The novel idea of short paperbacks in the social sciences was Frank Egner's, but his conception was a far cry from what emerged as Doubleday's "Short Studies in Sociology." Soon after I joined the firm, Egner presented his proposal: to publish pamphlets of ten to fifteen pages, each a watered-down treatment of a popular sociological topic, for which the author would receive an "honorarium" of no more than fifty dollars. I viewed this plan as both educationally atrocious and ruthlessly exploitative, voiced my consternation, and offered a counterscheme: that we bring out soft-covered books of modest length on themes of evident sociological importance written by men and women with strong scholarly credentials, several of which could be used in combination in general courses or individually could serve as "core" readings in more specialized subjects. I also urged that authors be paid decently, but managed merely to squeeze from Doubleday the paltry sum of $200 for each contributor.* In spite of this severe handicap, the "Studies" series was launched without mishap in 1953.

The almost immediate success of the series was the product of several circumstances plus a substantial measure of good luck. In the postwar years the large increase in college enrollments in general and the boom in academic sociology in particular guar-

---

* George Simpson, author of the first and most far-reaching number in the series, *Man and Society: Preface to Sociology and the Social Sciences,* 1954, fared much better, but hardly handsomely.

anteed an expanding market for textbooks—the series was riding a historical wave. At the same time, many teachers of sociology were highly critical of most of the "standard" texts as conceptually and theoretically thin, a shortcoming that the Short Studies were designed to avoid.* Moreover, the series encouraged instructors in introductory courses to put together "textbooks" in keeping with their own preferences by combining several studies, a flexibility that turned out to have wide appeal. And perhaps of some importance was Doubleday's extensive mailing campaign, far more effective than advertising in journals, although probably less so than word-of-mouth endorsement by sociologists themselves.†

Whatever the role of these favoring circumstances, of crucial importance to the early success of the Short Studies were the men and women who were persuaded to participate in this untested publishing project. Most of these adventurers were young scholars, not as yet members of an affluent professoriate, but all of them accepted their meager recompense with little audible complaint. Of far greater moment, they brought to their undertakings both sociological sophistication and skillful craftsmanship—qualities generally lacking in textbook writing at the time. Thus among the first dozen studies were several works that received critical acclaim and were widely used in various college courses for many years: Ely Chinoy's *Sociological Perspective* (first edition, 1954), Elizabeth Nottingham's *Religion and Society* (1954), Roscoe and Gisela Hinkle's *The Development of Modern Sociology* (1954), Wilbert Moore's *Economy and Society* (1955), Scott Greer's *Social Organization* (1955), Kurt Mayer's *Class and Society* (first edition, 1955), and Peter Blau's *Bureaucracy in Modern Society* (first edition, 1956).‡

* The Editor's Foreword in the first of the studies, includes the statement that both authors and the editor "must forego watered-down versions of sociology that serve neither the student—all too often underestimated by writers and publishers of textbooks—nor sociology itself" (C. H. Page in ibid., p. iii).
† Two additional circumstances favored the Short Studies: first, the fact that Doubleday, unlike other major publishing firms, owned its own printing plant in nearby Garden City, Long Island, meant efficient and quite speedy production of the studies shortly after manuscripts were edited; second, the idea of publishing inexpensive paperback books of nonfiction was "in the air" in the early 1950s, and Doubleday became the initiator of projects of this kind by introducing Anchor Books under the imaginative editorship of young Jason Epstein; my occasional meetings with Epstein were helpful for a neophyte editor.
‡ These seven volumes (and five others) were commissioned while I was con-

The Short Studies in Sociology, including these seven first-rate texts, were Doubleday's initial venture into the "college trade," and the series was followed soon by similar projects in psychology and political science—these new-style paperbacks were the primary concern of the text division of the firm. Doubleday, however, in conventional fashion, also published full-scale, hard-covered books in sociology which fell within my editorial domain—and some of which severely tested my newly acquired blue pencil. But only two of these, greatly contrasting volumes, proved to have the durability of the Studies: N. S. Timasheff's *Sociological Theory, Its Nature and Growth* (1955; fourth edition with George A. Theodorson, 1976) and Ely Chinoy's *Automobile Workers and the American Dream* (1955), a doctoral dissertation destined to become a minor classic.

Books of this promise, together with a unique and thriving series of paperback mini-texts, betokened a bright future for Doubleday's new department—or so it seemed to me in 1953. During that year the job of editing sociological works, undertaken as a raw beginner at what I soon learned to be a demanding task, absorbed much of my time and energy, and in 1954 both hard- and soft-covered publications were coming off the press. Thus when I went on sabbatical leave from Smith in February 1955, there was reason to assume that I would be resuming my editorial chores six months later. I did return to Smith, but not to Doubleday.

My leave of absence was spent vacationing in Europe happily ignorant of developments in publishing back home. Hence it came as something of a shock when, during a final carefree week in Paris, a message arrived announcing the forthcoming closure of Doubleday's college department and requesting my approval, by cabled reply, of a very modest sum "in settlement for your services." I responded cavalierly by noting my expected time of arrival in New York and indicating my willingness "to discuss the matter sometime thereafter." My shock was even greater when the ship was met by a pair of strangers who informed me that Doubleday's list in sociology was being bought by Random House and that their dockside mission was to lure me to the latter firm.

---

sulting editor at Doubleday, but only the first three—by Chinoy, Nottingham, and the Hinkles—were actually published by that firm. The Studies (and other books in sociology) were sold to Random House in 1955, as reported below.

Eager to rejoin Leonora after a lengthy absence and with only a slight bow to decent manners, I sent Jess Stein and Charles Lieber on their way. A few days later, however, like a baseball player in a package deal, along with the larger books and the Short Studies, I became a property of Random House.

Random House and the Ascension of Academic Sociology

At the time, in 1955, I knew very little about the commercial organization with which I was to be associated for a quarter of a century. I was aware of the reputation of Random House as a leading publisher of fiction and other books of general interest, occasionally I had read the column "Trade Winds" written by its president, Bennett Cerf, and almost weekly had encountered this celebrity's wise-cracking persona on television's "What's My Line," and, like many other nonaffluent academics, I had made ample use of the Modern Library's inexpensive classics. Clearly, none of this was helpful when I faced the job of consulting editor in the college department of this mammoth firm.

Of great help, however, were the guidance and friendship of the two men who managed this recently established enterprise: Jess Stein, the department's head and a long-time Random House principal,* and the relative newcomer Charles Lieber, the department's director and senior editor. Physically and in personality the two were opposites, Jess's humpty-dumpty stature, red-fringed pate, quiet speech and gentle manners standing in sharp contrast with Charles's slim six foot three, brigandish mustachios, hearty extroversion, and limitless supply of Jewish stories. But both of these men were serious intellectuals, political activists in their communities, and highly talented bookmakers devoted to the goal of producing profit-making works of quality. For a good many years this double aim was realized in the college department and in several "textbook" fields including sociology.

Random House's publications in sociology began with the

---

* Among Stein's accomplishments had been the editorship of *The American College Dictionary*, the development of an excellent reference department, and the management of The Modern Library; in subsequent years, as a vice president of the firm, he was editor-in-chief of *The Random House Dictionary of the English Language* (1967) and editorial director of *The Random House Encyclopedia* (1977). Jess Stein's impressive record receives high praise in Bennett Cerf's *At Random* (New York: Random House, 1977), pp. 281ff.

already well-established Short Studies and a handful of full-scale volumes, taken over from Doubleday in 1955. But under the leadership of Stein and Lieber, with an assist from a hard-working consulting editor, this modest list grew rapidly: within a very few years both soft- and hard-covered books were rolling off the press. With the merger of Random House and Alfred A. Knopf in 1960 several more volumes were acquired, as well as a second, distinguished imprint.* Thus by the mid-sixties the House had become a major publisher of works in sociology.

This could not have taken place without the large expansion of academic sociology and the mounting demand for textbooks. Contributing significantly to this development, moreover, was the move of Random House into the publication of paperbacks, which for a decade or so were primarily the Short Studies. In the wake of the earlier numbers in the series, cited above, appeared Gresham Sykes's *Crime and Society* (1956), Dennis Wrong's *Population* (1956), Michael Olmsted's *The Small Group* (1959), Charles Wright's *Mass Communications* (1959), Frederick Elkin's *The Child and Society* (1960), and Peter Rose's *They and We* (1963). Over the years extensive adoptions of the original and later editions of these first-rate texts brought profits to Random House, income to a consulting editor, and, in welcome contrast with Doubleday's paltry "honoraria," royalties to their authors.

By the early 1960s the wide use of the Studies ("Short" had been dropped) in college courses had given ample evidence of the commercial viability of concise paperback publications in the textbook market. It came as no surprise therefore when Prentice Hall launched a "Foundations of Modern Sociology Series" in 1964. Under the expert editorship of Alex Inkeles, who wrote the initial number (*What is Sociology?*), the Foundations followed the lead of the Studies by bringing out soft-covered booklets on major sociological themes, but on other counts the Prentice-Hall series was unique. On the one hand, all of its contributors were well-known leaders in their respective fields (in contrast with the younger and

---

* Among the Knopf acquisitions was Robin Williams's textual treatise, *American Society* (1951, 1960, 1970), the original edition of which I had reviewed (*American Sociological Review* 17, no. 5 [October 1951]: 726–27); as consulting editor for the second and third editions of this fine book, I profited educationally and materially. In later years the Knopf imprint was carried by a number of other works in sociology, including Robert Nisbet's superior text, *The Social Bond* (1970, rev. with Robert G. Perrin, 1977); again my editorial function paid dual benefits.

poorly paid authors of the early Short Studies)—a publishing coup
that alarmed some people at Random House.* On the other hand,
each number in the series, irrespective of the complexity of the
subject or the style of the author, strictly adhered to an overall
length of 128 pages (eight folios in printer's jargon), which may
have meant a saving in production costs. But this imposed conformity also may have reduced the appeal of the Foundations. In
any event, faced by a formidable rival, the Studies continued to
flourish.

The Studies, however, were a small part of "textbook" production during the years of the sociological ascension. In the 1960s
and for almost another decade Random House, together with
other firms, flooded the market with various kinds of publications—meritorious and otherwise. There were systematic introductions that were distinguished works of scholarship: Ely Chinoy's *Society* (1961, revised 1967), a winner in the commercial
sweepstakes; and Robert Nisbet's *The Social Bond* (1970, revised
1977), a succès d'estime. There were eclectic primers aimed at the
mass educational market, notably the lively and widely adopted
Sociology (1969) by David Dressler. There were hard- and soft-
covered texts in such fields as sociological theory, research methods,
race and ethnic relations, religion, urban sociology, and population. And there were a few of the ubiquitous "readers," including
the exceptional *Study of Society* (1967, revised 1970, 1973, 1977),
a skillfully integrated anthology edited and co-authored by Peter
Rose.

During these years the Studies continued to expand, reaching about thirty titles by 1970. These included paperbacks on a
wide variety of sociological themes: social movements, power,
racial conflict, blue-collar workers, the family, urbanism, delinquency, law, science, education, social research, and even works
on Mexican youth and "informal sociology." And two "series
within a series" were introduced, one in 1967 on modern national societies, which for lack of large sales was abandoned after
publication of well-received volumes on the Netherlands, Japan,
Sweden, Poland, and Israel; the other a few years later, an innovation edited by Peter Rose, on American ethnic groups (Jews,

* Contributors to the Foundations series include, among others, Wilbert E.
Moore (social change), Neil J. Smelser (economic life), William J. Goode
(the family), Melvin M. Tumin (social stratification), Theodore M. Mills
(groups), Talcott Parsons (societies, two volumes), and Albert K. Cohen
(deviance).

Italians, Japanese, Chinese, Mexicans, and white Southerners)*—
all first-rate books which also met the fate of a profit-defined "bottom line."

For several years before the imposition of this restraint,
however, marketplace considerations hardly seemed to govern the
college department at Random House. In the 1960s the prosperity
of the department, reported as the most solvent division of the
firm, encouraged the publication of scholarly works of distinction
but of limited sales potential. The sociology list included, for
example, Suzanne Keller's quasi-Parsonian opus on "strategic
elites," *Beyond the Ruling Class* (1963), Mirra Komarovsky's
monograph, *Blue-Collar Marriage* (1964),† Joyce O. Hertzler's
encyclopaedic *A Sociology of Language* (1965), and Robert Nisbet's collection of essays, *Tradition and Revolt* (1968). Working
with authors of books such as these was intellectually stimulating
and personally rewarding. But this time-consuming task, in addition to my editorial responsibilities for the Studies and a mounting number of larger textbooks, was more than a one-man job.

By 1964 the proliferation of publications in a variety of
sociological fields, reaching far beyond the capabilities of a single
adviser, led to the appointment of five additional consultants:
Marvin Bressler, Robert Nisbet, Peter Rose, Hannan Selvin, and
Dennis Wrong. These distinguished editorial colleagues lightened
my Random House load, to be sure, but this multiplication of consultants, as should have been foreseen, turned out to be more
ambitious than even a booming market could support. Bob Nisbet,
immersed in his own prolific writing, soon found editorial chores
distasteful, and in the following years personal scholarship greatly
outweighed editorial tasks in the working lives of Bressler, Selvin,
and Wrong. In the later 1960s and well into the 1970s, Peter Rose
and I were the activists in the Random House stable of consultants
in sociology.

The mid-sixties were a time of important events at Random
House. In 1964, after a dozen years of impressive editorial achievement as director of the college department, Charles Lieber left us
to become the founder and president of Atherton Press—thereby

---

* Written by an "insider," Lewis M. Killian's *White Southerners* (1970), a
widely acclaimed work, was a unique study in a series on ethnic groups.
Editor Peter Rose, with sociological sagacity, had hoped to bring out further
studies on Waspish minorities. Unfortunately the series was discontinued.
† This fine book, following its publication as a Vintage paperback, defied
prediction by enjoying large sales for many years.

fulfilling a long-standing but rarely voiced ambition. His successor, Theodore Caris, lacked Lieber's bookmaking expertise. Ted's pronounced success as head of the department (until his resignation in 1970) was in large part a product of his friendly cooperation with authors and fellow editors, his unrestrained pursuit of titles, and especially the massive growth of the textbook market. In 1966, as another surprise to most of us, Random House, until then a major "independent," became part of a conglomerate: the House was sold to the Radio Corporation of America for $40 million. Editors were assured, however, that RCA would impose no control of their selection of books or, generally, of the on-going operations of the firm—a stipulation that appeared to be honored for five or six years.* And in 1967, the premier money-making Random House book in sociology, Ely Chinoy's *Society,* appeared in its second edition, to continue to prosper as both a superior text and a commercially successful book.

Editorial association with books of this calibre advanced my sociological education; and working with their authors often led to lasting friendships. This experience also deepened my appreciation of painstaking intellectual craftsmanship and reduced my tolerance of careless or pretentious writing. As an editor, I learned at firsthand that most sociologists are indeed the dismal writers so frequently portrayed, and at times I struggled mightily with their sloppy efforts. But these literary horrors were far outnumbered by textual works marked by both fine scholarship and expository skill. On this score, the honor roll was lengthy: Peter Blau, Ely Chinoy, Frederick Elkin, Wilbert Moore, Robert Nisbet, Gresham Sykes, Robin Williams, Robert Wilson, Charles Wright, Dennis Wrong—to name ten authors whose manuscripts were a joy to edit.

The consulting editorship carried other benefits, including, after the first few years, a substantial supplementary income.† There were of course the standard perks of expensive dinners and

---

* Bennett Cerf refers to a "very important specification in the contract, spelled out clearly, that we kept absolute control of our business and that RCA had no right at all to interfere with what we published" (*At Random,* p. 287). This contractually established "absolute" independence, in my own view, is inconsistent with "bottom-line" practices that emerged at Random House in the 1970s.

† The 2 percent override on books under my editorship, in the late 1960s and early '70s, paid royalties sometimes exceeding $20,000 annually—a bonanza for a college teacher. By 1980 my Random House royalties had dwindled to about a quarter of this sum.

three-martini luncheons (my limit was two), traveling expenses and New York hotels when visiting headquarters, and even occasional coverage of trips to sociology meetings. And for several years, until the introduction of loot-curtailing economies, I exploited a bookworm's treasure house: free copies of almost any volumes published under the firm's multiple imprints, Knopf, Pantheon, Vintage, the Modern Library, and Random House itself.

Thus a consultant's job with a major publisher paid generously—but there were problems as well. One of these was the seemingly impenetrable barrier between the college department and the trade divisions of the firm. This conventional organizational separation, reputedly to a greater degree at Random House than elsewhere, meant that nontext books brought out by "college," however promising their sales potential in the larger market, received little or no attention in "trade." In some cases this neglect was costly to authors, their consulting editors, and Random House itself—highlighted in sociology by Wilbert Moore's *The Conduct of the Corporation* (1963) and Lewis Killian's *The Impossible Revolution* (1968), both nontechnical, gracefully written, and lively books on social themes of general interest.* This barrier also meant that such well-known volumes in sociology as Digby Baltzell's *The Protestant Establishment* (1968) and G. William Domhoff's *The Higher Circles* (1970), edited and marketed in a trade division, were given short shrift in the college department.

Within the department a more serious situation was brought about by the rapid turnover of personnel in sociology (and in other fields). I worked on books with ten different house editors in the 1970s.† Almost all of these men and women were

---

* *The Conduct of the Corporation* was praised for both its analytical and literary excellence by the sociological journalist William H. White and the sociological economist Eli Ginzberg, among others; it received very little attention by trade editors notwithstanding prepublication assurances to the author. The widely praised *The Impossible Revolution,* a study of "Black Power and the American Dream," edited by Peter Rose, was altogether neglected by trade; it was not even included in a full-page spread in the *New York Times Book Review* of April 14, 1968, which advertised presumably *all* recent Random House books on black Americans and race relations (including the anomalous *Growing Up Absurd* by Paul Goodman!)—an extreme case of organizationally induced blindness.

† In the following order: Ted Caris, Arthur Strimling, David Bartlett (for a lengthy stint of over three years), Lynn Farber, Murray Curtin (editor-in-chief of the college department), Walter Kossman, Barry Fetterolf (executive

very good at their jobs, overly tolerant of my compulsions, and delightful colleagues. But their sudden shifts from the sociology list to other subjects or, worse, their abrupt departures from Random House itself were often disconcerting. While occupational mobility was (and is) a well-known feature of the publishing world, unanticipated changes of the guard in the college department lowered group morale and sometimes aroused the ire of consulting editors. The most shocking episode of personnel replacement was the "Christmas purge" of 1974 when without warning and within a few days of an elaborate seasonal celebration of the "splendid achievements" of the department's editors, seven of these achievers, including the highly able sociology editor, were fired. Following this wholesale shakeup, and after what both authors and consultants judged to have been a year's excellent performance, the new house editor in sociology was also sacked.

These dismissals were not only unhappy events for the individuals involved. They were also symptomatic of what struck some of us at Random House as the deterioration of the college department. In contrast with the earlier, relatively trouble-free regimes of Charles Lieber and Ted Caris, in the 1970s changing departmental leadership encouraged internecine strife, editorial desks sometimes seemed to become musical chairs, and Peter Rose and I, as the principal consulting editors in sociology, were consulted less and less. These developments, especially the shrinkage of the academic adviser's role, were closely linked with a disturbing trend: the growing domination of the marketability of books irrespective of their quality.

Books and Nonbooks in the Academic Marketplace

For almost twenty years the college department at Random House earned the reputation as a publisher of praiseworthy texts and other works. By the mid-seventies, however, intense competition in a postboom textbook market, the developments within the department noted above, and quite possibly growing pressure from the parental RCA, had brought about important changes in policy and practice. Books of intellectual and scholarly merit but only modest sales potential were very rarely published, while sure-fire money-makers, whatever their deficiencies on other grounds, in-

editor), Glen Cowley, Jane Cullen, and Philip Metcalf. At this writing (1981), Fetterolf and Cullen are still at Random House; most of the others departed long ago.

creasingly became the department's chief concern. As in other large textbook firms, the bottom line at Random House was defined in profit-making terms.

Publishers of textbooks of course are engaged in business enterprise and must earn profits to stay alive. This primary interest moreover does not preclude publication of first-rate books, a conjuncture that had been amply illustrated for many years at Random House and elsewhere. But the sales potential of a huge textbook market and competition among publishers to capture as large a slice of it as possible are powerful incentives to substitute mass appeal for quality. This long-standing situation in the production of texts for heavily elected courses, especially introductory sociology, once prompted the following observation, written in 1958 but even more relevant today:

> The thinness, sometimes approaching stark superficiality, of textbooks designed for the introductory course (with a few notable exceptions) is in part a consequence of the authors' understandable effort to "cover the field," an effort that requires wide stretching. But there are other factors at work here, including the propensity of many publishers and some sociologists to seek popularity with intellectually inferior wares in the manner of vendors of much of "popular culture"; the pressure exerted by publishers upon young sociologists to write "student-oriented"—which all too often means watered-down—textbooks . . . ; and the related fact that many introductory textbooks are written by relatively immature sociologists or by textbook specialists, whose efforts often appear to be based upon other textbooks (a circularity of feeble, if not vicious, intellectual consequences) and written according to market-tested formulae.*

These comments were made in the light of my examination of numerous texts as a teacher and potential consumer and, as an advisory editor, my familiarity with publishing practices. But it was also evident, as I have noted, that introductory texts can be excellent or even outstanding scholarly works. Such a book, however, is a rare accomplishment and clearly is not merely "a compendium of accepted information about a discipline"†—it re-

* "Sociology as a Teaching Enterprise," p. 583 n.
† Mary E. Curtis uses this phrasing to describe the "successful text in the social sciences" in "The Informational Basis of Social Science Publishing," *Society* 17, no. 1 (November-December 1979): 28.

quires scholarly breadth and intellectual craftsmanship. These virtues distinguish a previously cited volume published by Random House twenty years ago, the foreword of which includes my effort to identify the chief ingredients of outstanding textbooks. Departing once more from propriety, I quote myself at length:

A good general textbook, first, requires an informed and judicious *selection* from sociology's mounting and frequently disparate materials. Clearly, an author cannot "cover the field": he must choose, from a wide assortment, a particular battery of conceptual working tools, certain specific theories, and a limited amount of substantive information. At its worst, this selection is based on an evaluation of what is currently most marketable—the textbook joins the grand parade of "popular culture." At its best, the choice of concepts, theories, and findings reflects a wide knowledge of sociology's persistent problems, accomplishments, and limitations; dedication to its potentialities; and consistent use of a single theoretical orientation together with an appreciation of alternative approaches. In a good textbook things hang together, but the synthesis, like society itself, is partial. Effective selection thus demands informed, meticulous, and mature stocktaking.

Second, a good general textbook promotes the *dual* educational function of sociology. It must be of course an effective introduction to the discipline itself—bringing out clearly the distinctive nature and principal features of sociological analysis and demonstrating how this mode of analysis helps substantially to reveal the major contours of social structure and social change. If the book performs this function ably it will be as well a stimulating and informative instrument of general education. For all readers—including the large majority of students who do not continue in the field—the textbook, to be sure, should enhance objective understanding of a changing social world, but it should also help the individual to relate *himself* to that world, to evaluate it, to make choices. Like the superior teacher, an outstanding textbook can be a guide to both knowledge and wisdom.

These high goals cannot be gained in any large measure if the guidance is obscured by murky or prolix writing. Therefore, a third requirement for a good textbook is *lucidity*. I do not refer to a breezy "style" or to routine interpolation of gay anecdote, nor am I suggesting that textbook authors should seek to rival the master essayists—sociologists have other fish to fry. But painstaking formulation and clarity of exposition . . . are an important part of scholarly craftsmanship. In the case of the introductory textbook, these qualities should merge with precise and consistent employment of technical terminology, on the one hand, and, on the other, sensitivity to conventional use of language. Sociological writing is prose of one sort or another—it should not be a barrier to communication.

Finally, a good textbook should be written for a literate and presumably educated readership: it should show *respect* for both student and teacher. Every point need not be hammered home relentlessly, nor need every passing reference be explicated for the benefit of the uninformed. If a textbook is to avoid being a dull tome, if it is to spur curiosity, it must not attempt encyclopedic dimensions, and it must leave some room "between the lines." A general work should not become for the student something he "has had"; it should be both an introduction to and an invitation to revisit an exciting intellectual enterprise.*

These proposed requirements of a meritorious textbook call for a breadth of knowledge and bookmaking skills that seemingly few sociologists (or other academics) possess. They also call for devotion to undergraduate education, in short supply among many able scholars, and dedication to a mode of professional work that adds little luster to bibliographies. Yet there is no more demanding task of craftsmanship and broad scholarship than the creation of a first-rate introductory text. The paucity of such volumes is not surprising.

Nor is the plethora of introductions that have appeared in recent decades. A huge (but now-shrinking) academic market, the siren calls of competing publishers, especially those made to younger sociologists, and the hope of handsome royalties have produced a multitude of textbooks. And in keeping with the variformity of sociology itself, there are many types. These include, for example, eclectic compilations of sociological ideas and findings, which provide readers with no theoretical approach to follow or to reject; similarly open-ended reader-texts, partial products of scissors and paste; books featured by particular theoretical perspectives, whether structural-functional, conflict oriented, symbolic interactionist, or even evolutionary (as in Gerhard Lenski's unique *Human Societies*); Marxist or neo-Marxist volumes, which have

* Foreword to Chinoy, *Society,* pp. vii–viii.

entered the textbook sweepstakes in recent years; texts built upon a limited number of "strategic" concepts (notably *The Social Bond* by Robert Nisbet); "humanistic" introductions, present-day manifestations of an ancient sociological tradition; and at least one text that presents "three sociologies" between single covers (Howard Boughey's *The Insights of Sociology*). These types are overlapping and the list is not exhaustive, as a random sample of available introductions would reveal, but they suggest the textual smorgasbord that confronts undergraduate teachers. Unless teachers forego textbooks altogether (my own practice for several years), the problem of selection is hardly simple.

This problem is complicated by the asymmetric relationship between the quality of introductory textbooks and their popularity. It is not always the case, as some observers have claimed, that the less the intellectual and scholarly strength of the book the more widely it is used. But during the last twenty-five years or so the list of best-selling texts, with very few exceptions, has excluded the volumes receiving the highest marks from reviewers in sociological journals. The chief appeal of market leaders, it sometimes seems, lies with exposition pitched at a grade-school level, sprightly anecdotes in goodly number, wide displays of photographs and cartoons, multiple type fonts printed in multiple colors, breath-taking book covers, and, all along, superficial treatment of complex and difficult problems of sociological analysis. This is a caricatured impression, of course, but these extrascholarly features mark numerous textbooks tailored for the "student reader" who all too often is taken to be, by publishers and apparently by many teachers, a participant in elementary rather than higher education. Probably most students entering college today are indeed ill prepared, but their learning is poorly served by substitution of vividly decorated primers for solid textual literature.

In earlier years almost all general texts, whether the "high level" rarities or the more simplistic and much more numerous introductions, were written by academics, although most leading sociologists had long eschewed this challenging but "elementary" form of publication.* Sociologists, however, can now be "authors"

* Textbook authorship was once a much more reputable form of scholarship, suggested by the fact that of the twenty presidents of the American Sociological Society, between 1921 and 1940 fourteen wrote introductory texts, while only one or two did so between 1948 and 1957. More recently the ASA presidents, Arnold Rose and Alfred McClung Lee, have written introductions. See Page, "Sociology as a Teaching Enterprise," pp. 583–84 n.

of introductory textbooks without undertaking the time-consuming labor that they demand. Recently several publishers, including Random House, have instituted the "managed" or "packaged" text. This conception, in the words of an editor of major studies in the social sciences, is "one of the most profitable lines in book publishing today. More and more often, college texts are being commissioned to meet actual or perceived demands or they are house-written. That is to say, the publisher hires a staff of professional writers to assemble material while some well-known academic puts his or her name on the book. Sometimes the 'author' submits outlines or raw manuscript which the publisher then rewrites extensively."* The managed text is an expensive team production, requiring a large investment in market research, writing, design, and marketing itself, and thus is restricted to books constructed for introductory and other heavily elected courses. But these packaged volumes are multiplying—and are posing questions of scholarly and professional concern.

One question pertains to the role of market analysis in the construction of textbooks. Authors, often in consultation with editors, traditionally have been the sole arbiters concerning the perspective, coverage, organization, and substantive details of their books. Although this worthy practice continues today with respect to most texts, introductions to sociology (and other fields) increasingly are being shaped in part by market research—by publishers' interpretations of instructors' responses to questionnaires and similar "objective" data. This trend, which goes hand in hand with the packaging of texts, shifts the responsibility for their contents from nominal authors to market analysts, from scholarly judgment to opinion polling. Such textbooks join other commodities in a consumption-oriented marketplace.

A related question refers to the authorship of managed texts. Until the emergence of these collective products in recent years, the scholars whose names appeared on title pages (except in known instances of misrepresentation) were assumed to be the books' authors—still a safe assumption with respect to the great majority of scholarly publications. Managed texts, however, are written by specialists in exposition, guided by outlines or raw copy provided by academics, with a large assist from market analysts. The writer's manuscripts may be subject to final approval by the nominal authors, as in the case of the highly successful

---

* Charles E. Smith, "Defining the Economics of Publishing," *Society* 17, no. 1 (November–December 1979): 32–33. Smith is editor-in-chief of The Free Press.

Random House text by David Light and Suzanne Keller,* surely
an essential professional safeguard. But a serious question remains,
in my tradition-laden view, concerning the de facto authorship of
managed texts.

Of course, publishers of managed texts proclaim their alleged virtues. Their coverage of subject matter, determined in
part by market research, reflects the views of teachers in the field—
a new kind of populism in bookmaking. Their "levels of difficulty" are matched with the readers for whom they are designed,
ranging from the rank and file in community colleges to carefully
selected students in schools of higher standards—an educational
disservice, surely, to many able youth. Their pages are graced by
jargon-free and clear-cut English—carrying the implications that
technical terminology is dispensable in scholarly disciplines and
that academics, sociologists or others, lack the incentive, time, or
ability to write decent exposition. This widespread view, encouraged by the "management" of texts, is a canard, as indicated
earlier by the lengthy list of sociologists whose finely crafted books
fell within my editorial orbit.

Few such works, however, reached my desk after the early
seventies. My role as consulting editor in sociology was shrinking
rapidly, due in part to the changes sketched above. And in some
ways the job at Random House had become distasteful. I was
distressed by the evident trend toward unbridled commercialism
that prevented publication of excellent works unless they promised very large sales, by the departure of able house editors who
displayed too much concern for the quality of books, and by the
move into key positions of single-minded hucksters. In contrast
with earlier years, in the words of a noted writer, "the same kind
of hustlers who run television and movies . . . run publishing
houses, and BIG is the word, concoction is the technique, . . . a
book isn't written, it is cooked up—and there are a lot of phone
calls involved."†

My unrestrained and frequently voiced criticism of these
developments may have contributed to the withering away of my
editorial duties—in my last few years at Random House they consisted largely of revisions of books that I had edited earlier. When
even these assignments vanished in the spring of 1980, and with
little regret, I ended what had become a merely nominal, non-
working editorial position.

---

* *Sociology,* published under the Knopf imprint; 1975, rev. 1979.
† William Saroyan, *New York Times Book Review,* June 8, 1980, p. 36.

But whatever the problems of these final years, my long-term job at Random House, as I have recorded earlier, was a rewarding journey. At its end, moreover, I looked upon my record as a job well done. The authors of five of the hundred or more books I edited—Peter Blau, Mirra Komarovsky, Wilbert Moore, Arnold Rose, and Robin Williams—have been presidents of the American Sociological Association; and among other leading scholars who also commended my editorial efforts, to name a foursome with contrasting intellectual styles, are Suzanne Keller, Robert Nisbet, N. S. Timasheff, and Dennis Wrong. The authors of two fine books, Elizabeth Nottingham and Michael Olmsted, overwhelmed me with dedications—these notwithstanding my ruthless editorial work. And the dozens of generous acknowledgments may indicate that over the years I fulfilled something more than the normal obligations of a consulting editor. These commendations have made a sometimes frustrating, quasi-scholarly task a source of lasting pride.

The American Sociological Review

My first five years of work at Doubleday and Random House must have brought my name before the Council of the American Sociological Society as a possible editor of the *American Sociological Review*. For on other counts I had no visible credentials: my connections with scholarly journals were limited to the authorship of a few essays and a flock of book reviews. Even so, as a bold gamble, in 1957 the Council invited me to edit the *ASR* for a three-year term. With misgivings to be sure, I accepted this surprising invitation—thus taking on, with no decent preparation, an important professional assignment.

This new venture carried far weightier responsibilities than those of an adviser in a commercial firm. An important similarity between these editorial jobs was time-consuming labor with sloppy manuscripts, an exercise referred to below. As editor of the ASS's official journal, my contacts with sociologists of all breeds would be extensive, I would play a gate-keeping role in the profession, and this function surely would call for more tact and fortitude than I had evidenced heretofore. But these initial concerns quickly diminished soon after "my" *ASR* was underway in the fall of 1957.

The move of the *Review* to Smith College was a homecoming event, for Frank Hankins had been its first editor more than twenty years before. But the return to Smith raised problems. Use of an office was approved by President Benjamin Wright, although with misgivings—as a historian of political thought he saw little scholarly virtue in the new-fangled "behavioral sciences." The office, a room of no more than 300 square feet, served as headquarters for my faculty activities as well as the *ASR*. It housed a secretarial desk, a small table and a few shelves for the book review editor, a filing cabinet, some ancient kitchen chairs, and a child's desk for the editor himself. A greater handicap, or so I assumed at the outset, was the location of the journal at an undergraduate college that lacked the institutional facilities and ready supply of sociologists available at larger universities. On both counts, however, these anticipated difficulties proved to be of little consequence: the cramped quarters became a jolly center of magazine production and the Valley supplied a corps of able men and women who helped run the enterprise.

The local editorial staff began with a Smith College contingent of the sociologists Ely Chinoy, Neal DeNood, Allen Kassof, and Margaret Marsh, the anthropologist Alfred Harris and the demographer George Mair, plus Mary Goss who was then a non-affiliated resident of Amherst; later they were joined by the urban historian Eric Lampard of Smith and the sociologists Edwin Driver and Thomas Wilkinson of the nearby University of Massachusetts. These ten scholars included representatives of various subfields in sociology and of related disciplines as well as specialists on the Soviet Union (Kassof), Africa (Harris), India (Driver), and Japan (Wilkinson). Here was a highly valuable diversity of expertise. A great deal of the staff's work for the *ASR*, however, consisted of such unrewarding tasks as reading galley proofs, writing brief reviews of marginal publications, refereeing what appeared to be inferior papers, and, from time to time, attending staff meetings called by a demanding editor. These dreary chores were carried out efficiently and with few complaints. The nonglamorous work of these volunteers was essential for the welfare of the journal and, indeed, my own well-being.

But most of the day-to-day labor on the *Review* was done by the editorial secretary Betty Vogel, Michael Olmsted, and their nominal boss. Mike Olmsted was much more than a first-rate book review editor: he evaluated papers in his special fields with sagacity, he designed an attractive cover to replace what had long been the dismal front of the *ASR*, and, until the final days of his fatal illness in 1960, his warmth and wit brightened our lives.*

* Michael Olmsted's professional accomplishments and his stalwart character receive attention in chap. 4, pp. 132–34.

Our office companion was the journal's anchor woman and, like Mike Olmsted, a great deal more. Under my lucky star, I found Betty following several interviews with unimpressive candidates; qualified editorial secretaries were in short supply locally. Betty herself had had no such work experience, but her keen intelligence, adaptability to novel circumstances, and enormous energy soon gave her mastery of the job. If the *ASR* office was something of a sweatshop, moreover, it was also blessed with Betty's vivacity, infectious sense of humor, and tension-breaking sallies. Betty Vogel was deflator of any signs of self-importance and guardian of our morale.

In bringing out a scholarly journal, Betty, Mike, and I, with periodic help from the local editorial staff, were a busy threesome. Meeting bimonthly deadlines, regularly working on two or three future issues, and, by no means least, coping with a huge correspondence were something of a struggle. The *Review*'s budget, in contrast with the less skimpy budgets of later years, permitted no copy editors or other supernumeraries—in some respects we were on our own.* But we also had the full cooperation and strong support of two ASS keystones: the society's esteemed executive officer, Matilda White Riley, and Henry Quellmalz, the splendid and indomitable publisher of the *ASR* whose continuing friendship I prize.

Quite apart from budgetary considerations, much of my own work on the journal was self-inflicted, based upon the conviction, as I alleged, "that painstaking formulation should be an important part of scholarly craftsmanship."† Whatever its source, my compulsion to tidy up the prose of fellow sociologists led to lengthy stints with the blue pencil in hand. It also brought commendation from some authors and, to be sure, aroused the ire of others. But this extensive copy-editing was well intended: I sought to improve the readability of the *ASR*.

This was a minor aim, however. In the fifties, according to many of its critics, the *Review* was theoretically thin, overloaded

---

* I managed to wrangle part-time assistance for Betty Vogel during her final year as editorial secretary. Beginning in 1963—and consistent with a recommendation of my final "Report of the Editor . . . ," *American Sociological Review* 25, no. 6 (December 1960): 942—the *ASR* has received budgetary support for copy-editing and other editorial functions. In recent years, the *American Sociologist, Contemporary Sociology,* the *Social Psychology Quarterly* (formerly *Sociometry*), and the *Journal of Health and Social Behavior,* all ASA publications, enjoy similar editorial assistance.
† Ibid.

with small-scale research reports, and neglectful of important social and sociological issues—charges with which I agreed. Thus, as
the incoming editor in the fall of 1957, I hoped to expand the
journal's theoretical content, to widen its substantive scope, to
give more attention to controversial matters, and, in general, to
heighten its intellectual tone. To attain these goals in any perceptive measure, I believed, would require fuller exercise of editorial authority than seemingly had been the practice in recent
years. Accordingly, I was prepared to take such daring steps as
changing a long-established format, requesting articles by leading
scholars, and, when convinced of their faulty judgment, overriding recommendations of referees. Solicitation and independent
evaluation of submitted papers by the editor, if practiced extensively, would be contrary to operating policy and, indeed, in my
view, would justify powerful protest by members of the ASS. But
limited and judicious use of these unilateral procedures, I felt,
might help to revivify the society's official journal.

As it turned out, there were no more than two or three
cases of disagreement with the referees. Several solicited articles
were published, however, including pieces by Robert Bierstedt,
William Goode, Everett Hughes, the anthropologist A. L. Kroe-
ber, Robert Merton, Wilbert Moore, Talcott Parsons, and David
Riesman. These requested contributions may have prevented
publication of a few submitted papers, but they brought to the
readers of the *Review* leading voices of American sociology.*

Solicitation of papers by prominent sociologists, a very rare
practice in earlier years, helped to upgrade the *ASR* as a scholarly
journal—or so I was convinced. Another change was the introduction (in the issue of June 1958) of a division of the *Review* on
"The Profession" which included not merely the obituaries, the
dull but useful official reports of the ASS, and communications
pertaining to the sociological guild, but both solicited and submitted articles on the occupation itself.† This innovation was

---

* My effort to enlist the mighty and "deviant" voice of C. Wright Mills was
unsuccessful. Mills, author of *White Collar* (1951), *The Power Elite* (1956),
and *The Sociological Imagination* (1959), was perhaps the most influential
American sociologist of the times—more so, in my view, *among rank and file
sociologists, as well as nonsociologists,* than Talcott Parsons.

† Among these were two especially notable (and solicited) scholarly papers:
Talcott Parsons, "Some Problems Confronting Sociology as a Profession,"
American Sociological Review 24, no. 4 (August 1959); and William J. Goode,
"Encroachment, Charlatanism, and the Emerging Profession," *American Soci-
ological Review* 25, no. 6 (December 1960).

consistent with my own growing interest in the sociology of sociology; of far greater importance, it was made with a view to the likely establishment of a separate journal on the profession, a frequent proposal that was realized with the first issue of *The American Sociologist* in 1965.

There were other innovations: the introduction of "review articles" on presumably major works in sociology, the publication of numerous reviews of sociologically relevant books in adjacent fields, the longer length than in earlier years of a good many of the papers. These various editorial changes, tolerated by the Publication Committee and the Council of the ASS (A), required expansion of the journal—the *ASR* grew almost twofold during my three years as editor.* This growth also required the budgetary support made possible by the boom in academic sociology and the large increase of dues-paying members of the society. Here was another instance of the important role of luck in a professional career: my reputedly successful editorship had the strong support of history.

Fortune also favored me in the selection of associate editors, the *Review*'s principal referees. Among them, as a nostalgic blessing, were the City College alumni Alvin Gouldner, Peter Rossi, and Louis Schneider, together with such other fine scholars as Wendell Bell, Albert Cohen, George Homans, Mirra Komarovsky, Morris Janowitz, Philip Rieff, Melvin Seeman, Gresham Sykes, and J. Milton Yinger. Few inferior papers survived the evaluations of these sociologists. I had only two criticisms of two or three of the associate editors: what I viewed as their overindulgence of awkward or pretentious exposition (a carry-over from my editorial labors at Random House); and occasional delays in the return of papers, a standard complaint of both contributors to and editors of scholarly journals.

No editors, I would suppose, escape at least some difficult confrontations with irate authors of rejected or even accepted papers. I was fortunate on this score: today I recall only four cases that threatened editorial and psychological trauma—and none of these, as it turned out, had drastic consequences.

On one occasion, the author of a rejected piece strongly condemned a long-standing practice of the *ASR* (and of other journals). To my great surprise, Rudolf Heberle responded to my lengthy letter that included quotations from the reports of the

---

* Explanation and tabular presentation of several of these changes are presented in "Report of the Editor. . . ."

referees by vigorously protesting the fact that the authorship had been unknown. How could readers, he asked, properly judge a paper when unaware of the identity and the scholarly prestige of its writer? In a further letter I tried to defend the policy of "blind" evaluations, but presumably this distinguished political sociologist of European background was not convinced. Our correspondence ceased.

Another case of a rejected paper prompted no protest by its author, but by her husband. After reading my explanatory letter, he was moved to write a four-page condemnation of the referees' evaluations, their ignorance of the virtues of factor analysis (central in the research for the paper), and the decision-making incapacity of the editor. I was floored by this mighty blast from my former student, Alvin Gouldner. Yet I managed a reply that concluded with an "old teacher's" and dutch uncle's admonition of this brilliant—and hot-tempered—scholar. This hard-hitting exchange of more than twenty years ago, praise be, was a mere moment of discord in my long-time friendship with Al Gouldner.

A "loyalty" case of a different order involved the indignant reaction of a group of sociologists to a highly critical appraisal of a book written by Stanley H. Udy, then of Yale. Udy's volume, a comparative study of the "organization of work" in a large number of nonindustrial societies, was reviewed by the eminent anthropologist Edward R. Leach who, in a letter accompanying the review, suggested that his severe commentary might be withheld from publication and that he would understand such a decision. The suggestion was rejected. But soon after his review appeared,* I received a telephone call from Udy's departmental chairman, August B. Hollingshead, whose tirade included the startling news that he and fellow sociologists at Yale, after serious consideration, had decided against a visit to Northampton and a face-to-face confrontation with an editor so injudicious as to publish Leach's allegedly scurrilous attack; for that I was grateful. Later I was relieved, although not surprised, to learn from the judicious Stan Udy himself that at the time of the collegial conference he was unaware of this contemplated act of ill-considered loyalty.

Of the several instances of careless proofreading during my tenure, only one case haunts my memory. The victim of this slip

---

* E. R. Leach, review of *Organization of Work: A Comparative Analysis of Production Among Non-Industrial Peoples* (1959) by Stanley H. Udy, Jr., *American Sociological Review* 25, no. 1 (February 1960): 136–38.

was the distinguished scholar Howard Becker,* a man of both great learning and terrible temper. On the latter score, I had confronted Becker's wrath in earlier years, as a consulting editor at Doubleday when George Simpson's short study *Man in Society* was published, only to learn soon thereafter that Becker had given this title to a volume prepared for his undergraduate students. In a ferocious letter he threatened suit against the officers of Doubleday, the printer of Simpson's book, Simpson himself, and me—presumably unaware of the fact that titles are not subject to copyright law. I weathered the storm—and indeed enjoyed Howard's warm friendship in subsequent years. But when his "Culture Case Study and Greek History" appeared as the lead article in the October 1958 issue of the *Review,* I failed to catch a printer's error: the substitution of "Harold" for Howard on the cover page. About two hundred copies of the issue had been printed and mailed to subscribers—including Becker's copy—before the blunder was noticed and a telephone call stopped the press. In another call to the offended author, I apologized for my delinquency. In place of his fury, a fearsome prospect, Howard Becker responded with gentle amusement and gracious toleration of my editorial folly.

Episodes of this kind were hardly earthshaking, and in historical perspective they appear as trivial editorial events. Far more troublesome than such rarities were regularly occurring situations faced by the *ASR* staff. One of these was the all-too-frequent and prolonged procrastination of reviewers of books, a distressing matter for anxious authors and a vexing problem for editors.† (This long-standing problem was transferred to the editors of *Contemporary Sociology* in 1972.) Another, but quite different, difficulty was the bimonthly scramble to meet the *Review*'s publication schedule. The tiny team of Betty Vogel, Mike Olmsted, and I, sometimes with the aid of all-night sessions, somehow managed to put the *ASR* together for Henry Quellmalz's printers

---

* Not to be confused with Howard S. Becker, of current fame. Howard Becker of the University of Wisconsin (and formerly of Smith College) was president of the American Sociological Association in 1959–60 and died midway during his term of office.

† It should be recorded that in later years, in contrast with my punctuality as a frequent reviewer in the 1950s and '60s, I was guilty of procrastination on three or four occasions—thereby disconcerting editors of *Contemporary Sociology* and the *American Journal of Sociology.* Confession, of course, is no excuse for delinquency.

in Albany—with only a slight delay of one of the eighteen issues of the journal. These victories against the odds were occasions for both self-congratulation and indulgent celebration.

We struggled with other problems of journal production, of course, most of which have faded from memory. But I recall, with immodest pride, our successes—"our" because they were the product of a collective effort. As the editor, however, I received the kudos. These included a batch of congratulatory letters, preserved in my otherwise skimpy *ASR* file, from associate editors and other sociologists, including Clarence Schrag, J. Milton Yinger, and Bennett H. Berger. Supplementing these personal—and often hyperbolic—messages, came official commendation: "Be it resolved that the American Sociological Association expresses its sincere appreciation to Professor Charles H. Page for his distinguished and discriminating service as Editor of the Association's official journal, the *American Sociological Review,* during the period 1957–1960. . . ."*

An indication that my editorship met the approval of at least some members of the sociological "establishment" was a proposal by the ASA officialdom, conveyed by Secretary Donald Young, that I continue as editor for a second three-year term. This surprising—and, I believe, unprecedented—invitation was gratifying, of course, but was declined on various grounds. One was my forthcoming departure from Smith—I could hardly move the *Review* to Princeton where I was to assume the duties of the chair. Another was my incapacity to take it easy on an editorial job—my three years with the *ASR*, given my compulsions, had been enormously demanding. But they had also brought very large rewards.

In later years, and in some small measure, I kept my hand in the publishing ventures of the ASA. Following my ex-officio membership while editor of the *Review,* I served on the association's Committee on Publications in the early 1960s and, again, from 1972 to 1975. This period saw the proliferation of its journals (and of others in sociology, both regional and specialized) and the severance of large parts of the *ASR* with the introduction of *The American Sociologist* in 1965 and *Contemporary Sociology* in 1972. Today I see as a kind of historical irony the fact that both of these worthy periodicals—one primarily concerned with the profession, the other with reviews of books—give more and more

* From a resolution voted at the second New York Business Meeting of the association, August 31, 1960, and published in the December 1960 issue of the *ASR*.

space to theoretical and broad intellectual themes. It may be an ancient's egocentric observation to suggest that there would be less reason for this trend if in recent years these important themes had received greater emphasis in the *American Sociological Review.**

Five years after my editorship of the journal an episode occurred marked by both delayed irony and serious professional delinquency. In 1965, while I was summering in Vermont, President Thomas Mendenhall of Smith College telephoned about an urgent matter: he declared that I must remove at once the several boxes of *ASR* files that had been stored in Tyler Annex, a small colonial building that had housed the *Review*. (In 1961, both the ASA executive officer and the new editor of the *ASR* had declined to take over the files.) The space was needed, Mendenhall explained, for the production of *Who's Afraid of Virginia Woolf?* which was being filmed on Smith's hallowed grounds. I hastened to comply; without encountering Burton or Taylor (alas) and with the help of friendly grips, I managed to shift the heavy boxes from Tyler Annex to my car—but then I faced the problem of their disposition. As I drove northward toward Vermont, Ashfield's town dump, burning on that rainy day, suggested a solution. Thus the routine files of the twenty-third, twenty-fourth, and twenty-fifth volumes of the *ASR* met a fiery fate. The ironic aftermath of this heedless act did not emerge until 1971 when I became chairman of the association's Committee on Archives—notwithstanding my report of this disqualifying crime of desperation.†

The Academic Editor as a Marginal Man

One would suppose that a sociologist, after almost three decades on the job, would be able to enunciate general principles concerning the role of academic editor. I can do so, however, in only tiny measure, and then only by citing what must be obvious

* As this book went to press, the Council of the ASA announced the discontinuation of *The American Sociologist* and the "direction" to the Committee on Publications "to intensify its efforts to find ways of restructuring the . . . ASR so as to 'enlarge and diversify its scope'" (*Footnotes* 10, no. 3 [March 1982]).

† The seriousness of the crime was lessened only slightly by an earlier action: my removal from the files of several nonroutine documents, some of which were turned over to Talcott Parsons, then the chairman of the ASA Committee on Publications.

features of this marginal position. There is no more adequate single answer to the question, "What makes a good editor?" than to the all-too-frequent one, "What makes a good teacher?" Both roles are performed expertly by men and women of varying talents who use quite different methods. Even so, I'll risk some generalizations about the role and functions of the editor in academic dress.

One requirement of editorial competence is simply a keen appreciation of felicitous writing. This means that highly useful preparation for editorial work is reading, and reading widely. Probably most good editors are bookworms. For sociologists with (or without, surely) editorial aspirations, reading far beyond the literature of their field is a sine qua non, or should be, I believe. Contrary to a tiresome canard, among present-day sociologists are a good many first-rate writers—Peter Berger, Robert Bierstedt, George Homans, Robert Merton, Robert Nisbet, and Dennis Wrong, to name only a half-dozen, and these scholars are wide-ranging readers, as their erudite works attest. That some of them—including Merton, whose editorial prowess is noted below—are also superior academic editors is hardly surprising.

Unlike editors of fiction and poetry, academic editors, particularly in the social sciences, work with a single literary form, exposition. Some sociologists, as I have indicated, are skillful exponents of expository writing, and indeed the works of a gifted few—for example, Kai Erikson—are graced with literary artistry. But many, perhaps most, sociologists, like many or most scholars in other fields, pay far too little heed to the ancient canons of decent exposition: lucidity, simplicity, parsimony. An important editorial task, therefore, consists of alerting writers to their awkward, needlessly complex, and inflated or even pretentious formulations. In my experience, most authors of both books and journal articles have welcomed, or at least accepted, the changes suggested by my often-times over-active editorial pencil.

Others of course have looked upon these proposed changes as ill-conceived, damaging, or, as a contributor to the *ASR* once put it, "crimimal." Editors deeply concerned with the quality of exposition should expect such complaints, and should be prepared to face the wrath of offended authors. Probably most writers regard their prose as beyond severe editorial criticism—writing rarely comes easily and usually carries a large psychological investment. And some authors are prone to condemn editors who seek to modify what the former view as a unique, hard-won "style." But very few sociologists, as I have noted, are literary artists—or so aspire. A more frequent charge against editorial interference invokes the argument that preoccupation with expositional niceties is misplaced with respect to "scientific" writing. Rejection of this claim was axiomatic in my editorial efforts over the many years.

The foregoing comments on the writing of sociologists and the editing of their works apply to both articles of limited scope and full-scale books. Working with books, however, is a far more complex and challenging task—it is apt to involve problems of organization, stylistic strategy ("reading appeal" is a major, sometimes an overriding, concern of publishers), and substantive detail, as well as exposition. Prospective materials, sample chapters, and "final" manuscripts enable ambitious editors to spread their wings—which at times they do too widely. Thus, as a Random House editor, in addition to making extensive suggestions concerning format, contents, and formulation, I spent many, many hours rewriting parts of untidy manuscripts and composing proposed new paragraphs or pages. The time spent was also, I suspect, a kind of compensation for a sociologist of limited "production."

A few academic editors, as in well-known cases of successful general editors, indeed may be frustrated authors. But this is not a prevailing pattern: most editorships are held by able scholars. (In sociology, the field's foremost editor, surely, is none other than Robert Merton.)* Scholarship, however, is only one facet of this multisided job. The competent editor, as I have suggested, is adviser to both author and publisher, eagle-eyed critic of manuscripts, and at times a de facto collaborator. In some measure, he may even be, to use my wife's hyperbole, a "midwife."

However successfully these tasks are carried out, according to the conventions of the world of scholarship the academic editor is a marginal man. As in the exceptional case of Merton, he may also be a scholar of great distinction, but his editorial role and status are marginal in two respects. While his advice and criticism often benefit the work of authors (their recorded testimony on this score is extensive), these contributions, although frequently substantial, lie on the edge, not at the center, of the scholarly process itself. An editorship may bring high rewards—psychological, educational, professional, even financial—but very limited scholarly stature.†

---

* An excellent account of Merton's voluminous and spectacular editorial work is provided by David Caplovitz in his review of Merton's *festschrift* in *Contemporary Sociology* 6, no. 2 (March 1977): 144–49.

Occupationally, however, the academic editor holds a second kind of marginal position—one that is apt to enhance his professional, though not his scholarly, status. As a consulting editor, he stands between authors and publisher, much as a departmental chairman mediates between colleagues and administration. Or, as a journal editor, he stands between authors and vita-building publication. In both cases, this interstitial marginality gives the academic editor a gate-keeping role in his profession. Fulfilling this role without ever arousing the enmity of one's fellow academics must be a rare achievement—and one beyond my own experience.

Afterword: Obiter Dicta of a Battle-Scarred Editor

As noted above, fewer and fewer of my working hours have been taken up with editorial tasks, which by today have almost ceased. Looking backward on what for decades was a demanding and time-consuming activity may be advantaged by perspective. In any case, I am prompted to end the present chapter with some incidental comments about the prosaic efforts of sociologists.

One comment pertains to the frequently voiced charge that unclear writing betokens unclear thought. This unhappy relationship, I am convinced, obtains in many, possibly most, cases, and in sociology, as in other fields, illustrations are legion. But at least two criticisms of the charge, when made without qualification, are cogent. The implied obverse of the generalization surely doesn't hold: lucid writing need not indicate an unmuddied mind. Moreover, the misleading nature of the naked proposition is evidenced by important exceptions. In sociology, Max Weber and Talcott Parsons, for example, have produced tortuous exposition (in *some* of their work), but few would impute mediocre intellect to these eminent scholars. Graceless or execrable prose, clearly, is not monopolized by dullards.

Yet sociological writing as such is a popular target of critics who spread the myth that sociologists are a common breed of

---

† This comment refers primarily to contemporary American sociology. It may not hold for other fields, and clearly does not apply to European tradition, as the editorial careers of Durkheim and Max Weber illustrate. Note, however, as Caplovitz, ibid., points out, that *The Idea of Social Structure: Papers in Honor of Robert K. Merton,* ed. Lewis A. Coser (New York: Harcourt Brace Jovanovich, 1975) includes no reference to Merton's masterful editorial work.

literary delinquents. They are accused especially, and ad nauseam, of jargon-laden exposition that allegedly offends the sensibilities of educated readers. Many sociological publications, to be sure, are overburdened with the discipline's technical terminology. But every developed field, scientific or technological or humanistic, has its specialized vocabulary—an insider's language. The widespread condemnation of sociological jargon derives in large part from the fact that everyone has a working knowledge of social life and thus is something of a "sociologist"—there are no outsiders. Self-proclaimed insiders are suspect.* Here is a situation that calls for a more judicious use of jargon by sociologists than, say, by physicists or literary critics.

Sociologists, like representatives of other fields, differ greatly in their capacity for or concern with felicitous prose. More than a few, as I have stressed, are highly accomplished writers. But there are others who place heavy burdens on editors. Overuse of jargon, syntactical curiosities, neologistic abominations, and tiresome repetition of words or phrases (neglect of synonyms and antonyms suggests limited vocabularies) mark their manuscripts. More important are the contrasting sins of pretentious writing, on the one hand, and, on the other, especially in some market-oriented textbooks, a breezy "style" deriving from the dregs of popular culture.† That these malpractices, however, are more prevalent among sociologists than among other academics—say, psychologists—is problematic.

The preceding comments refer to questions of craftsmanship in communication, often a large editorial concern. There are other problems faced by editors, of course, including the writer's management of substantive and analytical matters. On this count, academic editors, in some small measure, become the scholarly colleagues of authors.

A quite different problem involves personal ties between editors and authors. It is frequently held that judicious editors avoid working with the manuscripts of close friends—the risk of damage to cherished relationships is far too great. The fact that I have rarely heeded this wise counsel, but with few unhappy

* This and related problems concerning the language of sociology are discussed in MacIver and Page, *Society,* pp. 3–5.
† These and other features of sociological writing are discussed in my unpublished paper, "Sociologists as Craftsmen in Communication," used by Ely Chinoy in his excellent essay on "Popular Culture," chap. 5 in *Sociology and Contemporary Education,* pp. 127–34.

consequences, is one more instance of the role of good fortune in my professional life. For over the years, I have edited numerous works written by men and women with whom I enjoy warm bonds. In only two cases, however, have my editorial criticisms seriously threatened long-established friendships. But all friendships are precious, and now, as my editorial journey approaches the end, I endorse the admonition.

Approaches the end because, as my Random House duties have faded away in recent years, editing nevertheless has consumed a good many of my working hours. Prompted perhaps by the questionable assumption that emeriti have little to do, a seemingly growing number of authors, both friends and strangers, have asked me to read and comment upon their manuscripts. I cannot resist most such requests, and they are apt to release my editorial compulsions. Among the sociologists whose books I have edited since my retirement from teaching in 1975, are my former departmental colleagues at the University of Massachusetts, Jack Hewitt, Paul Hollander, Christopher Hurn, and Mike Lewis, as well as my one-time student Howard Boughey—all authors of highly commendable volumes.

7

Santa Cruz and Massachusetts,

1965–1975

MY FIVE YEARS in the chair at Princeton had ended under less than glorious circumstances, which encouraged me to give up a faculty post that I had assumed to be my last. But much stronger than this push was the pull of Santa Cruz. In 1964 I had spent some time on the beautiful site of the campus-to-be as a consultant—with no expectation of joining this future university, a possibility suggested by Chancellor Dean McHenry. With further visits, however, the notion of heading a "school of my own" seduced me. Thus, on July 1, 1965, I became the founding provost of Adlai E. Stevenson College. This tenure was short-lived, but it was packed with educational excitement, personal victories and failures, hilarity and tragedy.

Thus, the Santa Cruz campus of the University of California was my provostial home for a brief period. During that time my role as a teaching sociologist received scant attention, but my occupational identity was retained—with a large assist from carry-overs from earlier years. With the approval of Chancellor Mc-Henry, I continued as consulting editor at Random House—but only by burning some midnight oil. And during my first year in California, 1965–66, I served as president of the Eastern Sociological Society, in absentia.* In that same year, in keeping with the

* When elected in the early spring of 1965, I had no inkling of my forth-coming departure from the East. My proffered resignation of the presidency, following acceptance of the Santa Cruz position later that spring, was rejected by the generous, but perhaps unwise, action of the executive committee of the ESS.

custom of bestowing "California" status on newcomers, I was elected representative of the Pacific Society to the Council of the ASA. To hold office in regional organizations separated by a continent may have been unprecedented, was certainly silly, and called for more time, energy, and flexibility than my job at Santa Cruz allowed.

Experimental Interim at Santa Cruz

Among many academics throughout the country, the guiding concept of the Santa Cruz experiment had powerful appeal. This was a vision of a school that would combine the presumed virtues of small liberal arts colleges (close relations between students and faculty, their joint participation in an educational "community," dedicated teaching) with the advantages of major universities (graduate study, research centers, scholarly output). Stevenson was to be the second of twenty or more colleges projected in the original plan for Santa Cruz.*

The faculty of each college, according to this utopian plan, would consist of a united group of Fellows who would also be members of campuswide "Boards of Study," in fact conventional departments undisguised by English title. And the undergraduate program of each college would emphasize, in some unspecified degree, certain disciplines or a cross-disciplinary theme, giving it a distinctive character. Thus Santa Cruz began (and continued for almost fifteen years) with two problem-making features: a two-hat role for its teaching personnel, and a built-in inconsistency between colleges of liberal arts and collegiate specialization.†

These two problems were faced by all colleges at Santa

---

* In later years this plan was all but abandoned. By 1980 only eight colleges had been built, the originally contemplated figure of a student population of 26,000 had been reduced to less than 10,000, and there were rumors of the forthcoming demise of the Santa Cruz campus.

† Both of these features became troublesome after the first few years. Identification of Fellows with their colleges weakened and faculty members often changed college affiliation. More important, and in keeping with the frequent complaint of educational reformers, the departmentalism of the boards of study increasingly dominated the Santa Cruz campus. By 1981 the multicollege system, as envisioned by Dean McHenry, had been drastically altered. Gerald Grant and David Riesman in *The Perpetual Dream: Reform and Experiment in the American College* (Chicago: University of Chicago Press, 1978), in chap. 8, comment on "The Cluster Colleges at Santa Cruz," but say very little about Stevenson College.

Cruz, but less at Stevenson than elsewhere. The original faculty, which at the outset was a diversified collection of strangers, soon developed a strong allegiance to Stevenson that persisted long beyond the early years; there were few departures for other colleges or other schools. And, although the social sciences were designated as Stevenson's forte, I gave close attention to the recruitment of first-rate scholar-teachers in all fields in an effort to build a rounded faculty of liberal arts. In contrast with my fellow provosts, Cowell College's Page Smith, who concentrated on the humanities and history, and Crown College's Kenneth Thimann, who gave first place to the natural sciences, my ambition for Stevenson was balance.

At the time, widespread interest in Santa Cruz, which was receiving nationwide publicity, greatly aided faculty recruitment. Another important attraction was the location of the campus on the California coast seventy miles from San Francisco. But to enlist a faculty of almost fifty members in a large variety of academic fields within a six-month period was no easy task. It was managed only with the help of my able assistant, the sociologist Dennis McElrath, and the support of Chancellor McHenry. McHenry approved my extensive travel that, along with voluminous correspondence and many hours on the telephone, produced almost a full faculty by January 1966.

In that month a mixed array of men and women traveled to Santa Cruz, met for three days in their first assembly as a collegial body, and hammered out an educational plan.* Their enthusiasm, the lively give and take, and the rich display of expertise at the conference gave promise that Stevenson would have a strong, creative faculty and that its provost would have as colleagues few academic milquetoasts. This turned out to be the case.

This preliminary conference also brought out the superior talents of the two individuals whose contributions to the college would be unsurpassed by those of any other Stevensonians. Sheila Hough, my newly acquired and comely administrative assistant, demonstrated from backstage the organizational sophistication, adaptability to almost any situation, and sympathetic understand-

---

* The Stevenson faculty, both senior and junior rank, was drawn from many schools, including Berkeley, Cornell, Harvard, Northwestern, Oxford, Pennsylvania, Pittsburgh, Princeton, University of California, Davis, UCLA, Wisconsin, Williams, and Yale. Its diversity was also increased, and its quality enhanced, by five women—four more than the first and "rival" Cowell College could boast.

ing of human foibles that soon made her Stevenson's beloved anchor woman. The political scientist Glenn Willson, Oxonian recently arrived from the University of Rhodesia, a master of administration, and a leading voice at the conference, became my unrivaled choice for deputy provost. In personal style, they were opposites: Sheila's Western informality, salty speech, and uninhibited demeanor stood in sharp contrast with Glenn's British decorum, impeccable rhetoric, and quiet dignity. Working closely together, however, these two were indefatigable colleagues, superb trouble-shooters, powerful guardians of the college's welfare, candid critics of an inexperienced boss, and protectors of his sanity. For several years, Sheila, who later became a counselor and teaching member of the faculty, and Glenn, who succeeded me as provost, together with an excellent group of Fellows, were largely responsible for whatever triumphs Stevenson enjoyed.*

But Stevenson's successes, like those of the other colleges, could not have been accomplished without the leadership of an extraordinary chancellor. At Santa Cruz, Dean McHenry fulfilled a goal that he had shared with Clark Kerr when both young men were graduate students at Stanford and later Berkeley—to build a multicollege campus within a major university. He came to this challenging job with good credentials: scholarly stature as a political scientist, a chair and a deanship at UCLA, and head of planning activities for California's multiversity as an assistant to President Kerr. McHenry was a virtuoso in its bureaucratic hierarchy. Of greater importance, I believe, were his personal strengths: enormous energy, impressive public presence, easygoing friendliness in face-to-face encounters, and especially, an iron determination to succeed. He was dedicated to the Santa Cruz plan and its educational ideals, he appointed as administrative officers some highly capable individuals and, not least, he raised substantial supplementary funds needed by the individual colleges. Physically powerful, bald-headed, of ramrod carriage, and neatly groomed, in local circles Dean earned the name of "Mr. Clean."

The chancellor was a vigorous advocate of experimentation in college education, an institutional area in which he scored im-

---

* Sheila Hough continues as a Fellow of Stevenson today (1981), as Santa Cruz suffers its decline. F. M. Glenn Willson, who during his final years was both provost of Stevenson and vice chancellor of Santa Cruz, became Principal of the University of London in 1975 and, a few years later, moved to Australia as administrative head of Murdoch University.

portant victories at Santa Cruz. He was less successful, however, in adjusting to the innovations that were taking place in the way of life of both students and faculty. In the face of the counter-cultural changes of the 1960s, he fought what was bound to be a losing battle in his attempted imposition of traditional parietal rules. And he seemed to be outraged by the fact that some members of the faculty, like many students, were caught up in the drug taking and the "sexual revolution" of the times. On strictly educational matters, Dean and I were apt to see eye to eye. But on other questions we sometimes clashed.

With California in the vanguard, a new life-style for a sizable segment of middle-class youths was rising when Stevenson College opened in 1966. Sex seemed to be newly discovered, the psychedelic age was underway, both "doing one's own thing" and communal living were proclaimed. These paradoxical goals, so ran a refrain, could not be realized without the riddance of "bourgeois," hypocritical morality. All established authority and all bureaucracies, moreover, were condemned as social evils. And folks over thirty could not be trusted. While many, perhaps most, students at Santa Cruz (and elsewhere) gave only faint voice to this youthful creed, it was sounded loudly by a highly visible minority. The latter's ranks included several of the brightest Stevensonians. At times these able youngsters posed a challenge for a middle-aged provost whose own unorthodox beliefs had been formed in the 1920s.

Yet, I seemed to manage with both the "turned on" and the more conventional of Stevenson's 750 students. All but one or two of them even went along with the provost's authoritarian regulation against bare feet in the college's finest building. "Fellows Dinners" were held in this stunning dining hall and theater, when we were served by others, tables carried cloths and flowers, and rules of attire were in effect. But the main purpose of these weekly departures from the prevailing informality at Santa Cruz was enrichment of our cultural life—with music, drama, or, most often, addresses by distinguished guests. During Stevenson's first year, these visitors included, among others, an impressive but incongruous trio: Eric Hoffer overwhelmed all of us with his spectacular erudition, Allen Ginsberg shocked some among us with his powerful reading of "Howl" and other poems, and Robert Nisbet enlightened us with his brilliant lecture on conservatism.

The initial year of Stevenson's full-scale operation (1966–67) was my final year as provost. It began with a near-tragedy on the eve of the school's opening when the irreplaceable Sheila

Hough and the philosopher-anthropologist Bob Scholte were badly hurt in an auto accident. Both were hospitalized for several months. And this hectic year was marked by what at the time seemed to be threatening crises. These were brought about by such unrelated events as a scary drug-related episode,* a temporary breakdown of a required college course, and, from time to time, heated disputes with Chancellor McHenry. But we survived. Moreover, during that year, as a collective achievement, Stevenson was launched as a successful enterprise in college education.

I had hoped to survive as titular head of Stevenson until 1970, the graduation year of "my" first freshman class. What I defined as compelling circumstances, however, led to my resignation at this early stage. The demands of the provostship, leaving little time or energy for personal and domestic affairs, were far greater than those of my previous jobs as teacher and sometimes chairman. A related consideration was the growing urge to return to the classroom where students are close at hand and psychological rewards are the highest in academic life. Finally, although our personal relationship was friendly, periodic quarrels with Dean McHenry concerning administrative policy strongly suggested that continuation as college head would be a rocky road. My decision to resign as Stevenson's provost was announced in early May 1967.

A folder in my files marked "Stevenson College—Personal" contains a batch of letters, written in that month, from members of the faculty, students, and other colleagues at Santa Cruz. Protocol precludes quotation from these dearly prized reminders of my short-lived tenure there. But eight years later, upon my retirement from teaching in 1975, the artistic talents of Stevenson's Fellows produced a ballad, beautifully enscrolled, which decorates my study and cheers my life. Distorted memories and shocking hyperbole notwithstanding, herewith their poetic account of my administrative fling:

Here's to California Charles
Out of the East came he,
Unto the kooky shore.

---

* This episode involved the newly elected governor, Ronald Reagan. In response to wide media publicity, Reagan journeyed from Sacramento and requested an explanation of my ejection of two police officers from a student-sponsored, closed meeting concerned with the medical and legal aspects of drugs. After an hour or more together, the explanation was accepted and, rather to my surprise, the governor and I parted without acrimony.

He stood amidst the alien redwoods
And builded him he a college.

Crafty, cunning, coy, and cagey,
Cranky, charming, cute, and canny.
Founder, Solon, Primal Father,
Lawgiver, Totem, clever Prince.

Scouring the country with eagle eye,
Drew he unto him forty odd fellows.
Buildings arose, eight hundred students materialized,
Adlai E. Stevenson College of the University of
        California, Santa Cruz, was born, A. D. 1966.

He provosted the preceptors and proctors,
Contained the Chancellor and sedated the Senate,
Foxed the faculty and startled the students,
Saw through College Nights and University Days.

Too soon, two years, he left us.
(His timing was rarely off.)
But well begun is half done,
Especially when it was such fun.

Puppet-Master, we salute you,
Your creatures and heirs in our cage.
There's history yet to be written,
But only from the first Page.

In the years following my departure from Santa Cruz I returned almost annually to the arena of these mighty deeds. In 1968 I was elected Honorary Fellow of Adlai E. Stevenson College, a distinction I share with the artist-photographer Ansel Adams, the college's fine architect, Joseph Esherick, and Stevenson's superb second provost, Glenn Willson. In 1970 I was privileged to give the commencement address, facing for the final time a student class that began its undergraduate career during my own brief tenure.* In the fall of 1980 and after a five-year absence, together with Leonora, I rejoined the Stevensonians once more for a splendid celebration in the scene of my "experimental interim" in California.

---

* Following the delivery at Santa Cruz on June 14, 1970, the paper on "Utopian Hopes for the Future" (by no means a conventional graduation exercise) received wide circulation in California and elsewhere; it is buried in the archives of both UCSC and the University of Massachusetts.

A Teacher's Return to the Classroom

Rather than an "experiment," I had assumed that Santa Cruz would be the last stop of a long academic journey. Leonora and I, like thousands of other adventuresome immigrants, would become transplanted easterners in the booming wonderland of California. As in the earlier "final" move to Princeton, however, a far different fate awaited us—we were to return to staid New England.

I had also assumed that my return to the classroom would take place as a member of the Santa Cruz faculty. This turned out to be the case for only a single academic quarter in the fall of 1967.* For shortly after the announcement of my resignation as provost, I received unforeseen invitations from universities in the West and East. In mid-May, visits to three eastern schools didn't tempt me to leave California or Santa Cruz. But upon return from this whirlwind trip, a telephone call from Amherst persuaded me to cross the continent a second time to confer with sociologists and officials at the University of Massachusetts. Following brief negotiation, I joined the Massachusetts faculty, the appointment beginning in 1968. Various considerations led to this decision.

The move to Massachusetts would mean that Leonora and I would return to our beloved Northampton, would rejoin old friends, and would be only a short distance from my ailing mother in Vermont. Professionally, the university itself had a strong appeal. As I had learned at Smith, "Mass" had long been viewed as little more than the "cow college" of its agricultural origins by many of the faculty and students in the nearby, ivy-clad schools. By the late 1960s, however, this distorted image clashed with the reality of a neighboring institution rapidly becoming a major university. Like other departments, sociology at Massachusetts was growing apace—a strong attraction. And my own role in this development, as it was projected, would be in keeping with my aspirations for this final tour in academic life.

After fourteen years in departmental chairs followed by a short but rugged stint as a college head, I wanted no part of

---

* During these final months at Santa Cruz, my duties were minimal—thanks to Stevenson's new provost, my former deputy Glenn Willson. I taught a single seminar and, in an unconventional reversal of roles, served as Glenn's acting deputy. In contrast with a work load of seventy or eighty hours a week of the previous two years, and as a wonderful restorative, I spent many hours at the shore and in the water—thus returning to Massachusetts in mid-winter with the tan of a California beach boy.

further administrative work. At Massachusetts, it was agreed not only that I would be protected on this score, but that I would not be asked to serve on extradepartmental committees. My primary responsibility would be teaching—in the area, moreover, of my principal curricular interest, social theory. At Smith and Princeton, and briefly at Santa Cruz, I had taught courses in this subject with some success. Although this was hardly a strong credential, my major assignment at Massachusetts would be graduate seminars in classical and contemporary theory. Such a proposed program, it seemed to me, was ideal.

As matters turned out, there were inevitable departures from this restricted schedule, some of them demanding. As a fairly well-known and experienced academic, I was appointed to ad hoc search committees from time to time, put in some grueling weeks as adviser to the board of trustees in its quest for a president of the multicampus university, and, with shaky knees, even gave the speech of welcome to the board's appointee, Robert Wood.* For six of my eight years on the faculty, I was also a member and sometimes chairman of the governing committee of the University of Massachusetts Press, thereby learning new lessons about the world of books while working with this small but excellent publisher. But these duties were incidental to my paramount concern.

This was teaching, as noted above. In what must be an unusual case of curricular stability, my initial classroom schedule persisted until my retirement in 1975. It included a graduate seminar in theory each semester, an undergraduate lecture course, again in theory, in the fall, and a springtime senior seminar in which the yearly change of subject encouraged the exploration of such fashionable topics as youth and social change, sex and changing sex roles, and the sociology of sport. This two-course "load" and the concentration in theory were a teacher's boon. Moreover, this lineup of courses, all of which carried firm prerequisites or the instructor's permission, also meant that most of my students, graduate and undergraduate, were in the upper intellectual echelons—greatly easing the job of instruction, especially in a public

---

* The persuasive power of Provost and (later) Chancellor Oswald Tippo led to these assignments. A distinguished botanist, Tippo had held important faculty and administrative posts at the University of Illinois, Yale, the University of Colorado, and New York University before returning to his alma mater in 1964. Until his resignation as chancellor in 1971 "Oz" Tippo was in a class by himself as a senior administrative officer at Massachusetts—where, alas, able administrators were in short supply.

school. I had further educational responsibilities, of course, largely in the graduate program. These are reported later in the chapter.

Here, in this account of my "return to the classroom" in 1968, the important role of Everett Lee, then departmental head, warrants attention. Lee's initiative triggered my move to Massachusetts and my first months there were warmed by his cordiality. His vigorous leadership and comradely disposition, however, went hand in hand with an appalling administrative laxity. This seemingly compulsive and what turned out to be self-destructive trait disfigured the appointment or near-appointment of several sociologists—including my own, as I discovered only recently. Even so, Everett Lee's accomplishments at Massachusetts were substantial.

An excellent demographer from the University of Pennsylvania, Lee had been brought to Massachusetts in 1966 as head of the department with the expectation that he would take the lead in its anticipated growth. He did so—but for a surprisingly brief time. During the two and a half years of his stewardship Lee's goal, as he enthusiastically expressed it, was to create a "Berkeley of the East." This worthy ambition surely was utopian, but among the sociologists whose recruitment got underway while he was in office were Hans Speier, Lewis Killian, Paul Hollander, and Michael Lewis. This foursome's diversified scholarly interests suggested that Lee planned, as he claimed, to build a multifaceted department. At the same time, in an unsuccessful effort to establish a major center of population studies at Massachusetts, he also overstacked the department with fellow demographers, already in good supply.* This miscalculation, however, played no part in Lee's departure from the chair.

That unexpected event was brought about by his disregard of institutional regulations concerning faculty appointments. Lee's determination to build a strong department of sociology, single-handedly if needs be, was coupled with a naive conception of administrative responsibility and a grave misreading of collegial norms. Disclosure of his derelictions led to his resignation as de-

* T. O. Wilkinson, Edwin Driver, David Yaukey, and Hilda Golden (part time) were established members of the department when Lee arrived in 1966. This supply of demographic talent, with Lee's own appointment, was more than doubled when he recruited Albert Chevan, Surinder Mehta, Gordon Sutton, and Thomas Burch (Burch, with Lee's letter of appointment in hand, unsupported by departmental action, was persuaded not to join this assembly of demographers).

partmental head in January 1969.* Lee's reluctant successor, Thomas O. Wilkinson, took up the far from finished business of bringing strength to sociology at Massachusetts.

Sociology and Sociologists in a Booming University

Unlike recollections of earlier times memories of my adventures at the University of Massachusetts are fresh in mind and thus unfiltered by perspective. A related limitation of this account stems from the fact that several of my recent colleagues are nearby friends and neighbors, imposing a restraint unleavened by time and distance. My continuing participation in local professional and social activities, as an emeritus professor, may also inhibit the following pages. Finally, in contrast with a good many alumni of City College and Princeton, only a few of my former students at Massachusetts have as yet reached full blossom as professionals. The paucity of success stories prevents any authorial claim of conferred prestige—an unabashed boast of former chapters.

A further caveat is very much in order. The sociology faculty and the departmental student enrollment were much larger at Massachusetts than at the schools where I had taught previously, a demographic fact that also handicaps this chapter. For in order to avoid a lengthy catalogue of personnel and professional achievement, I must exercise a painful selectivity which ignores or gives short shrift to several faculty and student colleagues. These include men and women who helped to make my final teaching job a professorial delight.

During the two decades following World War II the Massachusetts sociology department, headed by Henry Korson, had grown from a tiny group to about fifteen members. Between 1968 and 1974 this number more than doubled—in keeping with both the boom of the university and the continuing expansion of sociology in American schools. This was a busy and exciting period: courses multiplied, curricular innovations flourished, the graduate program was overhauled, more and more able graduate students enrolled, and the Social and Demographic Research Institute got underway. But it was also a period of growing pains.

* Lee's resignation was requested by the administration immediately following a report of the department's executive-personnel committee. His derelictions included by-passing this elected committee concerning the specific terms of faculty appointments, unauthorized granting of tenure to appointees, and withholding critical letters from candidates' files.

In contrast with the earlier, gradual growth of the department when the occasional arrival of new colleagues caused no alarm, the sudden invasion by a swarm of sociologists was bound to challenge established procedures, threaten vested interests, and arouse anxieties. In the three years following my own appointment in 1968, the invaders included, among others, the established scholars Hans Speier and Lewis Killian plus a flock of such younger, fast-rising sociologists as Robert Faulkner, Anthony Harris, John Hewitt, Paul Hollander, Christopher Hurn, Michael Lewis, Gerald Platt, Clark Roof, and Randall Stokes. Between 1972 and 1974 this assembly was joined by Nicholas Jay Demerath III, the statistician Robert Leik (to be succeeded by Andy Anderson in 1975), and in political and medical sociology, respectively, James Wright and Richard Tessler. The talents and achievements of all these scholars merit more attention than that given to only a few of them in the following pages.

In the early 1970s, then, a large-scale sociological enterprise replaced the modest undertaking of preceding years. Speedy growth, a crowd of new faces, and programmatic proposals by newcomers induced different reactions among the department's veterans. Henry Korson, under whose leadership sociology had originally developed at Massachusetts, had turned to full-time teaching, research, and writing; Henry took the new dispensation in easy stride. T. O. Wilkinson, at the university since 1953, a superb teacher held in affection by students and by old-timers and newer colleagues alike, held the chair from 1968 to 1972 and thus played an important role in the recruitment of the latter including Speier, Killian, and his successor Jay Demerath; although he professed reluctance to take on the job, T. O. handled it ably—and, I suspect, took pride in the ascent of his old departmental home.* In striking contrast, Edwin Driver, although he applauded the upgraded status of sociology, allegedly expressed concern about the "takeover" by such unprincipled power-seekers as Wilkinson, Killian, and Page—a view consistent with Ed's reputed, long-time alienation from most of his colleagues. John Manfredi, like Driver a member of the faculty since 1948, was quite a different case: a learned and witty eccentric whose publications (unlike Driver's substantial bibliography) were skimpy, John had taught sociological theory for many years and probably resented my own move

---

* Wilkinson's administrative skills were demonstrated on a larger scale in later years: in 1976 he became dean of the Faculty of Social and Behavioral Sciences, an office he continues to hold today (1982).

into the choicest courses in the subject,* and he was outspoken
in his condemnation of new arrivals engaged in what he viewed
as trivial but vita-building empirical research. A "veteran" since
only 1961, and as an author the most visible sociologist in the
group,† Milton Gordon may have been uneasy about possible in-
vasions of his established courses in theory, stratification, and
ethnic relations, but he endorsed wholeheartedly the rise of a
large and strong department—which was, and is, strengthened by
Milton's scholarship, wisdom, and collegiality.‡

A second contingent of sociologists joined the department
shortly before its mushrooming growth began in 1968. The demographer David Yaukey arrived in 1964, and a year later expansion increased with the appointment of Curt Tausky in the
sociology of industry and organization, Eugene Piedmont in medical sociology, and William Julius Wilson, a soon-to-be authority
on American blacks. Unlike their predecessors all of whom had
received doctorates from eastern universities (Columbia, Harvard,
Pennsylvania, Yale), these four newcomers, with degrees from
non-ivy schools, brought fresh perspectives and needed talents to
the department, and each has contributed substantially to its academic stature.

Tausky and Piedmont (as associate dean of the Graduate
School) have remained at Massachusetts; they are now old hands.
Bill Wilson, however, resigned from the university in the fall of
1971 to become professor of sociology at the University of Chicago.
Bill's departure was an enormous loss for the department and a
great gain for Chicago, but hardly unexpected. For Bill, although
a young man who had received the Ph.D. only a few years earlier

---

* Manfredi's resentment on this score reached me only second-hand; our personal relationship was and remains a cordial one.

† Milton M. Gordon's numerous publications include *Social Class in American Sociology* (Durham, N.C.: Duke University Press, 1958); the influential
volume *Assimilation in American Life* (New York: Oxford University Press,
1964); and *Human Nature, Class, and Ethnicity* (New York: Oxford University Press, 1978). Gordon was president of the Eastern Sociological Society in
1978–79.

‡ In addition to these five sociologists, "veterans" included Hilda Golden and
John O'Rourke. An able demographer-urbanist and a friendly colleague,
Hilda was a part-time lecturer for several years before her tenured appointment in 1974; she reacted to the expansion of the department with aplomb.
John, social psychologist and specialist in small groups, was a member of the
faculty from 1962 until his death in 1974; what often appeared to be his dis-
content with the department apparently was unrelated to its sudden growth.

(1966), was and is an excellent scholar with powerful credentials in race relations, social stratification, and the logic of inquiry, and an outstanding teacher.* He was also a tough opponent on the golf course, a fine fisherman, and a boon companion. During our three overlapping years at Massachusetts, Bill was a good friend; he remains so today.

My other close friends in the department included four of my former students, surely a teacher's blessing. Milton Gordon, whose scholarly and professional deeds are cited above, had been at Columbia during my brief time there in 1942. Paul Hollander from Harvard, Mike Lewis from Illinois, and Jack Hewitt from Oberlin College and later York University, all with doctorates from Princeton, came to Massachusetts within two years of my arrival in 1968.† From then until, and following, my retirement from teaching in 1975, strong ties with these one-time students, and with Hans Speier, Lewis Killian, and Randall Stokes, have enriched my life.

Following five years of research and teaching at Harvard, Paul Hollander moved to Massachusetts in 1968. Since then his record as a creative scholar has been matched by few sociologists at the university. Paul's first major work, *Soviet and American Society,* was a prolonged undertaking (two drafts of which survived my editorial efforts). This widely acclaimed, comparative analysis of social and cultural institutions includes tours de force on Soviet propaganda and American advertising, the treatment of death in the two societies, and the functions of physical beauty and publicity in the determination of social status—hardly conventional sociological themes.‡ With strong credentials in politi-

---

* Within a few years after his appointment, Wilson became chairman of the Department of Sociology and the Lucy Flower Professor of Urban Sociology at the University of Chicago. His publications include the comparative study *Power, Racism, and Privilege* (New York: Macmillan, 1973) and the influential and controversial volume *The Declining Significance of Race: Blacks and Changing American Institutions* (Chicago: University of Chicago Press, 1978).

† Another former student, Peter Rossi, a graduate of City College, as noted in chap. 3, joined the Massachusetts faculty in 1974, a year before my retirement; Rossi's important role in " 'Producing' Doctors of Philosophy" receives comment below.

‡ *Soviet and American Society: A Comparison* (New York: Oxford University Press, 1973) was republished in soft cover by the University of Chicago Press in 1978. It had been preceded by Hollander's *American and Soviet Society:*

cal sociology, Russian studies, and the sociology of literature, Paul is a broad-gauged scholar who brings both learning and imagination to his endeavors. These qualities, together with a propensity for hard-hitting polemics, mark his most recent volume, *Political Pilgrims: Travels of Western Intellectuals to the Soviet Union, China, and Cuba.** This controversial study of ideological "migrations" has gotten far wider attention than books by sociologists generally receive. Paul Hollander is a fine sociologist, perceptive social critic, and an intellectual of stature.

Mike Lewis came to Massachusetts in 1969 following five years at Illinois. Whereas scholarly research and writing dominate Hollander's professional undertakings, Mike is both an outstanding teacher and an activist in academic affairs. He has been, for example, a leading spokesman of unorthodox views in departmental deliberations, chairman of its personnel committee, director of the graduate program in sociology, and at times an outspoken critic of the university's administration. These activities, however, have not prevented the growth of Mike's bibliography, highlighted by the volumes *Urban America* (1973) and *The Culture of Inequality* (1978). Social criticism and pessimism strongly color the latter work, in which the analysis focuses upon the traditional "individualization of success and failure" in American life, a "sensibility" shared by the successful and unsuccessful alike; numerous illustrations of this theme are drawn from the author's field investigations in Illinois. *The Culture of Inequality* is a controversial book—reactions have ranged from high praise (for example, by Studs Terkel, who rarely endorses works in sociology) to severe criticism. But it shows Mike Lewis as an able and unconventional sociologist, a concerned member of his society, and a vigorous defender of humanistic values.

A year after Mike's arrival, Jack Hewitt, the third sociologist with a Princeton pedigree, joined the swelling ranks at Massachusetts. Jack had been a successful teacher at Oberlin and York, and he had also become a devotee of symbolic interactionism, at the time an unrepresented perspective in our multisided department. Jack's undergraduate and graduate courses in this subject enriched the curriculum, his publications mounted, and his scholarly and expository talents were effectively exploited in

A Reader in Comparative Sociology and Perception (Englewood Cliffs, N.J.: Prentice-Hall, 1969).

* New York: Oxford University Press, 1981. This work was undertaken with the support of Hollander's Guggenheim Fellowship in 1974–75.

producing *Self and Society: A Symbolic Interactionist Social Psychology.** This excellent volume (which I was privileged to edit) not only elucidates the goals, concepts, and propositions of symbolic interactionism superbly, but clearly brings out important interconnections between the construction of social reality by individuals and both social structure and collective behavior.†

Jack brings to his various professional activities large supplies of energy, efficiency, common sense, and social sensitivity—and much more decorum than often found in collegial circles. Appreciation of these qualities supported his election to the departmental chairmanship in 1977. This was also the year of his promotion to the full professorship: like his fellow Princetonians Paul Hollander (in 1974) and Mike Lewis (in 1976), Jack Hewitt's attainments as a scholar-teacher had propelled him into senior academic rank.

Lewis Killian had gained national stature long before his move to Massachusetts in 1969; he was the first of a half-dozen senior professors to be appointed during the department's great expansion.‡ With a Chicago Ph.D., he had taught at Oklahoma and then for sixteen years at Florida State University. While serving in the chair for a single year (1968–69) on the strife-ridden campus of the University of Connecticut, he was invited to join the growing ranks at Massachusetts. Killian's decision to do so was a victory for the department, the university, and the Valley community.

Killian's earlier works include *Collective Behavior* (with Ralph H. Turner, 1957), an outstanding, widely used text on crowds, publics, and social movements; *Racial Crisis in America* (with Charles H. Grigg, 1963); and *The Impossible Revolution* (1968), a prescient analysis of "black power and the American dream." At Massachusetts his scholarly output continued: *White Southerners,* an insider's historical and sociological portrait of an important but neglected ethnic group, was published in 1970; a

---

* Boston: Allyn and Bacon, 1976; a revised edition of *Self and Society* was published in 1979.

† Of course, other sociologists have dealt with these interconnections, but generally with limited success. An earlier major effort, made use of by Hewitt, is the too frequently neglected volume, Hans Gerth and C. Wright Mills, *Character and Social Structure* (New York: Harcourt, Brace, 1953).

‡ The others, in order of appointment, were Hans Speier, Jay Demerath, Robert Leik, Alice Rossi, and Peter Rossi. Accomplishments of Speier, Demerath, and the Rossis at Massachusetts are heralded below.

revised edition of *Collective Behavior* appeared in 1972; and three years later *The Impossible Revolution* was updated with the addition of "Phase 2." These publications give extensive evidence of his talents as sociologist and social psychologist, and they illustrate his belief (which I share) that good sociology requires careful attention to historical context. They also suggest, but do not bring out fully, his broad learning, critical acumen, and a rare candor about his profession and himself.

Killian's pronounced Southern accent, rugged physique, and military bearing (he is a retired colonel in the army reserves) can be misleading. For these outward traits go along with his cosmopolitanism, distinguished scholarly achievement, exemplary citizenship, and opposition to provincialisms, regional or academic, and to social discrimination in all its forms. Lewis Killian is also a highly valued colleague and, for the more fortunate among us, a cherished friend.

My close friends on the Massachusetts sociology faculty include Randall Stokes who joined the department in 1970. In terms of conventional criteria, Randy's credentials in several areas are impressive. His foremost field of specialization is social change and "development," buttressed by extensive field research in southern Africa. He is a keen student of classical and contemporary social theory, on the one hand, and, on the other, his expertise in empirical and quantitative research is amply demonstrated in his scholarly work. And as an essayist sensitive to the phenomenological side of sociology, he has made important contributions to symbolic interactionism.* This diversity pays large dividends in Randy's popular graduate and undergraduate courses and has enriched his recently completed introductory textbook scheduled for publication in 1982.

These accomplishments highlight the curriculum vita of an unusual academic man who is also blessed with nonacademic talents. Randy is a fine musician who, as a skilled craftsman, re-

---

* Stokes's theoretical sophistication is illustrated in "Afrikan Calvinism and Economic Action: The Weberian Thesis in South Africa," *American Journal of Sociology* 81 (July 1975): 62–81; his quantitative skills are on display in "The African Industrial Entrepreneur and African Nationalism," *Economic Development and Cultural Change* 22 (July 1974): 557–79, and in the unpublished volume *The White South African* (with Edward Feit); and his work in symbolic interactionism includes the evocative essays (in collaboration with John P. Hewitt) "Disclaimers," *American Sociological Review* 40 (February 1975): 1–11, and "Aligning Actions," *ASR* 41 (October 1976): 838–49.

stores stringed instruments. He shines in racquet sports and on the baseball field. And, to speak of my own favorite outdoor recreation, he is the best fisherman I know.

Each of these personal friends substantially aided the development of sociology at Massachusetts in the 1970s. However, the major contributor to this growth, and especially its direction, was Jay Demerath who became chairman of the department in 1972. Although Jay and I had corresponded in earlier years, we had met only once, at a conference on sport in Madison. A year or two later, on leave from the University of Wisconsin, he became executive officer of the American Sociological Association, an office he held when he was named as one of several "outside" candidates for the post at Massachusetts. Receiving the endorsement of a dean's search committee, Jay's appointment was supported by departmental vote, but not without a minority of dissidents—some members decried what they saw as his over-ambition and his breezy verbal style. Thus Jay began and indeed continued his five-year tenure in the chair with something less than full support.

Within a few months after taking office, Jay was also criticized for "loading the department with Demerath people," an accusation sometimes heard in faculty and graduate student circles. The flimsy basis of this charge was the fact that the highly promising youngsters Jim Wright and Rick Tessler, both appointed as assistant professors in 1973,* were Wisconsin Ph.D.'s. Like all appointees, Jim and Rick had been "on trial" by presenting papers at Massachusetts and, of course, had been approved by an elected personnel committee. Except for Sonia Wright who became a part-time lecturer, during Jay's chairmanship the only additional sociologists to join the department were Alice Rossi, Peter Rossi, and Andy Anderson—all fine scholars, but hardly protégés of Demerath.

The professional qualifications of the "Demerath" appointees, however, were in keeping with Jay's aspirations for the department. During two visits to the university when his own candidacy was under consideration, he had spelled out his programmatic objectives: a large increase of empirical studies; the development of collaborative research by faculty and graduate students—he saw too many "lone-wolf scholars" in the depart-

---

* These proved to be excellent choices: Wright moved through the ranks rapidly, becoming a full professor in 1979; in the same year Tessler received tenure as an associate professor.

ment; and an emphasis on evaluation research, heretofore largely neglected by sociologists at Massachusetts. Although some members of the department questioned one or more of these goals, their successful attainment in a very few years was a triumph of Jay's chairmanship.

But this notable achievement was clouded by Jay's proclivities. Generally a friendly fellow who wore his office without pretension, in personal relationships with some of his colleagues he became a hard-boiled "realist" in a way that lent credence to the charge of cold bloodedness. His polished public manner and his name-dropping (a widespread practice in academia, as elsewhere) were sometimes seen as signs of ruthless ambition. And his weakness for questionable quips, manifest in both speech and writing, was viewed by some of us as a wiseacre's folly. However, these were minor matters. For Jay was a hard-working and efficient chairman, a strong guardian of the department's welfare, an able negotiator with the university administration, and, on a different level and in tandem with the warm and gracious Judy Demerath, a genial and generous host.*

Some members of the department probably would question this assessment. My own relations with Jay have long been marked by both cordiality and mutual respect—perhaps encouraged by my status as a senior untouchable. But we disagreed strongly about "main-line" sociology and desiderata for the Ph.D.

"Producing" Doctors of Philosophy

Throughout my tenure at Massachusetts I was heavily involved in the "production" of Ph.D.'s in sociology. As early as 1968 I drafted a plan that incorporated certain features of Princeton's graduate program: the elimination of stipulated or a specific number of courses; the introduction of new "special fields" from which students would elect two for examination; and the upgrading of the comprehensive examination, written and oral, which would include theory and methods as well as the special fields. Although objections were voiced concerning the proposal with respect to courses, the plan was adopted by the faculty with minor modifications. The program emphasized student independence and initiative, on the one hand, and, on the other, demanding

* Recognition of his leadership abilities was signaled in the spring of 1981 when Demerath, after four years out of office, resumed the chair with departmental support.

examination and dissertation requirements. Doctoral candidates sometimes complained, but most of them survived.

The program itself lasted little more than a year beyond Jay Demerath's arrival in 1972. Unlike the ongoing, Princeton-oriented enterprise with its permissive and eclectic features, Jay's proposals for "reform," based largely on the Wisconsin model, stressed schooling in research methods, apprenticeship and collaborative publication, and examination in what he saw as the two major areas in the discipline. To overstate the contrast, here was a clash between a conception of appropriate study for doctors of *philosophy* and the training of *professionals* in conventional sociology. Following hot dispute in the graduate studies committee (of which I was a member) and subsequently in the assembled faculty, the existent program was overturned in favor of Jay's plan—a victory, as he put it, for the department's "Young Turks." The plan—including comprehensives in "social organization" and "social psychology," a bewildering bifurcation of the sociological domain—had a limited existence: it was scrapped in 1976.

Reshaping graduate programs is a continuing exercise in all academic fields, but occurs with conspicuous frequency in sociology. This instability is brought about by shifts in faculty personnel, new leadership, graduate student demands, and by the changing fashions of a fickle discipline. All of these causal circumstances were present at Massachusetts. Thus the short-lived Demerath plan was succeeded by another that replaced "comprehensives" with heavy course requirements in theory and methods and, as a foretaste of the student's professional career, certification in one special field with a review essay and in a second field with a presentation at a departmental colloquium. And after only four years of this unique and seemingly successful scheme, study of the doctoral program was underway in 1980 with a view to further alterations.

But these organizational changes, although the subject of extended departmental debate, played a secondary role in the development of a strong graduate program at Massachusetts in the 1970s. This achievement was primarily the product of an expanded faculty of able sociologists who attracted a large number of excellent students—students who would have coped successfully with almost any programmatic formalities. During my final eight years in the classroom, I was privileged to teach, and to be taught by, these talented men and women.

In my seminars in sociological theory, I came to know all but a very few of the doctoral candidates, most of whom also had to face my questions and comments in the comprehensive examinations. As a member of some two dozen dissertation committees (the majority of which I chaired), I had a hand in the authors' scholarly efforts. As an adviser with editorial compulsions, I may have managed to improve some awkward exposition. And in a different role as a guest and sometimes host at student parties, I saw something of the social life of a much younger generation. These professional and extracurricular activities not only taught me a good deal about graduate student culture, but gave birth to a number of enduring friendships.*

My heavy involvement in the graduate program also made me keenly aware of an organizational and atmospheric characteristic of universities in the minor leagues. In contrast with such prestigious schools as Columbia and Princeton, where long-established self-assurance supports regulatory flexibility, preoccupation with bureaucratic procedures and formal requirements was manifest at Massachusetts. Departures from the "highest standards" were to be avoided at all costs. On this score anxieties were rife. Thus in the office of Graduate Studies assistant deans and their secretaries gave countless hours to the dreary task of making sure that the numerous and often silly regulations concerning the format and timing of doctoral dissertations had been followed to a T. In this office and in other administrative headquarters, there seemed to be relatively little interest in the *quality* of dissertations.

Within departments, of course, this was not the case. Nevertheless, the *type* of dissertation elected by most graduate students in sociology was influenced, I believe, by the fact that we were a department "on the make." Without the confidence engendered by the lofty status of, say, Harvard or Chicago, many on the faculty saw safety lying in the sociological mainstream. Students were encouraged, sometimes in the name of doing "real science," to undertake empirical investigations of modest scale, to analyze "data" rather than confront broad theoretical issues, and to avoid his-

---

* In addition to Richard Martin, Beate Riesterer, Alan Sica, Alan Ingham, and Richard Gruneau, some of whose exploits are recorded below, former graduate students with whom I maintain warm ties include Margaret Andersen, Michael Chernoff, Douglas Cooney, Yoon Mok Choe, Jan DeAmicis, Tom Dickey, Jeannette Gunner, H. Roy Kaplan, Rita Kirshstein, Wasyl Matveychuk, Steven Nock, Boris Popov, Mary Ellen Reilly, Daphne Spain (Nock), Eve Spangler, and Nancy Theberge. That the talents and achievements of these men and women are unrecorded may be a serious shortcoming of the present chapter.

torical, phenomenological, or essayistic studies. (This emphasis, although not because of departmental insecurity, became especially powerful following the arrival of Peter Rossi, a development reported below.)

Yet such studies were carried out, several with which I was closely associated. The dissertations of Richard Martin, Beate Reisterer, and Alan Sica, written under my direction, are illustrative:

Richard Martin's "Time and the Texture of Social Thought" (1976) is about as far from mainstream sociology as any department would tolerate. This unique study, in the author's words, "explores some of the implications of a philosophical investigation of time and temporality for sociological thought in terms of the relation between intellectual endeavor and social order." It also incorporates a sophisticated critique of scientism, "fascination for the numerical," and rationalism in the Western world. The study puts on exhibition—in graceful prose, a rare accomplishment in a doctoral dissertation—wide learning, analytical skill, and a creative bent. The unconventional nature of this work is consistent with Martin's professional nonconformity. Since 1977 and continuing today in a marginal academic role, Dick is the editor of a university press.

Beate Riesterer's "The Sociology of Freedom, A Study of Alfred Weber's Sociology of Universal History" (1980) could have been written only by a student with unusual qualifications. Beate had grown up in Germany and was thus bilingual, had studied at Heidelberg with Max Weber's brother, and was at home in the German philosophical tradition. This background prompted my suggestion that she undertake a dissertation on the sociology of this prolific author, which had received little attention in this country.* The study, which required research in Germany and consumed a good deal of Beate Riesterer's time for several years, is not only a meticulous exegesis of Weber's major sociological

---

* Although Alfred Weber's analysis of culture and civilization had informed works by Robert MacIver and Robert Merton, among others, only two selections of his voluminous writings had been translated and published in English: "Social Process, Civilizational Process, and Culture Movement," a mimeographed report of the Works Progress Administration and the Department of Social Science (sic), Columbia University, 1939; and Theory of Location of Industries (Chicago: University of Chicago Press, 1951). The Encyclopaedia of the Social Sciences (1930) has no article on Alfred Weber; one of the few articles in English is Edgar Salin's in the International Encyclopedia of the Social Sciences (1968).

ideas, but it also brings out important linkages between theoretical perspective, historical circumstances, and biography. This dissertation, clearly, is the work of a mature and able scholar.

Although written by a student almost twenty years younger than Beate, Alan Sica's dissertation is also an impressive piece of scholarship. "The Problem of Irrationality and Meaning in the Work of Max Weber" (1978) incorporates a study of the status of irrationality in classical social thought and modern philosophy, a detailed hermeneutic on much of Weber's work, a critique of Weber's treatment of irrationality and meaning, and an assessment of the latter's impact on theories of social action. Two volumes are emerging from this 670-page opus, one on the titular theme and a second, a revision of a long appendix, a work on hermeneutics. It is hardly surprising that the author of such a dissertation (as a member of the faculty of the University of Kansas) is a rising star in theoretical and historical sociology.

The primary concern with theoretical and philosophical problems of Alan Sica, Richard Martin, and Beate Riesterer, as suggested above, was atypical of the sociological interests of graduate students at Massachusetts. As at other universities, certification in theory was a requirement for all doctoral candidates, but most of them concentrated on one or two of sociology's numerous subfields and wrote dissertations on less ambitious subjects than "irrationality and meaning" in Max Weber, "time and the texture of social thought," and Alfred Weber's "sociology of universal history." The long-standing—and understandable—choice of relatively small-scale empirical projects became almost unanimous following the arrival of Peter Rossi in 1974. On at least one important count, Rossi's appointment (together with Alice Rossi's) placed Massachusetts somewhat closer to the major leagues of American sociology.

The capture of Pete Rossi from Johns Hopkins* was a victory for Jay Demerath whose primary goal as chairman, as noted earlier, was the large expansion of empirical, collaborative, and evaluation research. This was Pete's forte, evidenced by his imposing research accomplishments, mighty bibliography, and administrative record. As the new director of the Social and Demographic Research Institute (SADRI), Pete brought substantial research funds from Johns Hopkins. During the next few years

---

* Alice Rossi came from nearby Goucher College, where she had become one of the foremost scholars in women's studies and a powerful voice in her profession.

these grew enormously—grants for large-scale studies of disasters, natural hazards, recidivism, and weapons and violent crime ("hand-gun" research), plus smaller projects, reached almost $2 million by 1980. This bonanza in a heretofore underprivileged department has had various effects on sociology at Massachusetts.

In keeping with a nationwide trend—and, indeed, with a pragmatic tradition in American sociology—evaluational studies, of which there had been few in earlier years, rapidly became the dominant mode of research in the department. Pursued by a contingent of the faculty working with graduate students, joint publications mounted, decorating the vitae of beginners as well as those of established sociologists. A growing number of doctoral candidates received financial support from funded projects, bringing relief to a skimpy and shrinking university budget. And it is not surprising that more and more students, including highly talented young men and women, have followed the action in SADRI—where both income and "hard data" for empirical studies have been available. In recent years, only a tiny few have undertaken theoretical or "essayistic" dissertations. Several members of the faculty view this as a welcome change.

These developments were spearheaded by Pete Rossi, who soon became a powerful and highly influential figure in the department. SADRI, a modest and weakly financed enterprise in its initial years (1972–1974), under Pete's leadership became a thriving research center, a training ground in quantitative methodology, and an important source of income for graduate students. A coterie of younger, very able scholar-teachers—notably Jim Wright, Sonia Wright, Andy Anderson, and Rob Faulkner—became closely associated with SADRI and its director. And Pete himself—eminent sociologist, strong supporter of talented youth, workaholic, and caustic critic of lazier and allegedly soft-headed colleagues—became president-elect of the American Sociological Association in 1978,* as did Alice in 1981.

---

* Robert Faulkner's portrait, "Rossi: A Robin Hooding Heavyweight at the Helm" (*Footnotes*, August 1979, pp. 2ff.) includes a laudatory depiction of Pete's scholarly and professional talents, an account of his distinguished career, and a perceptive portrayal of his personal traits. Faulkner's extended use of the "heavyweight-lightweight" metaphor has been the subject of sharp criticism (because of its invidious implication) and considerable amusement. This unusually lengthy and informative portrait of an ASA president also strongly suggests Faulkner's unqualified admiration of "heavies." (In boxing this class includes both Joe Louis and numerous stumblebums.)

Pete and Alice Rossi had moved to Massachusetts in 1974, a year before my retirement from the department. I had little opportunity, therefore, to observe directly either the events depicted above or Alice's important contributions to both departmental and interdisciplinary studies. Nor did I, during this single year or later, take advantage of the presence of these two distinguished sociologists whose scholarship and leadership in their profession I had long admired. My neglect was a delinquency I continue to regret.

But I have not neglected one of my obligations in the "production" of doctors of philosophy. Upon retirement I was serving on twelve dissertation committees (none of them a SADRI project, to be sure), eight of which I chaired. This privileged assignment lasted until the fall of 1981. This is one of the ways that has made my emeritus years something less than a prolonged vacation. Another has been the continuation of my marginal role in the study of the world of sport.

Sociology and the World of Sport

My keen interest in sport goes back to high-school and college years when I competed in swimming and boxing. It was not until after World War II, however, that I became convinced that the sociological investigation of sport could be an important and exciting scholarly endeavor—a view strongly encouraged in my earliest contacts with David Riesman. Thus, in 1951 I applied to the Guggenheim Foundation for support to write a book on "Sport and American Life," which was rejected. Three years later Philip Rieff and I made rather elaborate plans to collaborate on a volume on the same theme; these plans were revived in 1963. Alas, none of these contemplated projects was realized.

Nevertheless, in the 1950s and '60s I enjoyed a minor role in the elevation of sport from an allegedly peripheral or trivial field to an important area for sociological study. From time to time I reviewed books on sport for journals in sociology, I became an active participant in national and international conferences on sport, and I presented what may have been the first paper on the subject at a meeting of the American Sociological Association.*

---

* "On the Sociology of Sport as a Research Field" (Boston, Mass., 1968). An extensively revised version of this paper appears in Gerald S. Kenyon, ed., *Sociology of Sport* (Chicago: The Athletic Institute, 1969).

In less than genteel academic circles, those activities earned me the unwarranted title, "Dean of American Jockologists."*

At Massachusetts the sociology of sport had a higher place on my agenda than it had had in former years. This came about through a combination of circumstances, the most important of which was my close relationship with John Loy. When he arrived at the university in 1969 at the age of thirty-one, John had already published extensively on sport and was soon to become America's best known sociologist in the field. With a joint appointment in physical education and sociology, he helped to establish the interdisciplinary Department of Sport Studies where, as both nurturing mentor and prolific scholar, he was the mainstay until he departed in 1977.† During our years as colleagues John and I organized and ran a conference on sport at Massachusetts (in 1970), shared a number of first-rate graduate students, served together on dissertation committees, read one another's manuscripts, and became firm friends.

Thanks largely to John Loy, Massachusetts emerged as an important center of the study of sport in the 1970s. In addition to the graduate students who earned M.A. and Ph.D. degrees in Sport Studies, several doctoral candidates in the Department of Sociology wrote dissertations in the field.‡ Rob Faulkner joined the department in 1971, bringing to the enterprise in the sociology of sport (and other fields) expertise in organizational and qualitative analysis. And publications by Massachusetts authors, especially those by Loy and his student collaborators, appeared with frequency. The most visible contribution of my own efforts on this score was an essay on "The World of Sport and Its Study."

* "Unwarranted" because this accolade belongs to the late Gregory P. Stone, author of the first influential publications on sport in American sociology. See esp. "American Sports—Play and Display," *Chicago Review* 9 (Fall 1955): 83–100.

† In that year Loy moved to the University of Waterloo; and in 1979 he became director of graduate studies in the Department of Physical Education at the University of Illinois.

‡ An outstanding sociological work, written in the Department of Sport Studies, is Susan J. Birrell's "Sporting Encounters: An Examination of the Work of Erving Goffman and Its Application to Sport" (University of Massachusetts, 1978). Dissertations on sport in the Department of Sociology include Erik K. M. Kjeldsen's "An Investigation of the Leadership Process in Organizationally Embedded Task Groups" (1976), Nancy Theberge's "An Occupational Analysis of Women's Professional Golf" (1977), and the studies acclaimed below by Alan Ingham and Richard Gruneau.

This piece was published as the first forty pages of the anthology, *Sport and Society,* a work originally planned by John Talamini. Following a meeting to discuss Talamini's proposal for such a volume, it was agreed that I would be its junior editor, write a general introduction as well as introductions to later sections, and seek an appropriate publisher. After a rather uneasy collaboration, the book came out in 1973.* *Sport and Society,* although it was well received by sportswriters throughout the country, got a friendly column in *Sports Illustrated,* and an enthusiastic endorsement by the veteran sage John Kieran,† had little success in trade. But as a textbook in college courses it was widely used for several years.

In the 1970s the study of sport, after a slow start in the preceding decade, became an academic industry. Most of its participants were physical educators or—to use the graceless term of an upgraded profession—kinesiologists. But a contingent of card-carrying sociologists also entered the field—the late Donald Ball, Harry Edwards, Rudolph Haerle, Janet Lever, Walter Schafer, Stanton Wheeler, plus a growing number of younger men and women. College courses and scholarly publications multiplied. The latter include studies in social history, works on present-day sport viewed as a major institution, and analyses of such diverse sports as baseball, boxing, cock fighting, hockey, horse racing, and soccer. In addition to sociologists, there have been historians, economists, anthropologists, philosophers, psychologists, and at least one psychiatrist (Arnold Beisser) who have contributed to the mounting literature. Impressive books by Michael Novak (*The Joy of Sports,* 1976), Allen Guttmann (*From Ritual to Record,* 1978), Jean-Marie Brohm (*Sport: A Prison of Measured Time,* 1978), and Christopher Lasch (*The Culture of Narcissism,* 1980) present contrasting and controversial theoretical interpretations of modern sport.‡ On a far lower intellectual level, several scissors-and-paste

* John T. Talamini and Charles H. Page, eds., *Sport and Society: An Anthology* (Boston and Toronto: Little, Brown, 1973).
† Kieran, clearly in a generous mood, wrote the following blurb for the dust jacket: "I would rate *Sport and Society: An Anthology* . . . the best survey of the function of sports in a civilized society that I have ever seen, and the editors have backed it up with the best collection of sports literature that I ever had the pleasure of reading."
‡ The volumes by Novak, Guttmann, and Brohm are ably analyzed and appraised by Richard Gruneau in "Freedom and Constraint: The Paradoxes of Play, Games, and Sport," *Journal of Sport History* 7, no. 3 (Winter 1980).

"readers" and three or four textbooks have been published in recent years.

Two further kinds of publications on sport gained the attention of sociologists and kinesiologists in the 1970s. A spate of muckraking books by Dave Meggysey, Johnny Sample, Curt Flood, and other well-known athletes exposed the authoritarianism, racism, sexism, brutality, and drug use in professional sport. These reports by participant observers gave some strength to a radical critique of modern sport, highlighted in the writings of Jack Scott, Paul Hoch, and Meggysey.* In Hoch's *Rip Off the Big Game* (1972) sport is portrayed as the product of a class-dominated society—exploitative, corrupt, playless, and the successor of religion as the opiate of the masses. This pseudo-Marxist tract was cited frequently in the publications of sport sociologists and was required reading in many college courses for several years. But Hoch's simplistic analysis seemed to have little impact on those students who were later to become leaders in the field.

Two of these students pursued the Ph.D. (and a good deal more) at Massachusetts. Alan Ingham and Richard Gruneau were dynamic and controversial figures in the department, both ran into difficulties in their graduate studies, and both spent far too many years writing dissertations. But Alan and Rick also possessed a rare combination of talents and interests. Both were superb all-round athletes, excellent teachers, and able young scholars who shared a penchant for Marxist, Weberian, and critical social theory. And while still in their twenties both were marked for success as specialists in sport studies and as sociologists.

Like many, perhaps most, sociologists of sport, Alan Ingham's interest in the field had its roots in his own athletic endeavors. As a young Englishman Alan was a star in football (soccer), track, and swimming. These agonistic accomplishments took place during his extensive training in physical education and undergraduate study at the University of Leeds. After moving to the United States in 1968, he earned a master's degree at Wash-

* Jack Scott's *The Athletic Revolution* (New York: The Free Press, 1971) is largely concerned with athletic programs in schools and colleges and the student movement of the 1960s; Scott wrote numerous articles for newspapers and magazines, studied and taught at Berkeley, directed athletics at Oberlin College for a brief period, and was widely viewed as the foremost radical sociologist in the field of sport. Dave Meggysey's *Out of Their League* (Berkeley, Calif.: Ramparts Press, 1971) combines muckraking with radical ideology.

ington State University, and the following year arrived at Massachusetts to continue graduate work in physical education. Soon thereafter Alan became a doctoral candidate in sociology.

During his three years in the department (1970–1973), Alan made effective use of his several talents in meeting a crowded agenda. Keenly intelligent, spectacularly articulate, a dynamo of energy, he breezed through courses and conquered the comprehensive examinations. He conducted research in experimental social psychology. He demonstrated pedagogical skill as a teaching assistant and later as an associate. His achievements on one count surpassed those of any of his fellow students: as a co-author, he completed six or seven scholarly papers all of which were published in books or journals. And, in weekly breaks from this heavy academic schedule, he coached at Amherst College and played soccer as a semipro.

Most sport sociologists, as in Alan's case, are former athletes, physical educators, and oftentimes coaches. But very few with this background have gained a reputation for high-level, innovative scholarship. Alan has done so (John Loy is also a notable exception). Alan's dozen or more published pieces and at least as many papers presented at national and international conferences have already gained him wide recognition as a foremost sociologist in the field of sport, and this output continues. His most ambitious work, however, is a less well known doctoral dissertation, a theoretically sophisticated and historically informed analysis of the impact on sport of the rise of industrial capitalism.* This impressive study required five years to complete, due in large part to Alan's responsibilities at the University of Washington, where he has taught since 1974, and his numerous writing projects.

His publications are sometimes overloaded with esoteric terminology that is apt to put off readers, and his lucid and often vivid exposition is not a model of parsimony. But these are trivial delinquencies. For as a man of learning and intellectual power Alan Ingham is a rarity among sociologists of sport. And so is his contemporary Rick Gruneau.

Although also an outstanding competitor in a variety of sports, Rick's earlier schooling, unlike Alan Ingham's submer-

---

* "American Sport in Transition: The Maturation of Industrial Capitalism and Its Impact Upon Sport" (University of Massachusetts, 1978). The theoretical orientation of this 350-page study is primarily Weberian, modified by Marxist conceptions, critical theory, and the work of Anthony Giddens.

gence in physical education, was centered in the liberal arts. He had studied sociology at the Universities of Guelph (B.A., honors) and Calgary (M.A.) and had had considerable experience in survey research before coming to Massachusetts in 1971 financed by a Canadian National Fellowship. With these credentials, Rick was viewed as an excellent prospect for the Ph.D. During two years of residence, however, his frequent off-campus journeys and a shaky performance in the comprehensive examinations hid from all but a few of us his scholarly potential.* In contrast with Ingham's impressive output while still a student, Rick's first important paper was written only after he returned to Canada in 1973.

"Sport, Social Differentiation, and Social Inequality" is one of three noteworthy essays in a volume edited by Donald Ball and John Loy.† This widely praised paper points up Rick's flair for theoretical analysis, his effective use of historical and empirical data, and his craftsmanship as a writer. It also initiated a continuing flow of meritorious publications. Most of these are marked by Rick's abiding concerns with theoretical issues, social stratification, and historiography—his mentors ranging from Marx, Weber, and Veblen to such contemporaries as Tom Bottomore, Anthony Giddens, Stephen Lukes, Frank Parkin, John Rex, and E. P. Thompson. His affinity for these British notables is due in part to his Canadian nationality, but has a stronger root in his admiration of radically inclined, theoretically sophisticated, historically informed scholars who write with skill and unpretentiousness.

The works of such authors are not the usual fare of specialists in the sociology of sport. But this is only one of Rick's preoccupations at Queen's University, his academic home since 1974. Held in high regard by both students and colleagues, he also teaches courses in social theory and social inequality, mainstays in the sociology department's curriculum. And, until its completion in 1980, he gave *some* attention to his doctoral dissertation.

As the director of this seemingly endless project, I pled

---

* "I'm afraid that I did more snow and water skiing than Sociology during my stay at U. of Mass." (letter to the author, February 16, 1981).
† *Sport and Social Order* (Reading, Mass.: Addison and Wesley, 1975), chap. 4. The two other outstanding essays also are contributions by Massachusetts sociologists: "Occupational Subcultures in the Work World of Sport" by Alan Ingham, chap. 8; and "Coming of Age in Organizations . . . Career Contingencies of Musicians and Hockey Players" by Robert Faulkner, chap. 11.

with Rick from time to time to wind it up, but with little result. He gave priority to other writing, changed the direction of the dissertation periodically, and, in keeping with an albeit fading British tradition, he appeared to disvalue the Ph.D. However, the long delay paid dividends for Rick Gruneau. For this study in social theory, social class, and the history of Canadian sport is the finest work to date of a youngster who is already an accomplished sociologist.*

The highest reward during my own lengthy flirtation with the sociology of sport has been and continues to be my close association with Rick Gruneau, Alan Ingham, and John Loy. In 1975–76 I spent the fall term with John as a visiting professor in the Department of Sport Studies, and since then the four of us have remained crosscontinental colleagues. Our common interests include the world of sport, to be sure, but a good deal more. In addition to being leaders in this field, Rick, Alan, and John are excellent general sociologists, warm companions, and scholar-teachers who indeed are also intellectuals.

A Notable Event: Intellectuals Descend on Massachusetts

Most sociologists are academics and many are highly competent scholars, but relatively few are men and women of intellectual stature. On this score, the sociologists at Massachusetts were no exception. In the early 1970s, however, our ranks included Hans Speier. As Hans approached retirement at the university we faced the problem of an appropriate celebration to honor an admired and beloved colleague held in high international esteem as scholar, policy-shaper, and full-fledged intellectual. Six of us as a self-appointed committee,† after considerable discussion agreed that a certain kind of conference might do the trick—if Hans himself concurred. His agreement (given with some hesitation by a modest man) launched an unusual interruption of the educational routines at Massachusetts.

The conference was planned with two considerations: first, its theme should be consistent with Hans Speier's major interests

---

* "Class, Sports, and Social Development: A Study in Social Theory and Sociological History" (University of Massachusetts, 1981), with minor revision, will be published as a book in the near future.

† The members of the original committee were Tony Harris, Paul Hollander, Lewis Killian, Mike Lewis, Randy Stokes, and me; later we were joined by Jay Demerath and the political scientists Peter Fliess and Gunther Lewy.

and achievements during his professional career; and second, it should be an event that would be rewarding for the university and for Hans himself. This was an ambitious undertaking, especially for a tiny group of academics with neither funds nor official sanction. But these handicaps did not deter us. A design for a conference on intellectuals emerged, as proposed by Tony Harris and developed by Mike Lewis, the committee's chairman. Mike, Tony, Randy Stokes, and Lewis Killian took on the most burdensome organizational jobs and far outworked the rest of us. My own contributions were hardly taxing, but one was crucial: my personal plea to President Robert Wood for financial backing produced $10,000. Wood's strong endorsement also guaranteed an important place for the conference on the university's official calendar.

Thus a conference on "Intellectuals, Knowledge, and the Public Arena" took place in early May 1973. This two-day meeting brought to Massachusetts some twenty notables who decorated the formal program and more than a hundred invited guests who witnessed a display of diverse talents, as well as some fireworks. In the first and most orderly session on "intellectuals and public policy" excellent papers by Reinhard Bendix, Harry McPherson, and James Q. Wilson were appraised by Arthur Schlesinger and Rita James Simon. The second session on "intellectuals and popular culture," focusing upon the gains and losses of celebrity status, was an explosive affair featured by what many of us viewed as a ruthless attack on Norman Podhoretz by Lewis Coser and by Podhoretz's own free-wheeling "paper," but saved from disaster by judicious and indeed eloquent commentaries by Daniel Aaron and Robert Nisbet. A centerpiece of the final session on "intellectuals and the academic public" was to have been a paper by Edward Shils who, alas, missed the conference. But our disappointment was lessened by a lengthy and learned presentation by Walter Metzger and the cogent observations of Daniel Bell, Tom Burns, and David Truman. The three sessions were expertly chaired, respectively, by Adam Yarmolinsky (the single exception to our rule against participants from the University of Massachusetts) and by Hans Speier's former Rand colleagues and longtime friends Herbert Goldhammer and Joseph Goldsen.

Apart from the formal program, unscheduled events spiced the conference. Especially in the evening hours when stimulants were close at hand, there were extensive and at times heated exchanges between conferees. These were prompted, if not guaranteed, by ideological and political differences; on this count, Bell,

Coser, Podhoretz, and Schlesinger, for example, are hardly bed-fellows. There was the active role played by Israel Shenker who covered the conference for the *New York Times*—as a busy gad-fly, he seemed to be everywhere at once. And at a splendid al-fresco dinner hosted by Jay and Judy Demerath, there appeared in the nearby woods a great white owl. Whether Minerva was hailing the wisdom or decrying its lack in this gathering of intel-lectuals posed an unanswered question.

The final meeting of the conference was Hans Speier's "response to the sessions," in the printed program's misleading words. Wisely avoiding comment on several lengthy papers and the ensuing discussions, Hans gave a brilliant address, in part autobiographical, on triumphs and agonies in the lives of intel-lectuals. Having no control over the uses made of their work, both personal heartache and historical irony may result from its ex-ploitation.* Hans's moving portrayal of this sometimes tragic process, a neglected theme in the earlier sessions, was a truly grand finale of a notable event at Massachusetts.

1975: A Year to Remember

When in 1968 the possibility of Hans Speier's move to Massachusetts became known, appropriate inducements included both a joint appointment and a named chair (a rarity at the uni-versity). Accordingly, in the following year and with the strong support of two departments, Hans became the Robert M. MacIver Professor of Sociology and Political Science. Upon Hans's retire-ment in 1973, my inheritance of this chair (but in sociology only) was an honor far beyond expectation and one I cherished—the chair carried the name of my famous mentor. The year of my own retirement, 1975, brought further unforeseen rewards.

In April I received the Merit Award from the Eastern Sociological Society. I had been a member of the society since 1933, had served on some committees, and had once functioned as

---

* As a historically important example, Speier cited Maurice Joly's *Dialogues in Hell,* a prophetic political essay written as an attack on the dictatorship of Napoleon III. Ideas that Joly condemned were preserved, perverted, and ultimately made a part of the repulsive anti-Semitic forgery, the *Protocols of the Elders of Zion.* This case was expounded later in Speier's essay, "The Truth in Hell: Maurice Joly on Modern Despotism," *Polity* 10, no. 1 (Fall 1977): 18–32, reprinted in Harold D. Lasswell, Daniel Lerner, and Hans Speier, eds., *Propaganda and Communication in World History,* vol. 3 (Hono-lulu: University Press of Hawaii, 1980).

a president in absentia—a rather feeble record for such a tribute. With no hesitation, however, and with delight I accepted the award. In response to Franklin Edwards's gracious presentation, I spoke about three distinctive merits of the ESS itself. Long before the organizational support of minorities by the ASA and before the rise of women's liberation, we had elected to our highest office E. Franklin Frazier, Gladys Bryson, Jessie Bernard, Ira Reid, and Mirra Komarovsky. Unlike several other regional societies, we had not added to the proliferation of sociological publications with an "Eastern" journal. And, in contrast with the national society, we had retained our long-standing and respectable acronym—we were not the ESA. What for me was both a happy and a lighthearted occasion was also, I assumed, a swan song for a veteran teaching sociologist.

But shortly thereafter this assumption was shattered. On the morning of my final day of teaching, May 15, what was planned as a professor's farewell message to his graduate students was halted by a startling invasion of the seminar. Shepherded by Mike Lewis, several dozen men and women from different stages of my journey in the academic world formed a grand parade around the room. It was led by Joan Bel Geddes from my entrance into teaching at Birch Wathen School, followed by former students and colleagues from City College, Smith, and Princeton. Even my early years at Random House were represented by Charles Lieber. I was overwhelmed. And all the more so when Mike announced the schedule for the day: after a post-parade informal gathering, I was to "relax at home in the afternoon" (how?, I wondered) so as to be ready for the "big event" to follow. Happily bewildered, I had become Mr. Chips.

Staging this event must have been a Herculean task, which was engineered and largely carried out by Ely Chinoy and Mike Lewis in collaboration with Leonora.* Somehow they managed this feat behind my back. This called for tight security during extensive preparations: writing letters, organizing a program, housing out-of-towners, securing facilities for what promised to be a sizable affair. These mighty efforts produced a gathering of some three hundred men and women who on May 15 arrived for cocktails on the beautiful grounds of the Lord Jeffrey Inn in Amherst. Only one person there knew all the others—a dazed but enraptured guest of honor.

* Ely Chinoy's death (reported in chap. 4) occurred on April 21, only a few weeks before the date set for the event. Thus Mike and his fellow planners proceeded with preparations for a celebration under tragic circumstances.

At dinner in the inn's crowded banquet hall Mike Lewis took over as an expert—and Hudibrastic—master of ceremonies. A series of speakers went to the rostrum, each of whom was familiar with the retiree's deeds and misdeeds during a period of his career. Joan Bel Geddes led off with an uproarious, inflated account of my salad days at Birch Wathen. In a more sober mood, Joe Goldsen spoke movingly of our time together at City College. Allen Kassof focused upon sometimes outrageous extracurricular activities at Smith, and Peter Rose, upon both the Smith years and my editorial propensities. From the Princeton period, Marvin Bressler brought down the house with a brilliant but hyperbolic depiction of my professorial and collegial proclivities, and Bob Cook, from a former student's viewpoint, expressed his affection for a one-time teacher. Finally, a contingent from Massachusetts— the graduate students Michael Chernoff, Dick Martin, and Boris Popov, and from the faculty Randy Stokes—deceived less than the others by the passage of time, spoke kindly about my final years in academic harness. My memory is hazy concerning the testimonials. But I do know that biography and history suffered severe distortion on this wonderful occasion.

Gifts included a splendid Orvis rod and reel from students alert to a fisherman's high aspirations, plus a can of worms. With less circumspection, old friends at Smith gave me a T-shirt emblazed with the centennial slogan "A Hundred Years of Women on Top." The greatest gift of course was the occasion itself together with scores of letters encased in a beautiful leather binding, presented by Mike. The letters were from former students and colleagues at City College, Smith, Princeton, and Santa Cruz. In replies, written over a period of many months, I recorded my heartfelt and everlasting thanks. But no words could convey the feelings of a time-worn teacher who had been given such a glorious departure.

Afterword

SEVERAL YEARS HAVE passed since I retired from teaching in 1975. I have spent a good deal of this time recording these recollections of a long—and indeed lucky—journey in the professional world of sociology. (But by no means "full time"—Leonora and I have traveled abroad frequently, my fishing days have multiplied, and I still give some attention to my calling.) As I approached its end, I faced the question of how to wind up this extended tale.

With little in mind for an afterword except that it should not be long, I sought suggestions from readers of the manuscript. Their consensus, as one of them put it, was the notion that I should "ruminate on the state of sociology, especially American sociology, as you observe it and reflect upon it in this year of our Lord (!) 1981."* I spent a good many hours at my desk trying to follow this suggestion. It became evident, however, that much of my attempt to write a conclusion of this kind was an exercise in hubris. The effort was abandoned in favor of the brief comments that follow.

Since my first encounter with sociology fifty years ago it has become a vast and complex enterprise. As a field of scholarly study (and in keeping with its "imperialism"),† sociology consists of a large and ever-growing number of subfields, to only a few of which have I attended closely. As a theoretical discipline, it includes an array of perspectives and methodologies in uneasy com-

---

* Robert Bierstedt, letter to the author, April 10, 1981.
† Page, "Sociology as a Teaching Enterprise," pp. 581ff.

petition; on this score, it has been claimed that there are several sociologies. As a curricular subject, it has burgeoned in academia, where it now appears to be on the downgrade. As a research technology (of which more below), it has grown spectacularly in recent years and continues to do so. And as a professional occupation, sociology has been an avenue of opportunity for thousands of men and women. I am one of the many beneficiaries of sociology's great growth who is now witnessing what, in some respects, seems to be its decline.

But only in *some* respects, in my optimistic view. To be sure, after many boom years, sociology is losing ground as a field of study in colleges and universities (and thus the multitude of textbooks face a shrinking market). As in other social sciences, financial support of research by governmental agencies has been severely reduced by the Reagan administration. Job opportunities for sociologists are becoming fewer, and there seems to be an oversupply of Ph.D. degrees. A threatening trend is the growing loss of sociology's traditional progressive-liberal constituency: both mounting conservatism and, to a lesser extent, resurgent Marxism are weakening what since early in this century have been important ideological allies.* On these counts, at least, sociology's heyday is over.

Yet, as a scholarly and intellectual undertaking, sociology continues to flourish. While too much trivia may appear in its journals and too many of its textbooks may be inferior primers, impressive works of various types abound. For example, books by the American scholars Daniel Bell, Reinhard Bendix, Barrington Moore, and Immanuel Wallerstein are faithful to what C. Wright Mills called the "classic tradition": whatever their thematic, methodological, and ideological differences, they are concerned with large-scale problems of social structure and social change and they are enriched by meticulous scholarship and theoretical sophistication. In theory itself diverse, exegetical, and innovative contributions have been made by Bendix, Richard J. Bernstein,† Peter

---

* Currently (November 1981), Christopher Hurn and I are planning to write an essay with the tentative title "Progressive Liberalism and the Decline of American Sociology" in which we suggest an explanation of sociology's loss of "constituency." A more wide-ranging discussion of sociology's recent problems is Arthur J. Vidich, Stanford M. Lyman, and Jeffrey C. Goldfarb, "Sociology and Society: Disciplinary Tensions and Professional Compromises," *Social Research* 48, no. 2 (Summer 1981): 322–61.

† The philosopher Bernstein's contributions to theoretical sociology are impressive, especially *The Restructuring of Social and Political Theory* (New

Blau, Randall Collins, Lewis Coser, William J. Goode, the late
Alvin Gouldner, George C. Homans, Robert Merton, Robert
Nisbet, and Dennis Wrong, among others. American versions of
phenomenological sociology are strongly represented by Peter
Berger, Aaron Cicourel, Erving Goffman, Joseph Gusfield, Maurice Natanson, and Edward Tiryakian. (The age of several of the
scholars named above, alas, handicaps the future of American sociology. But excellent scholarly and theoretical work in the years
ahead is assured, I believe, by such sociologists as Richard Gruneau, John Hewitt, Alan Sica, and Randall Stokes—to name only
young men whose writings were heralded in the preceding chapter. Of course, these four represent a tiny fraction of the similarly
talented men and women of their cohort.)

In sociology's special fields, moreover, first-rate research investigations multiply. Thus impressive studies have been made,
and no doubt will continue to appear, in social stratification and
mobility, race and ethnic relations, occupations and organizations,
social problems and "deviance," communications, demography,
and other areas of sociological concern. These are "empirical"
works, enriched by theoretical expertise.

Many of these studies make central use of a misnamed
"methodology" which, like other technologies, grows spectacularly.
Quantitative analysis, with the aid of ever-better computational
machinery, is the major research tool of such virtuosos as James S.
Coleman, O. D. Duncan, Peter Rossi, and Harrison White. I know
too little about this large and expanding instrument of sociological scholarship, which has received scanty attention in these recollections. But I am keenly aware of the fact that during my long
association with the enterprise, and increasingly so today, many of
sociology's ablest students have become exponents of what is often
viewed as an essential method in scientific work.

As a teaching sociologist, I have been far less concerned
with the field's *scientific* status than with its contribution as an
interpretive and, at its best, an artistic endeavor.* Thus a large

---

York: Harcourt Brace Jovanovich, 1976). Sociology is similarly indebted to
the phenomenological philosopher Maurice Natanson, cited below.
* A classic statement of this view is Robert A. Nisbet's "Sociology as an Art
Form," originally published in the *Pacific Sociological Review* (Fall 1962)
and reprinted in Nisbet's *Tradition and Revolt* (New York: Random House,
1968), chap. 8 and elsewhere. The conception of sociology as an artistic, not
a scientific, endeavor has recently been expressed by Lewis M. Killian in
"Sociologists Look at the Cuckoo's Nest: The Misuse of Ideal Types," *The
American Sociologist* 16, no. 4 (November 1981).

share of my preparatory study for the classroom has gone to certain kinds of sociological literature: the "classic tradition," works by modern-day followers of that tradition, and studies in social theory and my other teaching fields. But another share (as must be true of many sociologists) has gone elsewhere—to impressionistic essays, journalistic commentary, biography and autobiography, drama and fiction. Perhaps as a throwback to the nineteenth-century "dilettante" so despised by Emile Durkheim, I have viewed such writings as a source of sociological understanding—at times a more important source than numerous exhibitions of the "science of society."

As a conventionally certified sociologist, I have never found a permanent or livable theoretical home. For a short time in the 1930s I opted for what must have been judged an impossible theoretical mixture of Marx, Freud, and my mentor Robert MacIver. Later I became intrigued, but not captured, by functionalist doctrine of the Mertonian, not the Parsonian, variety. Still later I was mildly attracted by some of the work in symbolic interactionism, dramaturgy, and labeling theory—by the contributions of Howard S. Becker, Herbert Blumer, Erving Goffman, and Joseph Gusfield, for example, but not by Harold Garfinkel's opaque essays on ethnomethodology. None of these perspectives, however, provided firm theoretical anchorage. No doubt with too little discrimination, I see sociological virtue in all of them. As a teacher I became an advocate of what a good many others decried—a multiparadigmatic sociology. Little wonder, then, that students sometimes called me a "doctrinaire eclectic."

Former students, as well as former teachers and colleagues, have received far more attention in these recollections than have sociology's various orientations and its diverse achievements or failures. This may be the book's single vindication. But it also deals with other matters encountered in the journey. Recurring social themes, each a significant aspect of that journey, are friendship, collegiality, marginality, political ideology and sociology, and luck. (Two readers of the manuscript have accused me of exaggerating the role of luck. I do not think I have.) Additional themes of importance in the book, as in the journey, include graduate and undergraduate teaching, academic administration, and the role of editing works in sociology.

With the exception of teaching (over the years, my most important professional responsibility), these are marginal activities in the academic world of scholarship. Yet each of them, if pursued successfully, must be given serious attention. But not entirely, surely. For, as in most human endeavors, they have comic, at times hilarious, and indeed absurd dimensions. In this account of my travels as a teacher, chairman, and editor these could not be neglected. Thus I have tried to make *Lucky Journey* both a serious and lighthearted book.

Index

Library of Congress Cataloging in Publication Data

Page, Charles Hunt, 1909–

Fifty years in the sociological enterprise.

Includes index.

1. Page, Charles Hunt, 1909–   .   2. Sociologists—
United States—Biography.   I. Title.

HM22.U6P296   301'.092'4 [B]   82–7046

ISBN 0–87023–373–4   AACR2